Tomart's Price Guide to Saalfield and Merrill Paper Dolls

by Mary Young

Photography by the Author and Chris Hall

Also Includes Paper Dolls of **Artcraft** • **Dell** • **Simon & Schuster** • **Watkins/Strathmore**

Other books by the author:
Paper Dolls and Their Artists Book 1
Paper Dolls and Their Artists Book 2
A Collector's Guide to Paper Dolls - Saalfield, Lowe, Merrill
A Collector's Guide to Paper Dolls - Second Series
A Collector's Guide to Magazine Paper Dolls
Tomart's Price Guide to Lowe and Whitman Paper Dolls
Paper Dolls and Their Artists - Revised edition

Tomart Publications
division of Tomart Corporation • Dayton, Ohio

This book is dedicated to Elise, Ronald, Rebecca, Emil, Jonathan, Rachel, Peter and Lisa.

Acknowledgements

I wish to thank the following who have given so generously of their time and effort in lending paper dolls to photograph or sending information: Betsy Addison, Norene Allen, Marlene Brenner, Virginia Crossley, Rosemary Davidson, Mardell Davis, Peggy Ell, Rosalie Eppert, Angela Foust, Shirley Hedge, Marilyn Johnson, Pam Kalla, Judy Lawson, Louise Leek, Marge Meisinger, Wanda Myers, Madalaine Selfridge, Audrey Sepponen, Betsy Slap, Emma Terry, Florence Walker, Verlee Waterman, Jean Woodcock, Wynn Yusas and Henriette Zabin.

Special Thanks to Henry Saalfield and Alice McQuistion.

Extra special thanks to my husband George for his continued support and help with my hobby and writing.

Production of this book was made possible by the Tomart staff, most notably Marijke Shaffer, T.N. Tumbusch, Bob Welbaum, Nathan Hanneman, Rebecca Trissel and especially Tom Tumbusch for making it all possible. Separations and printing were performed by the Prism Color Group and Central Printing respectively.

Prices listed are based on the author's experience. They are presented as a guide for information purposes only. No one is obligated in any way to buy, sell, or trade according to these prices. Condition, rarity, demand and the reader's desire to own determine the actual price paid. No offer to buy or sell at the prices listed is intended or made. Buying and selling is conducted at the reader's risk. Neither the author nor the publisher assumes any liability for any losses suffered for use of, or any typographical errors contained in, this book. All value estimates are presented in U.S. dollars. All paper dolls are from the author's collection unless otherwise noted.

© Copyright 2000, Tomart Publications. All rights reserved

Published by Tomart Publications, Dayton, Ohio 45439

No part of this book may be reproduced, transmitted, or stored in any form or by any means, electronic or mechanical, without prior written permission from the publisher, Tomart Publications, 3300 Encrete Lane, Dayton, OH 45439-1944.

ISBN: 0-914293-45-1

1 2 3 4 5 6 7 8 9 0   8 7 6 5 4 3 2 1 9 0   Manufactured in the United States of America

Introduction

This book continues on in the coverage of the major paper doll producing companies. My last book covered the Lowe and Whitman paper dolls. This book covers two more of the major companies that produced paper dolls; Saalfield Publishing Co. of Akron, Ohio (including their Artcraft Division) and the Merrill Publishing Co. of Chicago. In addition a section at the end of the book covers paper dolls by Dell, Watkins/Strathmore , Simon and Schuster, and Pocket Books.

Coloring books that have paper dolls on the covers of the books with clothes inside in color or to be colored are pictured. However, if both dolls and clothes are inside the book in black and white, they will only be listed. (See special section at back of book for coloring books with paper dolls for companies other than Saalfield and Merrill.)

All known original paper dolls and their reprints are listed in the check lists for the Merrill and Saalfield companies including paper dolls from the Artcraft Division of Saalfield. All of the listed originals are pictured. Reprints having the same dolls as the original are not pictured but are listed. A special section showing reprints with re-drawn dolls has been added.

Books and box sets of paper toys are included in the check lists, when known, for each company but as they do not contain paper dolls with outfits, they will not be pictured.

All books are pictured and listed in the check lists in numerical order according to the publisher's number which appears on the book cover. If the book has no number, then the book is listed at the end of the list. Most numbers are 3 or 4 digit numbers. Sometimes you will find a number on a book reading as follows: 3446:10. The 10 is not part of the number but is the publisher's code for the price of the book: i.e. 10 cents.

The check lists for each company's paper dolls will contain all the original and reprint paper dolls. If a reprint, the number of the original book will also be included in parenthesis.

Price Guide

The prices in this book are based on mint, un-cut, original paper dolls. Reprints that are almost identical are just slightly lower in price. In the case of a reprint of a celebrity book where the dolls have been redrawn, the price is drastically reduced.

If the paper doll book is cut out then the price if usually half the lowest price given for the un-cut book. This is providing all the dolls and outfits are in very good condition and the set is complete. If not, then the price will be lower yet.

The prices in this guide were largely derived from many detailed studies of different sales lists of paper dolls and notes taken at paper doll conventions where paper dolls were sold. Information and knowledge from other collectors and personal judgement were other influencing factors.

Collecting Paper Dolls

If you are wondering how to get started in this fascinating hobby, a good idea would be to learn something about the different types of paper dolls and the prices they bring. You can attend toy shows, doll shows, flea markets, antique shows and antique malls. You may want to concentrate on paper dolls from a special era or one particular type of paper doll. If you are interested in just starting a general collection, begin by buying the paper dolls available in the stores now. Someday these too will be sought after.

Check the ads in the many magazines available that feature collectibles. Paper dolls are now available over the internet auction sites. As with every hobby it is wise to learn a little bit about the hobby first. Besides having a paper doll price guide it is also a good idea to subscribe to the paper doll newsletters. If you would like more information you can write to the author at Box 9244 Dayton, Ohio 45409. Please enclose a SASE.

Paper Doll History

It has long been thought that paper dolls began as pantins (jumping jacks) in Europe and evolved into the paper dolls we are familiar with now. Pantins were dolls made of cardboard with arms and legs that moved when a string attached to the parts was pulled.

During the 19th century, paper dolls were of famous dancers and of the opera star, Jenny Lind, plus many of the non-celebrity kind, all of which are very rare and hard to find now.

In the late 1800s advertising paper dolls were used by many companies to further the sale of their products. The ONT Thread Company, Lion Coffee, McLoughlins Coffee, Ceresota Flour, and Pillsbury Flour are a few examples. Many times the child could send away for a complete series of paper dolls after receiving the first doll with the product. This type of advertising continued into the 1900s and even today has not completely disappeared.

Women's magazines started to include a page of paper dolls around the turn of the century. Some of the more popular series of paper dolls appeared in Good Housekeeping, Ladies' Home Journal, Pictorial Review, Delineator, McCall's and Woman's Home Companion.

The type of paper dolls most familiar to us today is the paper doll book which features the dolls on the cardboard covers and the clothes on the inside pages. This type of book made its appearance in the late 1920s and the early 1930s and sold for a very reasonable price of either five or ten cents. This meant that children everywhere in the country could enjoy paper dolls with their saved pennies. Even during the depression years these books sold well and parents could buy paper dolls for birthdays and holidays for a fraction of what "real" dolls sold for.

The war years of the early 1940s saw the biggest surge of paper dolls which was never to be equaled again. Every company seemed to try to outdo one another with beautiful books of non-celebrity and celebrity paper dolls. Some celebrity books from those years are Alice Fay, Claudette Colbert, Judy Garland, Greer Garson, and Rita Hayworth, not to mention the child stars of Margaret O'Brien and Gloria Jean. Shirley Temple was a teenager by now; however, many paper dolls of Shirley as a child appeared in the 1930s and one set as a teenager in the 1940s. There were paper dolls of the stars of radio programs such as Hour of Charm, Glenn Miller, and Benny Goodman plus paper dolls from entire movies such as Ziegfeld Girl and Gone With The Wind. One book called Hollywood Personalities featured the stars from the Bing Crosby movie Holiday Inn.

Aside from paper doll books, children of the 1930s and 1940s also enjoyed paper dolls that appeared in the comic sections of their local newspapers. Blondie, Brenda Starr, and Jane Arden were very popular at that time, and children eagerly awaited the Sunday comics to get their new paper dolls.

In the 1950s, the advent of television was being felt and children were not quite as interested in sitting down to read a good book or cut out paper dolls as before. From the 1960s on, there has been a steady decline in the amount of paper dolls produced. However, you can still find some in your local stores in lesser quantity. Paper dolls of "real" dolls were made as far back as the 1930s. The Dy-Dee-Doll is one example. This type of paper doll seems to be what is found more readily now, with the Barbie Doll well out in front.

Reprints

Original paper doll books were often reprinted after they were first published. Sometimes the book was reprinted exactly like the original, but more often it was changed somewhat. The following typifies the many different ways an original may have been reprinted:

- The reprint and original may be exact duplicates.
- The reprint may be an exact duplicate but with a different price.
- The reprint may be the same but with no price on the book at all.
- The reprint may have fewer pages.
- The reprint may be printed on a lesser grade of paper.
- The reprint may have a new background on the covers; dolls and inside pages remain the same.
- The reprint may have completely new covers, dolls redrawn while inside pages remain the same.

- The reprint may have fewer dolls than the original.
- The reprint may have a different title than the original.
- The reprint may be a box set while the original was a book.
- The reprint may be a book while the original was a box set.
- The reprint may be made up of dolls from two, three or even four different paper doll books.
- The reprint may have dolls and outfits of reduced or enlarged size.
- The reprint may not have die-cut dolls though the original book did.
- The reprint may have coloring pages added or subtracted.
- The reprint may have a reprint of its own.
- The reprint may be an exact duplicate with a different trade name.

2596 The Well Dressed Girl

2793 Lucky Paper Dolls

One common type of reprint is better known in the business as a jobber book. The dolls and clothes in these books were the same as the original except that usually two or more pages were dropped and the covers were made of very lightweight cardboard, rarely die-cut. The jobber book was usually placed on the market at the same time as the original main line book; however, these less expensive books did not go to the big chain stores but rather to small toy and variety stores, drug stores, train stations, and bus depots.

An interesting example of a reprint that has a reprint is that of a Saalfield book The Well Dressed Girl #2596 also issued as #1574. These books are reprints of the Claudette Colbert book #2451. It was the usual reprint of a celebrity book made into a non-

2451 Claudette Colbert

celebrity book in which the dolls were redrawn using the outlines of the Claudette Colbert dolls and retaining the original clothes. Later, it was decided to reprint The Well Dressed Girl and this time the clothes of Claudette Colbert were not used but new outfits were created. So, all that was left now of the Claudette Colbert book were the outlines of the dolls. This new reprint was again called The Well Dressed Girl with a new number #1721 (This "new" Well Dressed Girl was also issued with the following numbers; #1771 and #2607) The story does not end here as another reprint was made. A new set of dolls was drawn, and a new title "Lucky Paper Dolls" (#2793 and #2693) was given to the book. The dolls still maintain the basic outlines of the Claudette Colbert dolls, and the outfits are those from "The Well Dressed Girl" #1721.

Because of the great number of reprints with redrawn paper dolls by the Saalfield Company, the author has grouped as many as possible together on eight of the color pages.

A reprint may appeal to the collector just as much as the original book, especially if it contains added material or if the dolls are redrawn by a favorite artist. Many collectors try to collect both the original books and all their reprints.

The above information on reprints refers only to reprints published by the original company within a few days, months, or years of the original. In

Introduction

recent years a number of paper doll books have been reprinted by companies other than the initial company and can still be bought today. These reprint books give the collector an opportunity to own copies of some beautiful early paper dolls which are now hard to find uncut. The books will usually be noted on the cover or on the wrapping that they are a reprint. It would be good if these new reprints also had some printing on the backs of the dolls to allow a collector to distinguish the new from the old in case the dolls are cut out, but unfortunately only a few do have this feature. However, collectors will find that most of the dolls, when cut out, will have a distinguishable white color on their backs.

Anyone with paper doll questions or information is encouraged to write the author at P.O. Box 9244, Wright Brothers Branch, Dayton, Ohio 45409. Please enclose a SASE.

The Saalfield Publishing Co.

The Saalfield Publishing Company was formed in 1900 when Mr. Arthur J. Saalfield purchased the publishing department of the Werner Company, a publishing and manufacturing enterprise in Akron, Ohio. Bibles, cookbooks, dictionaries, encyclopedias and home medical books were early best sellers for Saalfield.

In 1902, Mr. Saalfield published his first book for children. The book was titled Billy Whiskers. Written by Mrs. Frances Trego Montgomery, the book became the launching pad which propelled the Saalfield Company on its way to becoming one of the most successful publishers of children's books in America. Because of the success of the first Billy Whiskers book, Mrs. Montgomery was asked to write a series of Billy Whiskers books. Each of these books became a big hit with children everywhere. Other books for children, including the Auto Boys and The Campfire Girl series, were added to the Saalfield line. Mr. Saalfield's wife wrote stories for children, too, and these were published by the company under Mrs. Saalfield's maiden name of Adah Louise Sutton.

As the company grew, Mr. Saalfield began looking for more space. He also was keeping an eye out for equipment that could produce books made of cloth. He had learned of the "rag books" printed in England for very young children. Such books were just the thing for babies and toddlers because they were made of cloth and could not tear. When the Globe Sign Company in Akron went up for sale, this was heaven-sent as it not only had the larger space but also the type of equipment that Mr. Saalfield was looking for. When it was learned that the Globe Sign Company had produced advertising signs lithographed in color on muslin, Mr. Saalfield needed to look no further. The Globe Sign Company was purchased in 1906. The Saalfield Publishing Company was then moved from their old location in the Werner Company building to their new location in the Globe building. The early Saalfield muslin books soon appeared and were a big success. In 1908, a muslin book called Babies of All Nations was published. This was Saalfield's first "doll" book and it contained 12 dolls to cut out, sew and stuff. Muslin dolls were also printed on single sheets for many years, two of the earliest being Muslin Teddy Bear and Greenaway Muslin Doll. These sheets of dolls continued for many years, and eventually there were as many as forty different sheets listed in the Saalfield catalogs. The last one, Priscilla, appeared in the 1937 catalog.

Old print of the Saalfield Company from an early catalog

When chain stores began appearing across the country, Mr. Saalfield had the foresight to add less expensive children's books to his line. There were twelve books in the first series which included Jack and the Beanstalk and Cinderella, and they were all illustrated by Mrs. Frances Brundage. These books were published in 1908, and it was not long before Mrs. Brundage was also drawing paper dolls for the company. She drew many of the early paper doll sets published by Saalfield.

One of the biggest successes for the company came about by the appearance into the movie world of a little girl named Shirley Temple. A contract was drawn up in 1933 which gave the Saalfield Publishing Company the exclusive rights to produce publications on Shirley Temple. Coloring books, paper dolls, story books, activity sets and other items were placed on the market and carried the company through the post depression period. Shirley Temple items sold into the 1940s and then were discontinued until late in the Fifties when Shirley Temple had her TV show. At that time, new paper dolls of Shirley as a child were produced including one paper doll that was 18 inches tall and a "Play Kit" that included paper dolls with outfits that laced onto the dolls.

The Saalfield Publishing Company was bought by the Rand McNally Company in 1976. This marked the end of three generations of publishing leadership from within the Saalfield family. When Arthur J. Saalfield died in 1919, his son Albert George Saalfield took over the company. Albert was president for forty years until his death in 1959 at which time Henry Robinson Saalfield, the son of Albert and the grandson of the founder, became president. Henry held the position until the company closed in 1976. The Saalfield archives were purchased by the Kent State University Libraries in Kent, Ohio. Here, all manner of story books, paper dolls, puzzles and games produced by the Saalfield Company will be preserved for all time.

Saalfield sold some of their early paper dolls in boxes, envelopes and by the sheet. These items were numbered 1A, 1AA, 2B etc. and were referred to as "assortments" in the Saalfield catalogs.

The paper dolls (except for 3B, 5A and 5AA that had the movie stars) all originated with the paper doll book #1180 Dollies to Paint, Cutout and Dress, copyright 1918. The small 7¼" (approx.) and 5½" dolls are the same as the six dolls in the original book but the 12" dolls are re-drawn. Some of the 7¼" dolls were given new names and these names along with a number, were printed at the side of the dolls. When cut out, the name and number is lost. For the 12" dolls, the name and number is printed near the feet of the dolls.

Shirley Temple and Albert George Saalfield in 1938 when Shirley visited the Saalfield Publishing Company. Photo courtesy of Henry Robinson Saalfield.

Shirley Temple Black with Henry Robinson Saalfield at the time when the new paper dolls of Shirley were published in 1958. Photo courtesy of Henry Robinson Saalfield.

The dolls were given numbers and names as follows:

12" dolls: 201-Helen, 202-Jack, 203-Margaret, 204-Alice

7¼" dolls: 101-Jane, 102-Mary, 103-Pearl, 104-Bessie, 105-Elizabeth, 106-Jack

The dolls' outfits were also numbered. For example, Mary #102 would have outfits numbered 102-A, 102-B etc. Here again, when cut out, the information is lost.

The following is a list of the known paper dolls in this group of assortments:

- **1A** Two 7¼" dolls w/6 dresses & 6 hats (envelope)
- **1AA** One 7¼" doll w/3 dresses & 3 hats (envelope)
- **1B** Three 7¼" dolls w/9 dresses & 9 hats - "My Sweet Dollies" (Box)
- **1BS** Two 7¼" dolls w/6 dresses & 6 hats - "My Sweet Dollies" (Box)
- **1BS** "My Sweet Dollies" two 7¼" dolls with eight dresses and eight hats (box)
- **1C** "My Four Dollies" four 7¼" dolls with 12 dresses and 12 hats (box)
- **1D** Six dolls w/18 dresses & 18 hats (Box)
- **2A** One 12" doll w/3 dresses & 3 hats - "Little Playmate" (envelope)
- **2B** Two 12" dolls w/6 dresses & 6 hats - "Dolls I Love Best" (Box)
- **2BS** One 12" doll w/3 dresses & 3 hats - "The Doll I Love Best" (Box)
- **3A** Three sheets, 7¼" x 10" ea., one 5½" doll & outfits on each sheet. Sold by the sheet. Each sheet is marked 3-A.
- **3AA** "Five Dollies To Cut Out and Dress With 25 Dresses and 25 Hats in Colors" Envelope with five sheets of dolls and clothes. Dolls are 7¼" size. The sheets have no identifying number on them and are identical to pages in book #1180.
- **3-B** "Six Dollies To Cut Out And Dress" Box set with six 7¼" x 10" sheets. Dolls are 5½" size. Each sheet is marked 3-A.
- **3-B** "The Happy Family Paper Dolls" Box set with six 7¼" x 10" sheets. Same dolls as above 3-B set.
- **3-B** "Six Dollies To Cut Out And Dress" Box set with six 7¼" x 10" sheets. Dolls are movie stars such as Charlie Chaplin and Norma Talmadge. Each sheet is marked 5-A.
- **4A** Four 12" dolls w/12 dresses & 12 hats in double compartment box
- **4A** Eight dolls w/20 dresses & 20 hats in double compartment box
- **5A** Six sheets, 7¼" x 10". From set 3-B (Charlie Chaplin, etc.) Sold by the sheet. Each sheet is marked 5-A.
- **5AA** "Five Dollies To Cut Out And Dress" Envelope. Five Sheets 7¼" x 10". Each sheet is marked 5-A. From set 3B (Charlie Chaplin, etc.)

The Four 12" Dolls
Paper dolls courtesy of Rosalie Eppert

Helen #201 outfits 201A, B & C

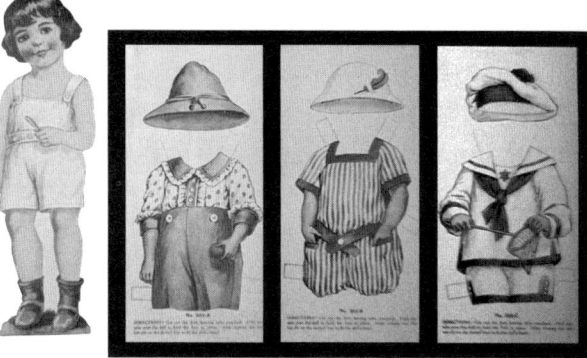

Jack #202 outfits 202A, B & C

Margaret #203 cut set

Alice #204 outfits 204A, B & C

Saalfield

The 7¼" Dolls:

Jane #101 outfit 101B

Jane has been found un-cut but only one of her un-cut out-fits with the accompanying numbers of 101-A, 101-B etc. has been found so far. (Paper dolls courtesy of Peggy Ell, Rosalie Eppert & Florence Walker.)

Mary #102   outfit 102A

outfit 102B   outfit 102C

Pearl #103   outfit 103A

outfit 103B   outfit 103C

Bessie #104   outfit 104A

outfit 104B   outfit 104C

Elizabeth #105   outfit 105A

outfit 105B   outfit 105C

Jack #106   outfit 106A

outfit 106B   outfit 106C

Saalfield

9

The following are some boxes and envelopes that were used in the assortments:

Envelope containing five sheets of paper dolls exactly like pages from the paper doll book #1180. This particular envelope had Helen's Trousseau, Alice's Trousseau, Elizabeth's Trousseau and two sheets of Mary's Trousseau. The sheets have no identifying number. Courtesy of Virginia Crossley

3AA Five Dollies to Cut Out and Dress $65 - 85

The 12" doll in this Box varied from box to box.

2BS The Doll I Love Best $40 - 60

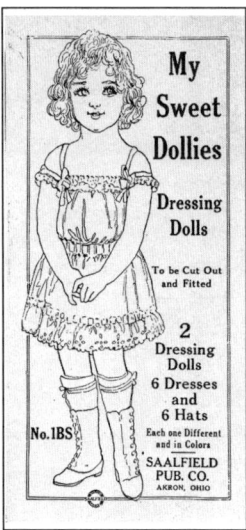

This box contained two 7¼" dolls. The doll's numbers are not listed on the box so the dolls could vary.

1BS My Sweet Dollies $40 - 65

The 12" doll of Helen & her outfits were included in this envelope and her number was printed on the envelope. Little Playmate envelopes have been found for the other three 12" dolls with their own number printed on the envelope. All have the same picture on the envelope including the boy. Courtesy of Louise Leek

2A Little Playmate $40 - 60

The four 7¼" dolls in this box vary from box to box. Courtesy of Florence Walker

1C My Four Dollies $60 - 85

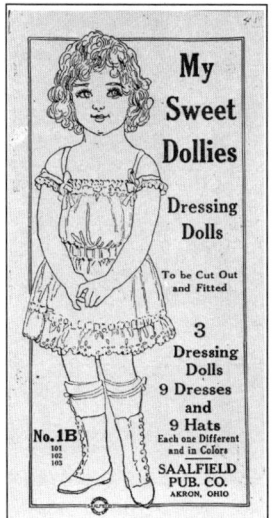

This box contained three 7¼" dolls; Jane, Mary and Pearl. Their numbers 101, 102, & 103 are listed on the box.

1B My Sweet Dollies $50 - 75

3-B (box) Six Dollies to Cut Out and Dress $75 - 95

This Box contains six sheets with six dolls from paper doll book #1180. One sheet (Alice's Trousseau) is also shown here on the box cover. Dolls are 5½".

(Another box 3-B with identical title and paper dolls has been found with the sheet of Mary's Trousseau pictured on the cover.)

(Still another box 3-B has been found with the same six sheets of dolls except the title for this set is THE HAPPY FAMILY PAPER DOLLS and the picture on the box cover is the same as the cover for book #1180.)

The six sheets inside box 3-B are numbered 3-A. This sheet is Elizabeth's Trousseau. The sheets were also sold separately. $12 - 15 a sheet.

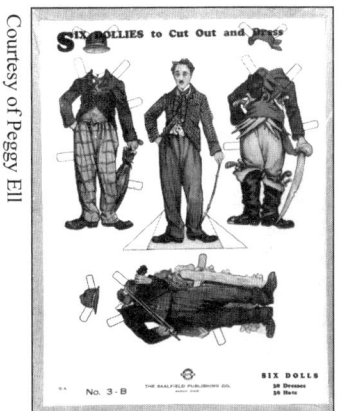

Courtesy of Peggy Ell

3-B (box) Six Dollies to Cut Out and Dress $150 - 180

 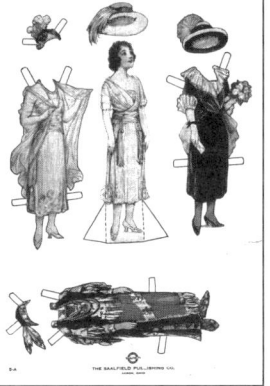 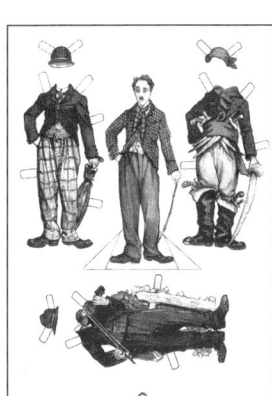 

Contents of Box 3-B Each of the 6 sheets is numbered 5-A

5AA Five Dollies to Cut Out and Dress (envelope)
This envelope contains five of the six 5-A sheets of movie stars shown above. The sheets may vary from envelope to envelope. $140 - 165

(Another box 3-B has been found with identical title and same movie star paper dolls except the box cover shows one of the other stars on the cover.)

The box states there are 30 dresses & 30 hats. This is true for the set with the six children. But the set with the movie stars had only a total of 18 dresses (and suits) and 21 hats.

Saalfield

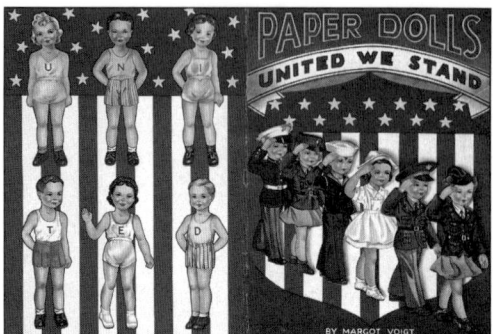

5 Boy And Girl Cut-Out Doll Book Original copyright 1932 by the Stecher Lithographic Company. Listed in the 1937 Saalfield catalog. $65 - 95

100 Bettina And Her Playmate Rosalie Original copyright by the Stecher Lithographic Company, no date. Listed and pictured in the 1931 Saalfield catalog. $75 - 90

113 United We Stand 1943 $50 - 65

Courtesy of Marlene Brenner

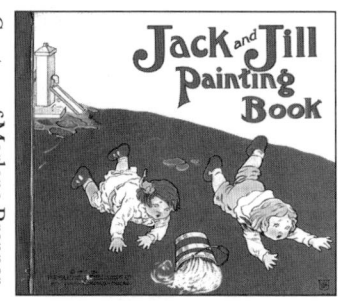

168 Jack And Jill Painting Book 1915 $45 - 65

168 Title page doesn't say Jack And Jill Painting Book Instead it has Nursery Painting Book.

168 Inside pages of paper dolls. The doll on right is in color, doll on left to be colored.

230 Paper Dolls To Cut Out - Ten Dolls With Dresses, Hats And Playthings 1932 This book was reprinted many times with a variety of different covers and also in box sets. One reprint used this same number 230, but is dated 1939 $75 - 95

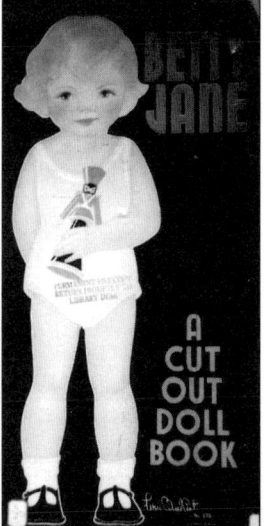

275 Betty Jane 1934 $75 - 95

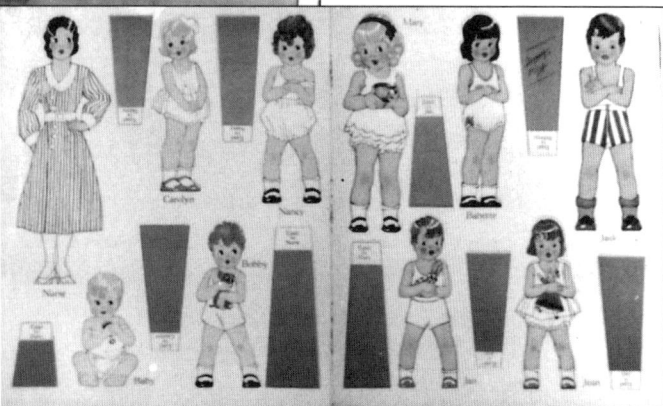

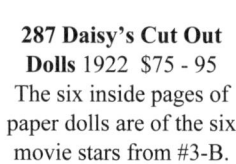

287 Daisy's Cut Out Dolls 1922 $75 - 95 The six inside pages of paper dolls are of the six movie stars from #3-B.

Courtesy of Betsy Slap

294 Little Mary Mixup And Her Friend Peggy 1922 $100 - 175

294 Inside pages

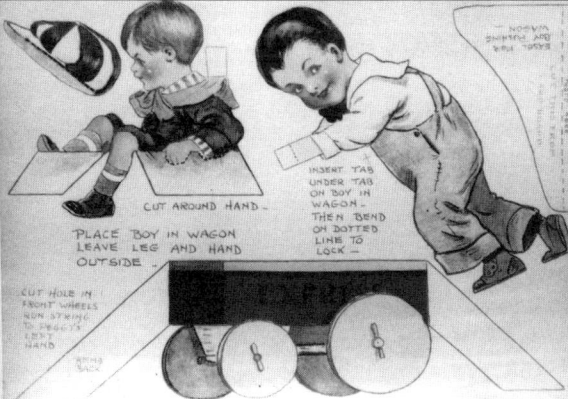

294 Inside pages

877 Dolly Jean - Her Paper Doll House, Furniture and Clothes 1932 $100 - 160

877 back cover

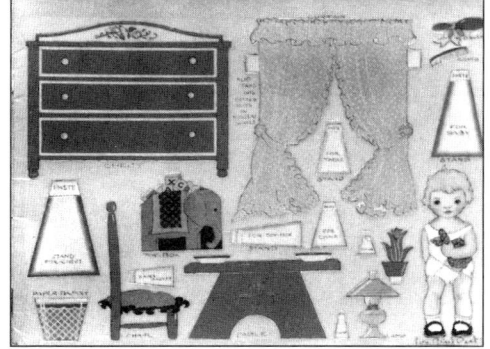

877 Inside front and back cover

Saalfield

13

 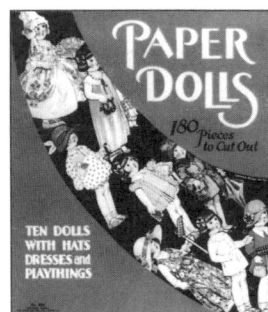 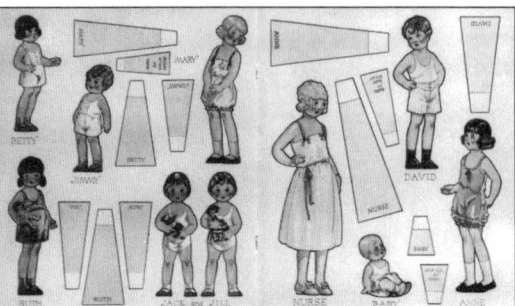

881 Many Things To Do 1932 (One page of paper dolls in color) $12 - 18

885 Paper Dolls - 180 Pieces To Cut Out - Ten Dolls With Hats, Dresses And Playthings 1932 $75 - 100

885 Inside pages of paper dolls

 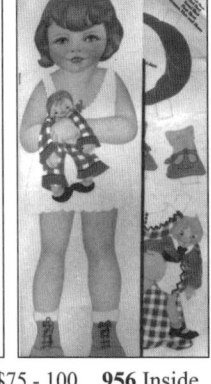 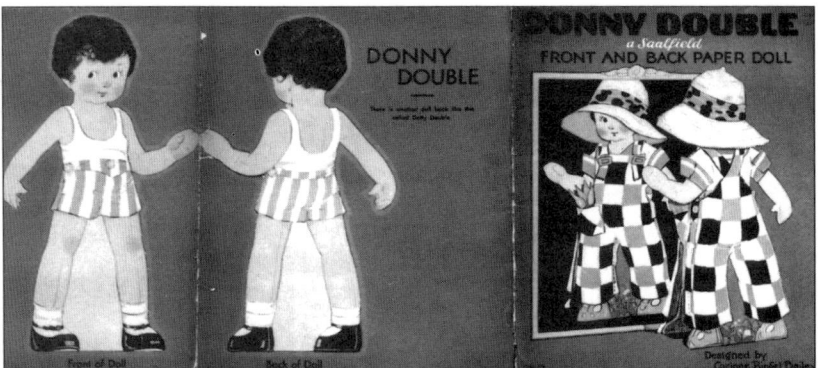

956 Sally Lou 1931 $75 - 100   **956** Inside

976 Donny Double 1933 $50 - 65

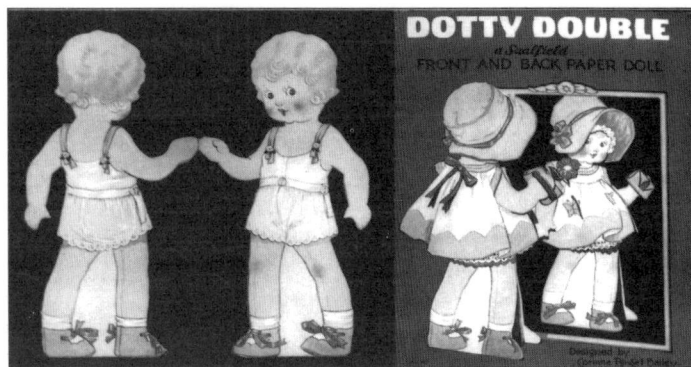 

977 Dotty Double 1933 $50 - 65

980 Mickey Mouse and Minnie Mouse 1933 $300 - 500

 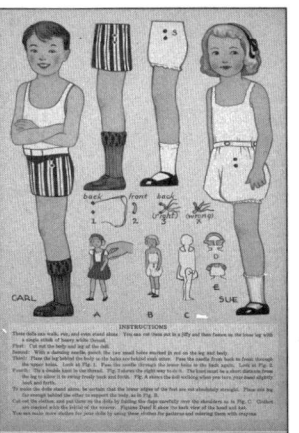

1074 Walking Paper Doll Family 1934 $75 - 90

1074 Inside front and back cover

Saalfield

14

1170 Cover   **1170 The Four Little Dolls** 1920 $65 - 95 Courtesy Verlee Waterman.

This is a story book with four pages of paper dolls. Shown are the pages with Saraphine and Gladys (she is Elizabeth in #1180). The other two dolls, Rose and Violet, are missing from the book.

1171 Cover view #1.

1171 Cover view #2.

1171 My Book Of Paper Dolls - Ready To Cut Out And Dress This book has no date, but was listed in catalogs of the 1920s and very early 1930s. In the 1931 catalog the number was changed to #1171-804, and in the 1932 catalog the number is just #804. The last time the book is listed is in 1933. Two different covers have been found for #1171 and are pictured. View #1 has a red background and is of very stiff cardboard. View #2 is of slick paper and is signed by Frances Brundage. A linentex version of this book, #936, appeared in the 1932 and 1933 editions of the Saalfield catalog and used the cover in view #1. These four dolls originated in the #1180 book but the dolls here, are re-drawn and made larger. $65 - 90

Saalfield

1180 Dollies To Paint Cutout and Dress 1918, Included in this book are six pages of paper dolls in color and duplicate pages in black and white to be colored. $75 - 100
Front and back cover are the same.
Courtesy of Betsy Addison.
Photos by Robert Addison.

1180 Elizabeth's Trousseau

1180 Alice's Trousseau

1180 Mary's Trousseau

1180 Margaret's Trousseau

1180 Jack's Wardrobe

1180 Helen's Trousseau

Saalfield

Courtesy of Shirley Hedge

1261 Gulliver's Travels 1939 $95 - 175

1330 Mother and Daughter 1962 $20 - 35
The dolls were meant to be Jackie and Caroline Kennedy.

1331 Gina Gillespie 1962 $35 - 50

1332 The Kewpies 1963 $50 - 75

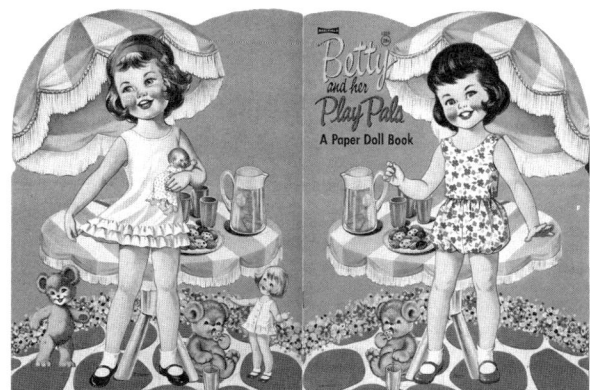
1335 Betty and her Play Pals $15 - 25
Originated from a foreign paper doll book.

1336 The Wonderful World of the Brothers Grimm 1963 $35 - 50

1337 Kissy Paper Doll 1963 $35 - 40

1339 Bonnets and Bows 1963 $12 - 15

Courtesy of Betsy Slap

Saalfield

Courtesy of Emma Terry

1341 Baby Paper Dolls 1963 $20 - 35

1342 Bridal Party 1963 $18 - 25

1344 Walter Lantz Cartoon Stars 1963 $25 - 40

1345 Little Women 1963 $20 - 35

1346 Pretty as a Rose 1963 $12 - 15

1352 The Quintuplets 1964 $50 - 75

1357 Karen 1965 $35 - 50
From the Karen segment of the Television series "90 Bristol Court" filmed at Universal Studios.

Saalfield

18

1357 **Charming** $10 - 15 Originated from a foreign book.   1357 Inside cover

1502 **Superman Cut-Outs Book** 1940 $100 - 200   1661 **Gloria Jean** 1940 $85 - 125

1664 **Gloria Jean** 1941 $100 - 175   1666 **Gloria Jean** 1941 $100 - 175

1710 **Shirley** $6 - 8 Originated from a foreign book.   1711 **Molly** $6 - 8 Originated from a foreign book.

Courtesy of Audrey Sepponen

1712 **Melissa** $6 - 8 Originated from a foreign book.   1713 **Judy** $6 - 8 Originated from a foreign book.

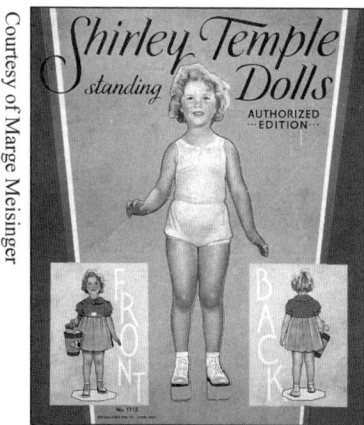

1715 **Shirley Temple Standing Dolls** 1935 $175 - 275   1715 Reverse side of front cover and first page of clothes.

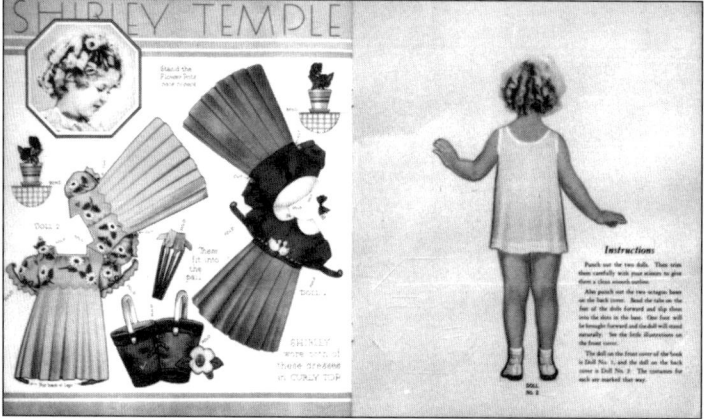

1715 Back cover   1715 Reverse side of back cover and last page of clothes.

1719 **Shirley Temple Standing Doll, box** 1935 $100 - 175   1727 **Shirley Temple Standing Doll, box** 1935 $100 - 200
Doll and clothes are front and back style.

Courtesy of Marge Meisinger

Saalfield

1733 My Twins $12 - 15 Originated from a foreign book. **1734 Sally** $12 - 15 Originated from a foreign book.

1735 Anne $12 - 15 Originated from a foreign book. **1736 Helen** $12 - 15 Originated from a foreign book.

1739 Shirley Temple Playhouse, box 1935 $175 - 275   Doll of Shirley, her doll carriage, and one page of clothes from the playhouse set.

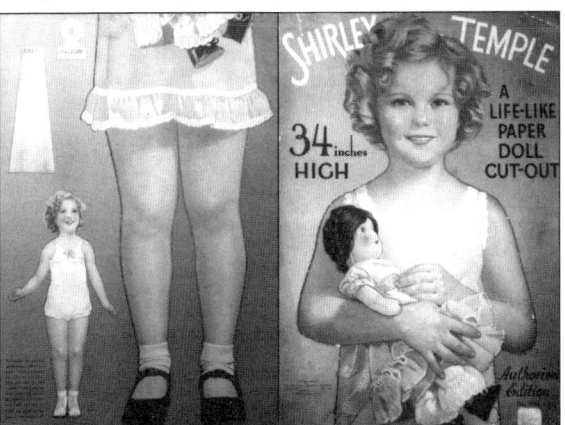

1761 Shirley Temple Dolls and Dresses 1937 $175 - 300   **1765 Shirley Temple** 1936 $200 - 350 (34" high)

Saalfield

Courtesy of Peggy Ell

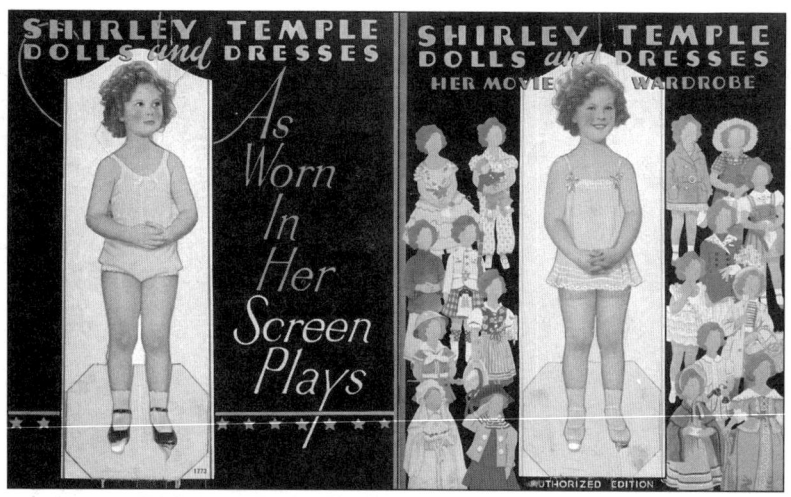

1773 Shirley Temple – Her Movie Wardrobe 1938 $200 - 300

1782 Shirley Temple 1939 $175 - 300

1787 Shirley Temple – In Masquerade Costumes 1940 $175 - 300

1954 Baby Dolls 1941 $25 - 40

2094 Paper Doll Family and Their House 1934 $75 - 100

2097 Comics Paper Doll Cut-Out Book 1935 $200 - 400

Saalfield

2106 Paper Dolls Around the World 1935 $35 – 50   **2109 Paper Doll Family** 1935 $75 – 90

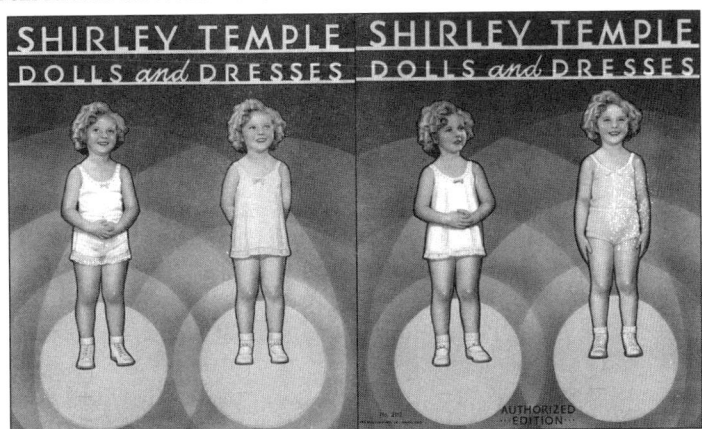

2112 Shirley Temple – Dolls and Dresses 1934 $175 – 300

2126 Polly Pepper Paper Dolls 1936 $75 – 100   The four dolls from Polly Pepper.

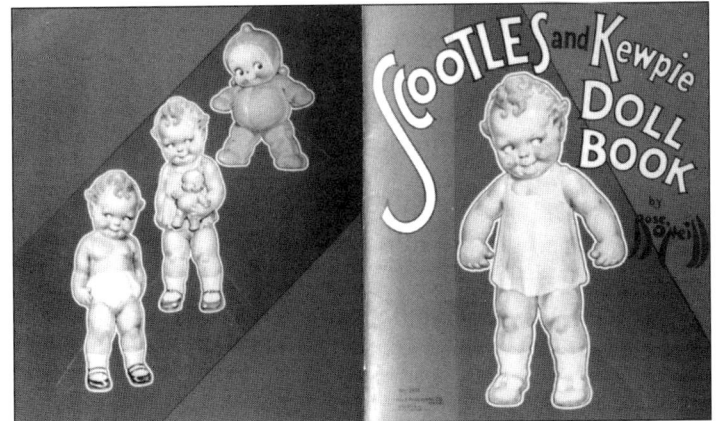 

2131 Scootles and Kewpie Doll Book 1936 $200 – 350   **2140 Housekeeping with the Kuddle Kiddies** 1936 $75 – 100

Saalfield

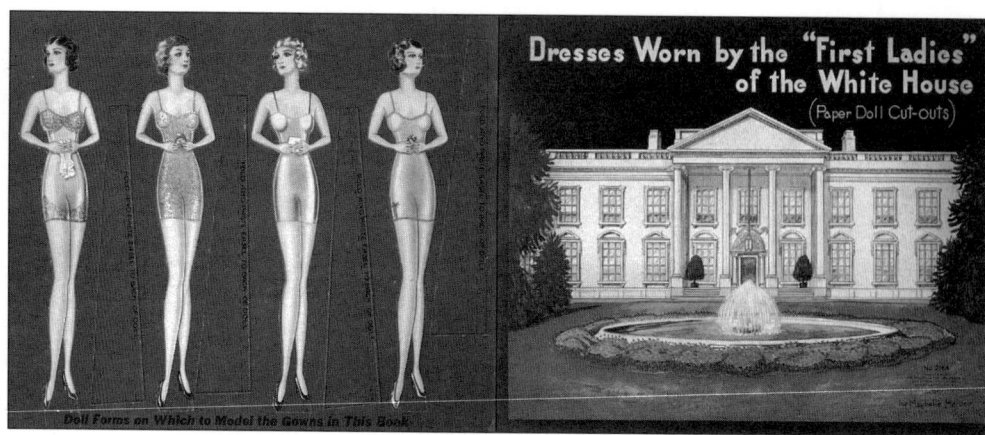

2160 Petunia and Patches 1937 $125 - 200   **2164 Dresses Worn by the "First Ladies" of the White House** 1937 $45 - 60

2176 Let's Play Doctor 1938 $65 - 90   **2176** Inside page of dolls

2183 Kitchen Play (with paper dolls) 1938 $25 - 35   **2185 Baby Dear** 1938 $65 - 90   **2189 Henry and Henrietta** 1938 $40 - 50

2193 Fashion Shop 1938 $65 - 100   **2193** Inside page of dolls

Saalfield

2194 Let's Play Wedding 1938 $75 - 100

2216 The Princess Paper Doll Book 1939 $150 - 275   **C2231 The New Zoo Revue** 1974 $10 - 15 (clothes to be colored)

2242 Hollywood Fashion Dolls 1939 $65 - 90   **2245 Goldilocks and the Three Bears** 1939 $100 - 200

2284 Ruth E. Newton's Paper Doll Cut-Outs 1940 $125 - 200

Saalfield

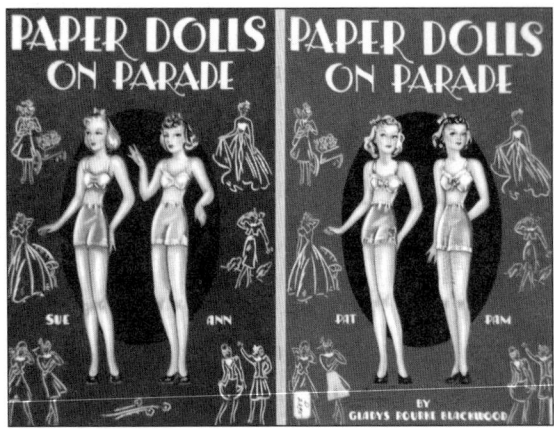

2295 Paper Dolls On Parade 1940 $60 - 85

Courtesy of Audrey Sepponen

 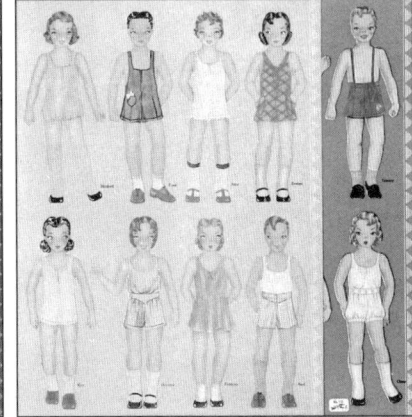

2313 50 Paper Dolls 1940 $50 - 85 **2313** Inside page

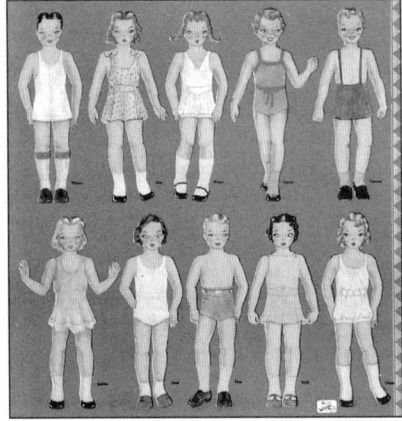 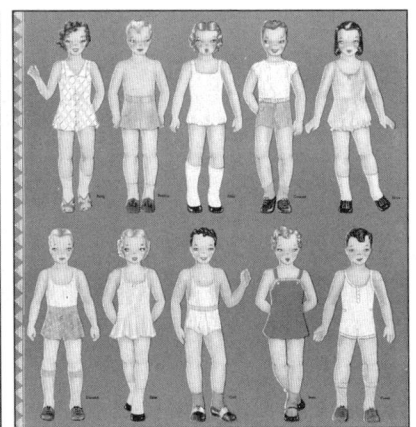 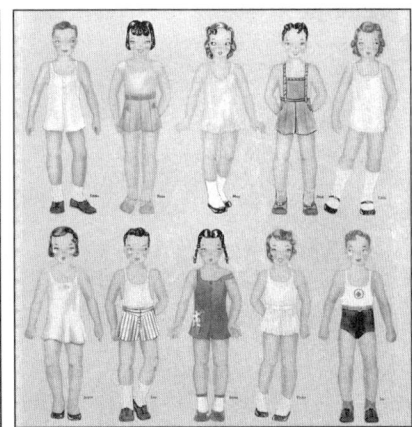

2313 Inside pages

2321 Tiptop Paper Dolls 1940 $85 - 150 **2328 Skating Party Paper Dolls** 1941 $40 - 60

Saalfield

2329 14 Good Little Dolls 1941 $40 - 60

2335 Children of America 1941 $25 - 35

2348 The Badgett Quadruplets 1941 $90 - 175

2348 Inside front cover

2356 Charlie Chaplin and Paulette Goddard 1941 $200 - 300

2358 Little Miss America 1941 $60 - 85

2360 Daisy Mae & Li'l Abner 1941 $100 - 150

2361 Debs & Sub-debs 1941 $35 - 50

Saalfield

2389 Daisy Mae and Li'l Abner 1942 $125 - 200

2397 The Modern Miss in Paper Dolls 1942 $35 - 50

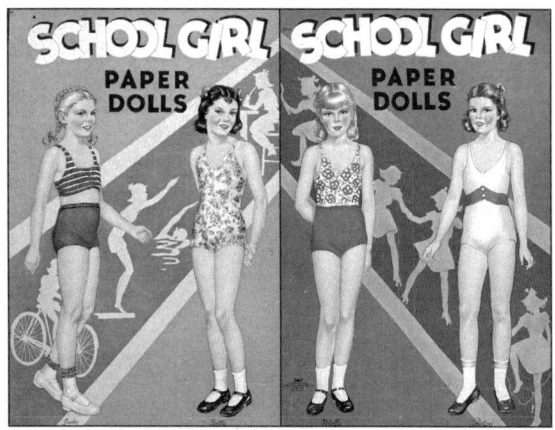
2400 School Girl 1942 $35 - 50

2408 Jane Arden 1942 $125 - 200

2410 Paper Doll Party 1944 $35 - 50

2421 3 Paper Doll Books
(in a partial box)
1942 $40 - 50

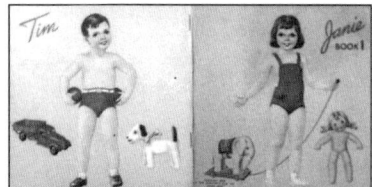
2421 Book one

2421 Book two

Paper Doll Party was completed in 1941 but the copyright date is 1944. In the three years between there were box sets using these dolls and a jobber book (#279) in 1943. Maybe the date on the book was misprinted or it was decided to bring this original book out at a later date.

2424 Mommy and Me 1943 $40 - 50

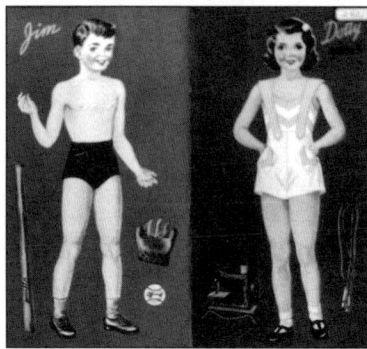
2421 Book three

Saalfield

2425 The New Shirley Temple in Paper Dolls 1942 $125 - 250

2426 Joan Carroll 1942 $75 - 125

2427 Mary Martin 1942 $100 - 150

2430 Quiz Kids 1942 $90 - 175

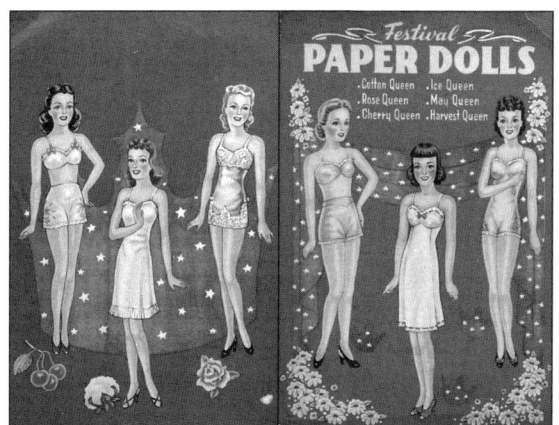

2431 Festival Paper Dolls 1944 $50 - 65

2436 Little Orphan Annie's Paper Dolls 1943 $125 - 200

2438 Ann Sothern 1943, 8 page $100 - 200, 6 page $75 - 150

2445 Victory Paper Dolls 1943 $85 - 125

Saalfield

Courtesy of Audrey Sepponen

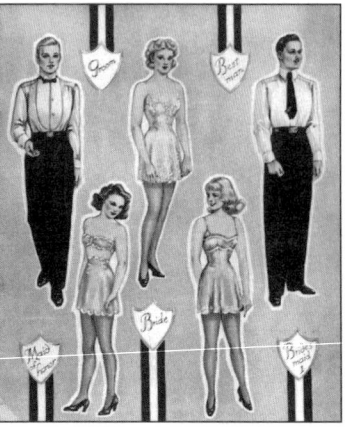

2446 Army and Navy Wedding Party 1943 $90 - 150   **2446** Inside front cover

Courtesy of Betsy Slap

2450 Uncle Sam's Little Helpers 1943 $75 - 125   **2451 Claudette Colbert** 1943 $125 - 200

2458 Sweetheart Paper Dolls 1943 $50 - 75   **2460 Boots and her Buddies** 1943 $90 - 160

2462 Betty Field 1943 $90 - 175

Saalfield

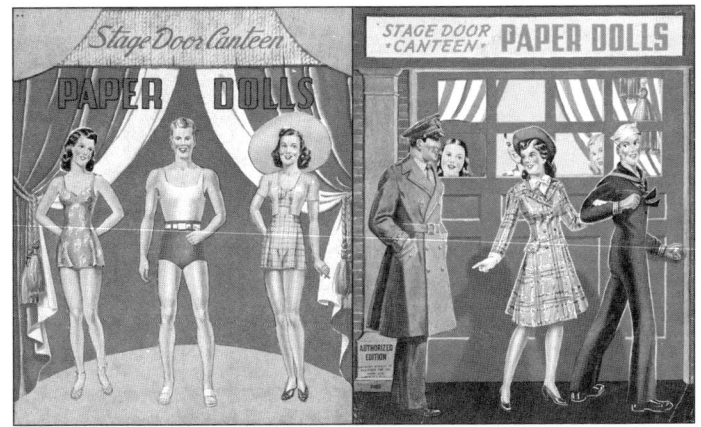

2468 Stage Door Canteen 1943 $60 - 90   **2468** Inside front cover

Courtesy of Emma Terry

2475 Lucille Ball 1944 **6 page** $125 - 200 **8 page** $150 - 275   **2478 Nancy & Her Dolls** 1944 $45 - 60

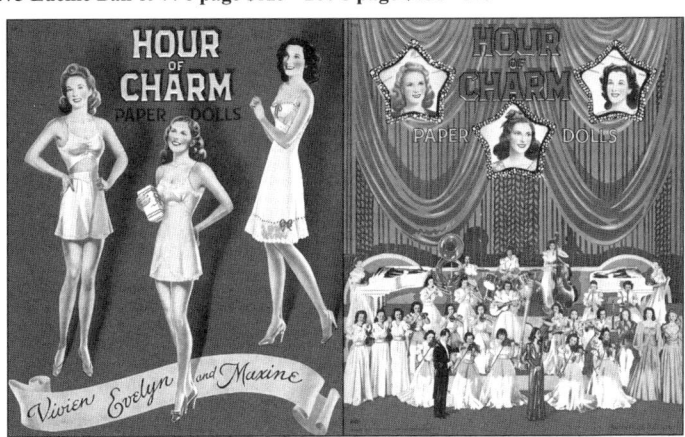 

2481 Hour of Charm 1943 $75 - 150   **2481** Inside front cover

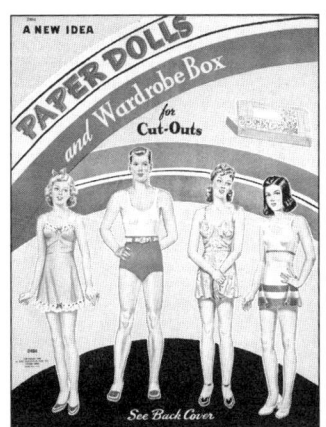 

2484 Paper Dolls and Wardrobe Box 1944 $35 - 50   **2485 Rock-A-Bye Baby** 1945 $35 - 50

Saalfield

2486 Bob and Betty 1945 $45 - 65   2486 Inside front cover

2487 Good Neighbor 1944 $35 - 45   2487 Inside front cover

2488 Carnival 1944 $35 - 45   2488 Inside front cover

2489 Artist Models 1945 $70 - 90   **2492 Mary Martin** 1944 $100 - 200

Saalfield

Saalfield reprints with redrawn dolls

Saalfield published many reprints with redrawn dolls but the clothes pages were the same as the original book. These paper doll books are grouped together on the following color pages. The stock number and title is given under each picture. The number in parentheses is the original book number and a picture of that book can be found in the main Saalfield section. If the book was dated the date is also given.

These same re-drawn dolls could appear in other reprints with different stock numbers and even different titles. Space does not allow for all these variations to be shown but all are listed in the Saalfield check list.

Prices for these reprints are 10% lower than the original book (original book number in parentheses)

Merrill reprints with re-drawn dolls are very few and are covered in the Merrill section.

711 Western (4448)

1324 Tina (6160)

721 Peggy Lou 1961 (4449)

1741 Romance (2732)

6181 Anne, Judy, Carol Darling Dolls with Wavy Hair 1955 (5180 & 5181 plus one new doll)

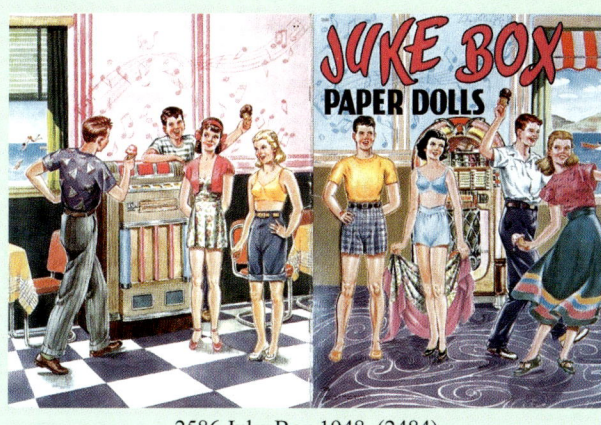
2586 Juke Box 1948 (2484)

2742 Posy Pals (6041)

1322 Mother Goose (2758)

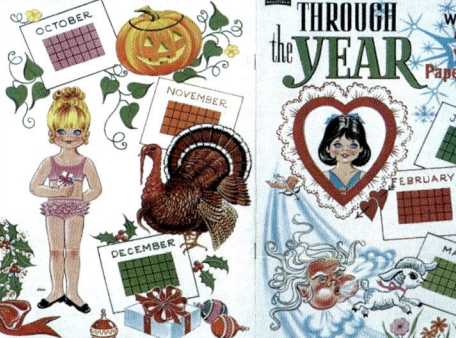
1220 Through the Year with 3 Paper Dolls (1346)

Saalfield

4418 Happiness is Babyland 1966 (1352)

2791 Mother and Daughter (2618)

2784 Robin Hood (2748)

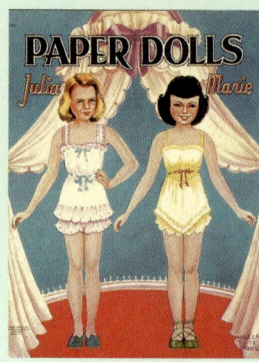
1530 Paper Dolls 1948 (2426)

1335 Round the Clock 1963 (2764)

4261 Susan Dey 1972/73 (4218)

2627 Wedding Day 1961 (2721)

1535 Hollywood Fashions 1949 (2427)

1724 Bonny Paper Dolls (6079)

1726 Leading Ladies (2733)

2795 Champion (2757)

2794 Paper Doll's with Early American Costumes (4411)

2796 Parade of Paper Dolls 1960 (2760)

Saalfield

1360 Fiesta 1965 (2487)

2179 Paper Dolls with Costumes of 21 Nations 1938 (2106)

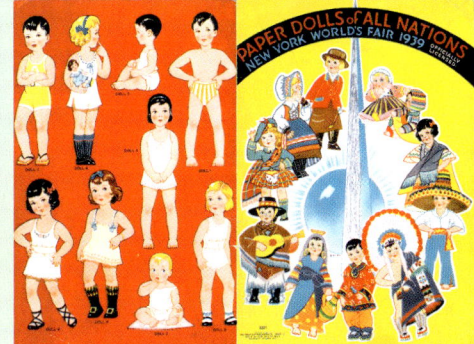
2227 Paper Dolls of All Nations 1939 (2106) Courtesy of Peggy Ell

2771 Fiesta (2487)

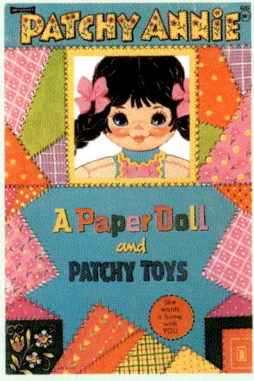
4282 Patchy Annie (6058)

2786 Indian Princess (4406)

2591 Five Baby Paper Dolls 1948 (2348)

1531 High School Paper Dolls 1948 (2425)

1544 Vanity Paper Dolls 1951 (2425)

2750 Polka Dot Darlings 1957 (6027)

4407 Butterfly Ballet (6093)

2705 Classmates 1948 (1664)

Saalfield

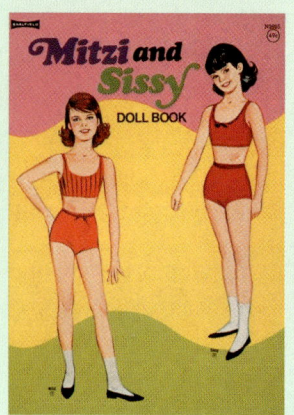
N3965
Mitzi and Sissy (4446)

1953 Four Cousins 1941 (2216)

128 Patty and Sue 1944 (2216)

4423 Mardi Gras (4408)

2704 Fashion Plate 1948 (2462)

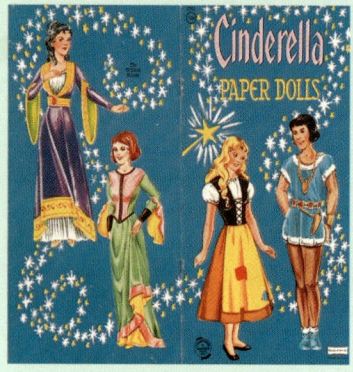
1731 Cinderella (2590)

1744 Pretty as a Picture (2739)

2589 Lovely Lady 1948 (2475)

2483 Juniors 1945 (2400)

304 The Kelly Sisters 1944 (1782)

274 Playtime Paper Dolls 1942 (885)

Saalfield

36

4478 Bubble Party (6092) Courtesy of Virginia Crossley

1355 Playtime Pals (6020) Courtesy of Virginia Crossley

2793 Lucky (2451) See page 5 for more information on this book

2596 The Well Dressed Girl (2451) See page 5 for more information on this book.

1742 Holiday (2737)

4351 Beautiful Models (from 2 books, #2739 & 2712) Courtesy of Virginia Crossley

4412 Pageant (4438) with inside front & back covers Courtesy of Virginia Crossley

2707 Ten of Us (2519) Courtesy of Virginia Crossley

2770 Career Girls (2731) Courtesy of Virginia Crossley

Saalfield

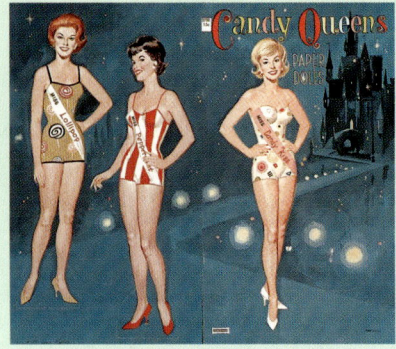
2732 Candy Queens (2737) Courtesy of Pam Kalla

1308 Star Bright 1960 (4420) Courtesy of Pam Kalla

1358 The Melody Four (4423)

2587 Summer Date 1948 (2518) Courtesy of Peggy Ell

1513 Outdoor Paper Dolls 1948 (2518)

1733 Calypso (2723)

2296 Paper Dolls 1940 (230)

4408 Pepe 1961 (2712 with Pepe doll added)

313 Air, Land and Sea (2445) Courtesy of Virginia Crossley

Saalfield

38

1520 Smart Paper Dolls 1940 (2242)

1521 Model Paper Dolls (2242)

2673 Lovely Lady (2722)

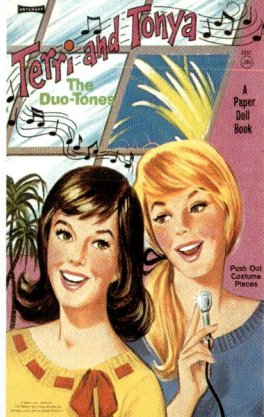
4241 Terri and Tonya 1966/70 (4469)

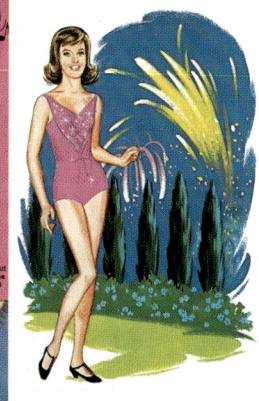

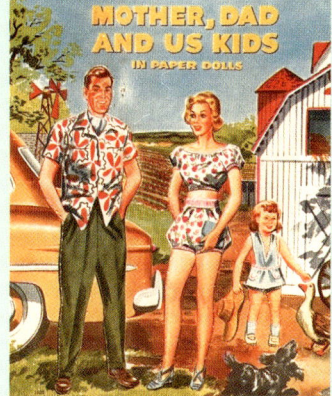
1503 Mother, Dad and Us Kids 1949 (2564) Front cover only, back cover same as the original book 2564

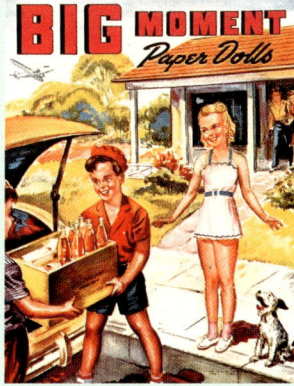
2585 Big Moment 1948 (2410) Just the doll on this front cover is re-drawn. The dolls on the back cover are the same as those in 2410

2592 Lots of Little Paper Dolls 1949 (2313)

1589 Dolls You Love to Dress 1949 (2438)

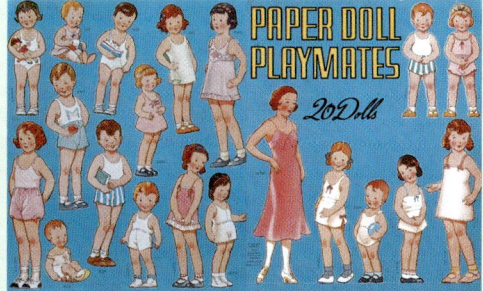
154 Paper Doll Playmates 1940 (885) Courtesy of Virginia Crossley

1588 Belle of the Ball 1948 (2492)

Saalfield

39

6050 The Partridge Family - Box set (5137) Doll of Chris is now blond & dressed differently. Tracy & mother are also dressed in different clothes

6055 Julia - Box set (4435)

259 Paper Dolls and Dresses 1940 (2242)

4442 Fashion Land (4407)

1720 Date Time (2740)

1757 Schoolmates (2759)

1350 Baby Brother (2783)

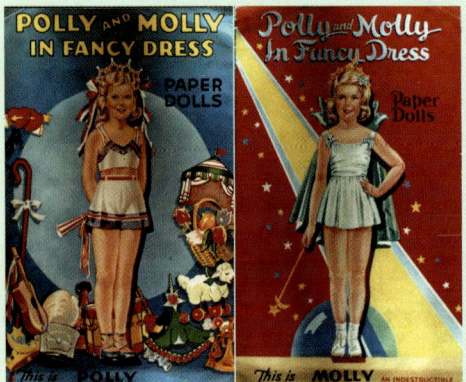
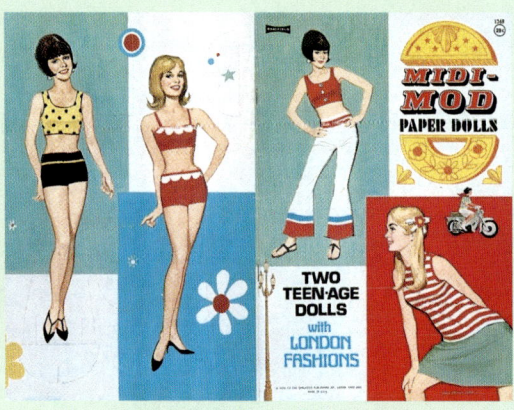

2467 Polly and Molly in Fancy Dress 1943 (1787) Courtesy of Betsy Slap

1348 Midi-Mod 1966 (4439)

2740 Happy Birthday (2743)

Saalfield

40

2497 Raggedy Ann and Andy 1944 $75 - 100   **2500 Baby Sparkle Plenty** 1948 $50 - 75

Baby Sparkle Plenty
Baby Sparkle Plenty #2500 (book), #1510 (four page soft cover jobber book) and #5160 (box set) were all published in 1948. The three dolls in the box set are heavy statuette dolls. (fig. #1, 2, and 3). The two books each use two of the dolls but have them in reverse. #2500 used fig. 1 and 3 (in reverse) and #1510 used fig. 2 and 3 (in reverse). Even though reversed it made no difference in the fit of the outfits which are the same for all three sets.

 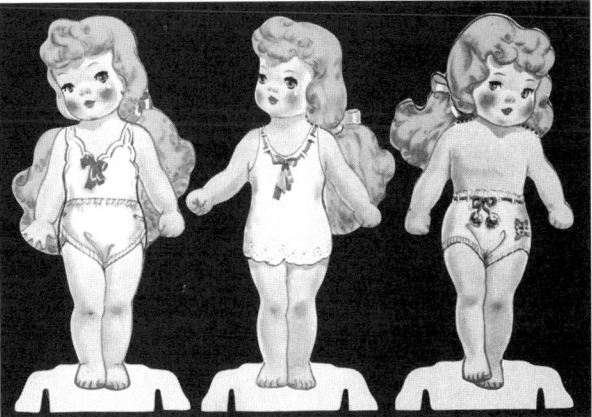

5160 Baby Sparkle Plenty, box 1948 $60 - 90   **5160** Figure 1, Figure 2, Figure3

1510 Baby Sparkle Plenty 1948   **2503 Claudette Colbert** 1945 $100 - 200

2518 Romance Paper Dolls 1945 $35 - 45   **2519 Dainty Dolls for Tiny Tots** 1946 $35 - 45

Saalfield

2520 Push-Out Paper Dolls 1946 $35 - 45

2546 Air Hostess 1947 $50 - 75

2550 Schoolmates 1947 $35 - 45

2564 Family of Paper Dolls 1947 $35 - 50

2576 Honey Kitten 1948 $35 - 45

2583 Stand-Together Dolls 1947 $35 - 45

2584 16 Paper Dolls 1948 $35 - 45

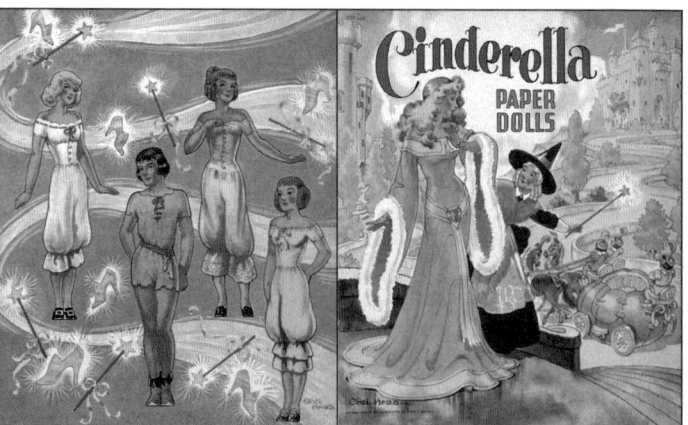
2590 Cinderella 1950 $65 - 90

Saalfield

2598 Animal Paper Dolls 1950 $50 - 75

2600 Hedy Lamarr 1951 $100 - 150

2604 Dora Grows Up 1951 $25 - 35

2605 Gigi Perreau 1951 $65 - 90

2608 Sweetheart 1951 $20 - 30

2610 Circus Paper Dolls 1952 $35 - 50

2611 Winter Girl Wendy, Summer Girl Sue 1952 $30 - 45

2612 Pals and Pets 1952 $25 - 35

Saalfield

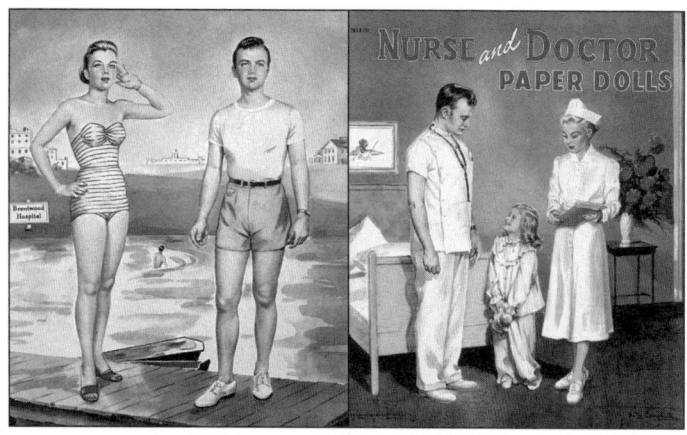
2613 Nurse and Doctor 1952 $40 - 50

2614 Picnic 1952 $25 - 35

2615 Happy Birthday 1952 $30 - 40

2616 Ballet Paper Dolls 1953 $25 - 40

2617 Merry Teens 1953 $20 - 30

2618 Southern Belles 1953 $25 - 35

2619 Best Friends 1953 $25 - 35

2620 Hat Box 1954 $20 - 30

Saalfield

2621 Pert and Pretty Paper Dolls 1954 $25 - 35   **2622 Town and Country** 1954 $25 - 35

2700 Doll House 1948 $25 - 40   **2701 Teen Shop** 1948 $25 - 30

2706 Prince & Princess 1949 $60 - 80

2708 4 Great Big Paper Dolls 1949 $40 - 55   **2709 Deluxe Mounted Dolls** 1949 $35 - 50

Saalfield

45

2712 Carmen Paper Dolls – Rita Hayworth 1948 $80 - 130   **2713 Pasting Without Paste – Little Dressmakers** 1949 $20 - 30

2715 Pasting Without Paste Paper Dolls 1950 $20 - 30

2716 Riders of the West 1950 $25 - 35   **2716** Inside front cover

2717 Square Dance 1950 $25 - 35   **2717** Inside front cover   **2717 Dutch Treat** 1961 $15 - 25

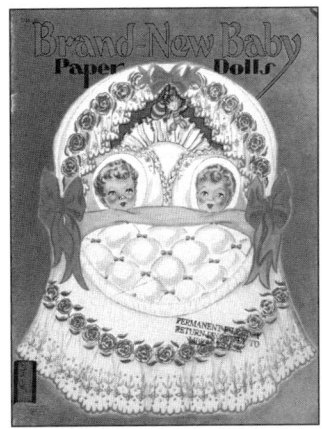 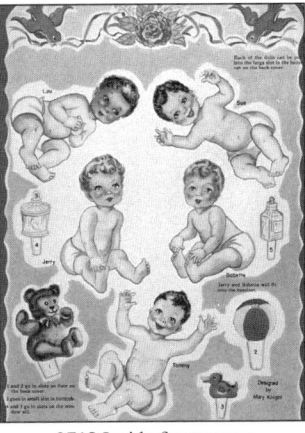 

2718 Brand-New Baby 1951 $30 - 40   2718 Inside front cover   **2721 Wedding Party** 1951 $40 - 50

2722 Faye Emerson 1952 $85 - 135   **2723 Carmen Miranda** 1952 $100 - 150

Courtesy of Betsy Slap

2724 Bonny Braids 1951 $75 - 100   **2725 Joan Caulfield** 1953 $85 - 135

2730 Calico Cut-Outs 1953 $20 - 30   **2731 Laraine Day** 1953 $75 - 125

Saalfield

47

2732 Diana Lynn 1953 $75 - 125 **2733 Linda Darnell** 1953 $85 - 135

2734 Judy Holliday 1954 $85 - 135 **2734 Penny and Her Pets** $15 - 25 (from a foreign book)

2735 June and Stu Erwin 1954 $85 - 135 **2735 Sandy** $15 - 25 (from a foreign book)

2736 Little Toddlers 1954 $25 - 35 **2737 My Little Margie** 1954 $85 - 135 (Gale Storm)

Saalfield

2738 Paper Doll Patsy and Her Pals 1954 $40 - 60

2739 Paper Dolls With Glamour Gowns 1954 $35 - 50

2740 Girl Friend – Boy Friend 1954 $30 - 40

2742 Beauty Queen no date $25 - 35

2743 Paper Doll Playmates 1955 $20 - 30

2747 Baby Sitter 1956 $25 - 40

2748 Robin Hood and Maid Marian 1956 $60 - 80

2749 Bridal Party 1956 $25 - 40

Saalfield

49

2753 Charming Paper Dolls 1957 $25 – 35

2755 Angel Paper Dolls 1957 $40 – 60

2757 Double Date 1957 $25 – 35

2758 Paper Dolls from Mother Goose 1957 $25 – 35

2759 Little Rascals – Spanky and Darla 1957 $50 – 75

2760 Majorette 1957 $25 – 35

2761 Story Princess 1957 $60 – 80

2763 Ice Festival 1957 $25 – 35

Saalfield

50

2764 A Day with Diane 1957 $15 - 25

2765 Petticoat Girls 1957 $15 - 25

2766 Fashions for the Modern Miss 1957 $20 - 30
Some books were dated 1952 by mistake.

2767 Around the World With Connie and Jean 1958 $15 - 20

Courtesy of Audrey Sepponen

2779 Lilac Time 1959 $20 - 30

2780 Sugar 'n Spice 1959 $15 - 20

2783 Baby Brother 1959 $20 - 25

2798 Storyland no date, circa 1960 $25 - 30

2882 Here Comes the Bride, box
1949 $20 - 30

Saalfield

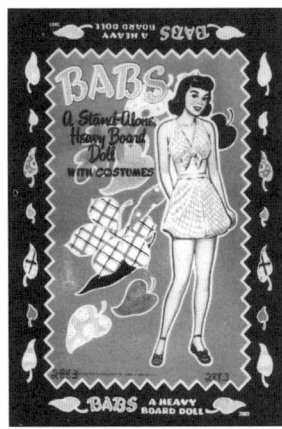  

2883 Babs, box 1949 $18 - 20   **2884 Peggy, box** 1949 $18 - 20   **2885 Sally, box** 1949 $18 - 20

P4041 Daddy's Girl 1974 $12 - 18   **N4042 For Miss America – Henrietta Hippo** 1974 $15 - 25

N4043 Colonial America 1974 $12 - 18   **N4043** Inside pages with dolls

R4112 Short-Stop Sue & Her Wardrobe, box 1975 $10 - 15   **R4113 5 Little Belles, box**
Picture from 1976 catalog $10 - 15

Saalfield

4186 My Bonnie Lassie, box 1957 $18 - 25

4187 Heidi and Peter, box 1957 $30 - 45

4211 Goldilocks and the Three Bears 1970 $20 - 30   **4211** Inside covers

4213 Nanny and the Professor 1970 $40 - 60   **4213** Inside covers

Saalfield

4214 Playmates $10 - 15   **4214** Inside covers

4217 Shamrock $10 - 15 Originated from a foreign book.   **4217** Inside covers

4218 Susan Dey 1972 $40 - 50   **4218** Inside cover   **4230 Mary, Mary Quite Contrary** 1972 $12 - 18   **4230** Inside front cover

4231 Amy Jo 1972 $12 - 18   **4231** Inside front cover   **4232 Holly** 1972 $12 - 18   **4232** Inside front cover   **4233 Ballet** 1972 $12 - 18   **4233** Inside front cover

Saalfield

4235 Sunbeam 1974 $10 - 15   **4236 Prints and Polka Dots** 1973 $10 - 15

4248 Tricia 1970 $40 - 50   4248 Inside   **4260 Teen Boutique** 1973 $10 - 15   4260 Inside

4262 Fave Teens 1973 $10 - 15   4262 Inside   **4263 Girlfriends** 1973 $10 - 15   4263 Inside

  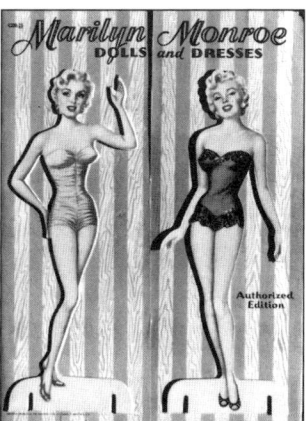

4280 Sleepy Doll 1971 $12 - 18   **4280** Inside front cover   **4308 Marilyn Monroe** 1953 $200 - 350

Saalfield

4309 Bonnie Bows 1953 $25 - 40

4310 Eve Arden 1953 $85 - 150   4310 Inside front cover   4310 Inside back cover

Courtesy of Audrey Sepponen

4311 Arlene Dahl 1953 $85 - 150   4311 Inside front cover   4311 Inside back cover

4312 Coronation Paper Dolls and Coloring Book 1953 $50 - 75

Saalfield

Courtesy of Audrey Sepponen

4318 Barbara Britton 1954 $85 - 150

4318 Inside front cover

4318 Inside back cover

4319 Ozzie and Harriet 1954 $85 - 150

4319 Inside front cover

4319 Inside back cover

4320 Rhonda Fleming Paper Dolls and Coloring Book 1954 $85 - 150

4321 Prince Valiant and Princess Aleta 1954 $85 - 150

4326 Juliet Jones Paper Dolls and Coloring Book 1955 $85 - 125

4328 Jane Russell Paper Dolls and Coloring Book 1955 $85 - 125

Saalfield

57

4343 Curiosity Shop 1971 $15 - 25　　　　4352 Loretta Young Paper Dolls and Coloring Book 1956 $85 - 150

4406 Indian Paper Dolls with Pictures to Color 1956 $25 - 40　　　4407 Ann Sothern 1956 $80 - 100

4408 Mardi Gras 1956 $35 - 50　　4408 Inside　　4409 Kim Novak Paper Dolls with Pictures to Color 1957 $85 - 150

4410 Little Miss Alice Paper Dolls – Pictures to Color 1957 $25 - 40　　4411 In Old New York – Colonial Paper Dolls with Pictures to Color
1957 $30 - 45

Saalfield

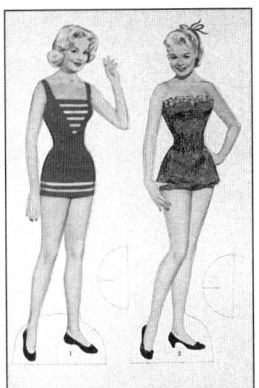

4412 Donna Reed 1959 $75 - 100   **4412** Inside   **4413 Sandra Dee** 1959 $60 - 75   **4413** Inside

Courtesy of Betsy Slap

4414 Baby Dears 1959 $20 - 25   **4414** Inside pages

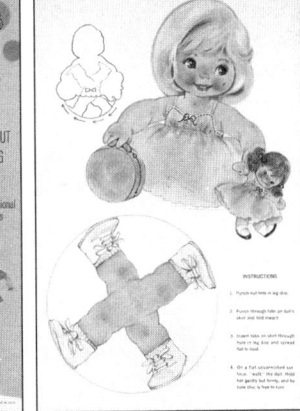

4415 Sally Twinkletoes and Peggy Twirl 1966 $12 - 18   **4416 Toodles the Toddler** 1966 $12 - 18

Courtesy of Emma Terry

4420 Sheree North 1957 $75 - 100   **4420 Here Comes the Bride** 1967 $20 - 30   **4420** Inside

Saalfield

59

4421 Gisele MacKenzie 1957 $75 - 100

4422 Virginia Mayo 1957 $75 - 125

4423 Martha Hyer 1958 $75 - 100

4424 Julie Andrews 1958 $75 - 100

4425 Evelyn Rudie 1958 $40 - 60

4428 Gisele MacKenzie 1958 $75 - 100

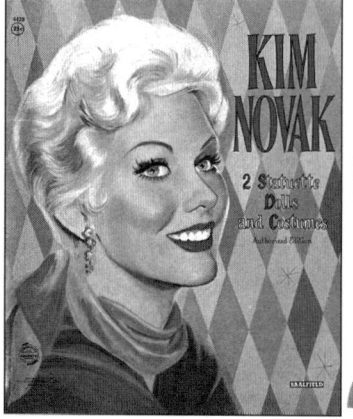
4429 Kim Novak 1958 $100 - 150

4430 Campus Sweethearts 1957 $18 - 25

Saalfield

60

4430 Kiddie Circus early 1960's $18 - 25   **4431 Flower Girls** 1957 $18 - 25

4431 Bonnets and Bows no date, circa 1960 $18 - 25   4431 Inside

4431 Ballet (A Double Doll Book) 1964 $25 - 40

4432 Tuesday Weld 1960 $60 - 75   4432 Inside

Saalfield

4432 Double Wedding (A Double Doll Book) 1964 $25 - 40

Courtesy of Audrey Sepponen

4433 Tammy Marihugh 1960 $40 - 60   **4433** Inside

4433 United Nations (A Double Doll Book) 1964 $25 - 40

4434 Polly Bergen 1958 $75 - 100   **4434** Inside

Saalfield

4434 Blondie 1968 $50 - 75   4434 Inside front and back cover

   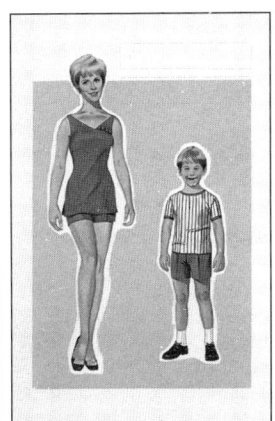 

4435 Shirley Temple 1958 $60 - 75   **4435 Julia** 1968 $50 - 75   4435 Inside front and back cover

4436 Joanne Woodward 1958 $75 - 100

4436 Finian's Rainbow 1968 $40 - 50   4436 Inside covers

Saalfield

63

4438 Brenda Starr 1964 $75 - 150   **4439 Judy Doll – Miss Teenage America** 1964 $30 - 45

Courtesy of Virginia Crossley

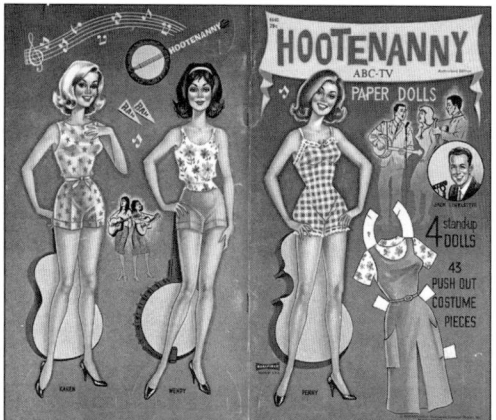

4440 Hootenanny 1964 $35 - 50   **4440** Inside front cover   **4440 Mini Moppets** 1969 $10 - 15

4441 Mini Mods 1969 $10 - 15   **4442 Sugar 'n Spice** 1969 $10 - 15

4443 Dolly and Me 1969 $10 - 15

Saalfield

4444 The Old Woman Who Lived in a Shoe 1960 $35 - 50   **4444** Inside front cover

4445 Little Women 1960 $35 - 50   **4445** Inside front cover

4446 Evelyn Rudie 1958 $40 - 60

 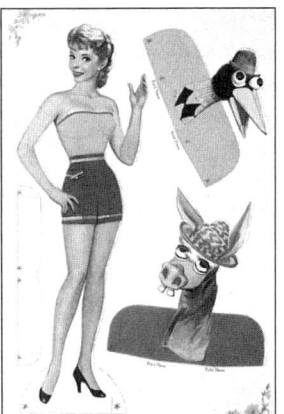

4447 Shari Lewis 1958 $60 - 75   **4447** Inside pages

Saalfield

65

 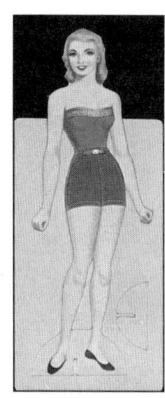  

4448 Texas Rose circa 1959 $35 - 50   **4449 Through the Year with Cindy** 1959 $20 - 30

4451 Paper Doll Playmates 1966 $20 - 25

4452 Sugar Plum Pals 1966 $20 - 25

  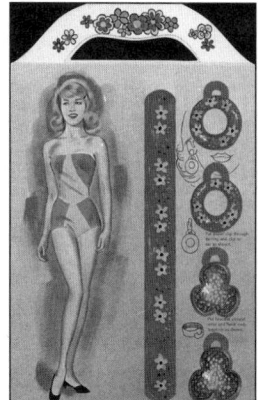

4469 Mod Fashions – Featuring Jane Fonda 1966 $45 - 60   **4469** Inside front and back cover

Saalfield

4475 White House Paper Dolls 1969 $40 - 50 **4475** Inside covers

4479 That Girl – Starring Marlo Thomas 1967 $45-60 **4479** Inside covers

4486 Wiggie the Mod Model 1967 $20 - 30 **4486** Inside front cover

4487 The Happiest Millionaire 1967 $50 - 75 **4487** Inside front and back cover

Saalfield

4488 Kewpie Kin 1967 $35 - 50   **4488** Inside front and back cover

5110 Shirley Temple 1958 $75 - 100   **5111 The Candy Stripers** 1973 $20 - 30   **5111** Inside front and back cover

5112 Lost Horizon 1973 $40 - 50   **5112** Inside front and back cover

5113 Classic Boutique $10 - 15 (from a foreign book)

Saalfield

68

5115 Dodie from My Three Sons 1971 $30 - 40   5115 Inside front and back cover

5120 Betsy McCall 1965 $35 - 45   5120 Inside

5121 The Flying Nun 1968 $40 - 60   5121 Inside front and back cover

5137 Partridge Family 1971 $40 - 50   5137 Inside front and back cover

Saalfield

5139 Hee Haw 1971 $40 - 50   **5139** Inside front and back cover

5180 Jeannette 1954 $12 - 18   **5181 Corinne** 1954 $12 - 18   **5214 Cradle Baby** 1948 $25 - 35

5225 Marie Osmond 1973 $40 - 50   **5225** Inside front and back cover

5229 Little Girls are Everything Nice $10 - 15 (from a foreign book)   **5229** Inside back cover

Saalfield

5246 Summertime Sue, Wintertime Wendy 1974 $20 - 30   **5246** Inside front cover

6020 Preschool 1958 $25 - 30

6027 Darling Dolls with Wavy Hair, box 1952 $25 - 35

6028 Lovely Dolls with Real Cloth Dresses, box 1952 $25 - 35

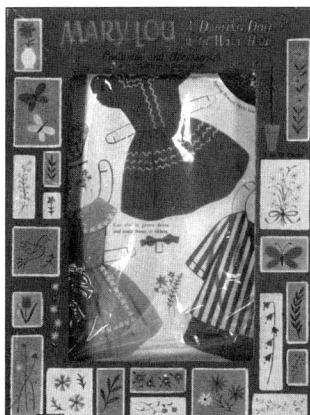

6041 Mary Lou – A Darling Doll with Wavy Hair, box 1958 $20 - 25   **6042 Little Audrey's Dress Designer Kit, box** 1962 $40 - 65

Saalfield

6045 Laugh-in Party, box 1969 $40 - 60   **6052 Sweetheart Dolls, box** 1954 $20 - 30

Elizabeth is the daughter of Mr. Henry Saalfield

6054 Elizabeth The Beautiful Bride, box 1966 $30 - 40   **6057 Fashion Whirl (game), box** 1968-1970 $30 - 50

6058 Patchy Annie 1962 $20 - 30   **6058 Inside**   **6058 The Holiday Twins Betty and Bobby, box** 1970 $10 - 15

6059 Patchwork, box 1971 $10 - 15   **6060 Shari Lewis and her Puppets, box** 1960 $45 - 65

Saalfield

6061 Make Believe and Play Stewardess, box 1970 $25 - 30   **6068** Paper Dolls with Lace-On Costumes, box 1955 $25 - 30   **6068** Janie, Sue, and Nancy

6068 All three sets of Paper Dolls with Lace-On Costumes were reprinted a number of times with new box covers.

6068 Paper Dolls with Lace-On Costumes 1964 $20 - 25 (Carol, Bunny, and Linda)   **6068** Michele, Carolyn, and Elaine 1969 $15 - 20

  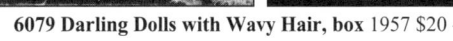

6078 Mother and Daughter, box 1963 $20 - 25   **6079** Darling Dolls with Wavy Hair, box 1957 $20 - 28

  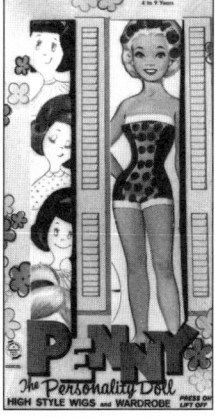 

6088 Kewpie Dolls, box 1963 $50 - 75   **6091** Penny, box 1964 $18 - 25   **6092** Connie Darling and Her Dolly, box 1964 $18 - 25

Saalfield

6093 Paper Doll Ballet, box 1957 $30 - 40

6097 Sweetheart Dolls, box 1957 $25 - 35

6116 Polly and Molly and Their Dollies 1958 $25 - 35

6117 Kathy and Sue, box 1958 $25 - 35

6128 Four Hi-Heel Standing Dolls, box 1959 $25 - 35

6160 You Are a Doll, box 1962 $25 - 40 The doll has a blank face for a child's picture.

Saalfield

6169 3 Darling Dolls, box 1964 $20 - 30

6189 6 Standing Dolls with Lace-On Costumes, box 1956 $25 - 35

6194 Darling Dolls with Wavy Hair, box 1957 $25 - 35

 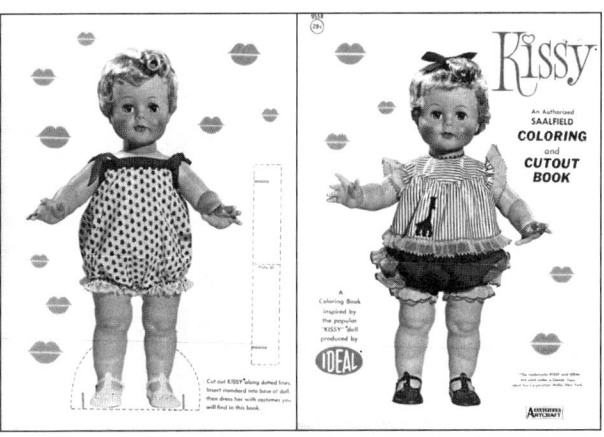

9553 Kewpies – A Coloring and Cut-Out Book 1962 $40 - 50   **9558** Kissy – Coloring and Cut-Out Book 1963 $15 - 25

Saalfield

A coloring and paper doll book. This book began as a coloring book in 1963 and paper dolls were added in 1964.

9568 Story of the Ballet 1963/1964 $18 - 25

9619 Once Upon a Wedding Day Coloring and Cut-Out Book no date $20 - 30

9632 Tressy Fashion Model $30 - 40 A paper doll and coloring book.

9859 Shirley Temple Play Kit 1958 $60 - 100

9859 Inside of the three part folder.

Saalfield

Saalfield Books Without Numbers:

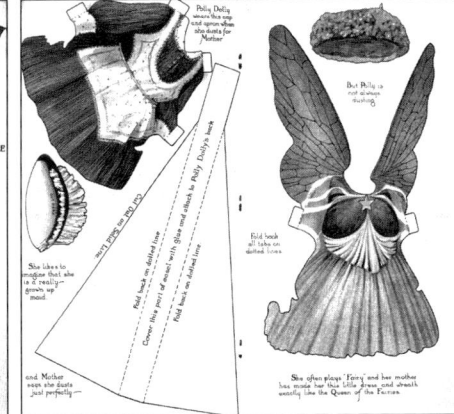

Polly Dolly Courtesy of Virginia Crossley $100 - 175

Paper Dolls, Bob and Judy no date, $15 - 18 This is a small book 6½ x 7½. It may have been in a box with other activity books.

Polly Dolly Inside pages

Some of the Saalfield catalogs of the 1920s list two books originally published by the Stetcher Lithographic Co., "Polly Dolly" and "Dolly Dimple." The listings state that the books include a doll, clothes, and story. They measure 7⅝ x 13¾. A book of "Polly Dolly" has been found which meets this description. There are 8 pages to the book which is also stated in the catalog. On the first page it reads, "Ask for Polly Dolly's Sister, Dolly Dimple." The story pages are printed on the back of the doll and clothes pages, so when they are cut out, parts of the story will show up on the back of the pieces. At the bottom of the first page of the story "Polly's Dolly's," it states, "Copyright by Stetcher Lithographic Co. Rochester, N.Y." The Saalfield Co. sold other Stetcher books as well. (See paper dolls #5 and #100)

Paper Dolls Published by the Saalfield Publishing Company:

This list also includes Artcraft books of paper dolls, Artcraft being a division of The Saalfield Publishing Company. Compiled through the help of old Saalfield catalogs, private collections and the Saalfield archives at the Kent State Libraries, this list contains both original and reprint books. All reprint books listed will carry a number in parentheses following their titles indicating the original from which the reprint is derived. Brackets without any numbers enclosed after the title indicate a reprint where the original is not definitely known. When dates are not given, either the book has no date or the date has not been verified.

1A	**Two 7¼" dolls** - envelope (Information from early Saalfield Catalog. Title not given.)	1BS	**My Sweet Dollies** - box (w/8 dresses & hats)	3AA	**Five Dollies To Cut Out & Dress** - box
1AA	**One 7¼" doll** - envelope (Information from early Saalfield Catalog. Title not given.)	1C	**My Four Dollies** - box	3B	**Happy Family** - box
		1D	**Six dolls** (information from early Saalfield catalog. Title not given.)	3B	**Six Dollies To Cut Out and Dress** - box
				3B	**Six Dollies To Cut Out and Dress** - box (different from above)
1B	**My Sweet Dollies** - box	2A	**Little Playmate** - envelope	4A	**Four 12" dolls** - box (Information from early Saalfield catalog. Title not given.)
1BS	**My Sweet Dollies** - box (w/6 dresses & hats)	2B	**Dolls I Love Best** - box		
		2BS	**The Doll I Love Best** - box	4A	**Eight dolls** - box (Information from early Saalfield catalog. Title not given.)
		3A	5½" doll on sheets w/# 3A on each sheet		

Saalfield

5	**Boy and Girl Cut-Out Doll Book,** (appeared in the 1937 Saalfield catalog) originally copyrighted 1932 by the Stecher Lithographic Company
5A	**Sheets with the movie star paper dolls** from set 3B (Charlie Chaplin, etc.) each sheet marked 5-A
5AA	**Five Dollies to Cut Out and Dress** - envelope
TR40	**My Peek-A-Boo Show Book,** stage settings, not paper dolls
VP41	**Let's Play Circus,** circus settings, not paper dolls
100	**Bettina and her Playmate Rosalie** (appeared in the 1931 Saalfield catalog) originally copyrighted by the Stecher Lithographic Company
112	**Paper Dolly Coloring Book** (2335)
113	**United We Stand** 1943
115	**Style Shop** 1943 (2397)
116	**Judy and Joyce** 1943 (2424)
128	**Patty and Sue** 1944 (2216)
129	**Paper Doll Babies** 1944 (1954)
143	**Five Paper Dolls** 1937 (230) This book came in the activity box #610
154	**Paper Doll Playmates** 1940 (885)
155	**Paper Dolls Around The World** (2106)
156	**Gloria Jean** 1940 (1661)
165	**Modern Paper Dolls** 1940 (2295)
167	**School Friends** 1940 (2313)
168	**Jack and Jill Painting Book** 1915 (1 paper doll in color & the same doll in black & white to be colored. This book has also been found with no number)
177	**Superman cut-outs** 1940 (1502)
180	**Jack and Jill Painting Book** 1915 (see description for #168)
185	**Play With Paper Dolls** 1941 (2329)
188	**Paper Dolly Book** 1941 (2126)
193	**Gloria Jean** (1664)
197	**Happy Paper Dolls**
199	**Charlie Chaplin and Paulette Goddard** (2356)
200	**Paper Dolls Painted From Life** 1941 (2358)
203	**Up To Date Paper Dolls** 1941 (2295)
204	**Ten Little Neighbors** 1941 (885)
212	**The Badgett Quadruplets** 1941 (2348)
215	**Li'l Abner and Daisy Mae** 1941 (2360)
218	**Dollies to Paint, Cut-out and Dress** (1180)
218W	**Dollies to Paint, Cut-out and Dress** (1180)
S218	**Dollies To Paint, Cut-Out and Dress** (1180) Some books have been found to contain an extra doll from 1171
X218	**Dollies To Paint, Cut-Out and Dress** 1918 (1180) Some copies of X218 have been found to have the paper dolls printed back to back so if you cut out one page you cut into the doll on the other side of the page!
222	**Country Club** 1941 (2361)
223	**Gloria Jean** 1941 [1666]
227	**Paper Dolls of All Nations** 1939 (2106)
229	**Seven Standing Dolls With Wooden Bases** 1939 - Box (230)
230	**Paper Dolls To Cut Out,** 10 dolls w/dresses, hats & playthings 1932
230	**Paper Dolls To Cut Out,** same as above but w/a different cover and dated 1939 (pages in color & to be colored)
231	**Paper Doll Box** - 10 dolls, 170 pieces - 1932 catalog
231	**Polly Pepper Paper Dolls** 1936 (2126)
232	**Doll Box** - 15 dolls, walls for nursery, 50 pieces of furnishings, 148 pieces for costumes - 1932 catalog
233	**Front and Back Paper Doll Box** 1933 (976 and 977)
235	**Play Box of Farm Cut-Outs** - stand-ups
236	**The Whole Family In Paper Dolls** - box - 1939 catalog
239	**Polly Pepper Paper Dolls** - Box (2126)
239	**Play Box Of Grocery Store Cut-Outs** - stand-ups
240	**Toy Soldiers** - Box - stand-ups
241	**The Manger Scene** - Box - stand-ups
242	**Beautiful Paper Dolls** 1941 (2358)
244	**Wild West Cut-Outs** - stand-ups
245	**Army Cut-Outs** - stand-ups
246	**Army Cut-Outs** - stand-ups
246	**Cut-Out Play Book,** dolls & nursery - 1934 catalog
247	**Firemen Cut-Outs** - Box - stand-ups
247	**Paper Doll Cut-Outs** - 1934 catalog
248	**Fireman Cut-Outs** - Box -stand-ups
249	**Cut-Out Boats** - Box - stand-ups
250	**Cut-Out Boats** - Box -stand-ups
250	**Junior Miss** 1942 (2400)
253	**Twenty Standing Dolls,** 180 pieces no box (885)
254	**Gloria Jean** 1941 - Box (1666)
254	**Kitchen Play Box** - 1939 Catalog
255	**Princess Paper Dolls** 1939 - Box (2216)
256	**Henry and Henrietta** 1939 - Box (2189)
257	**Five Paper Doll Books** - Box (2242)
258	**Paper Dolls Of All Nations,** New York Worlds Fair Edition - Box (2106)
259	**Paper Dolls and Dresses** - Box 1940 (2242)
259	**Paper Dolls At Beachside** - Box 1941 catalog (2242)
266	**Skating Paper Dolls** 1942 (2328)
268	**Paper Dolls On Parade** (2295)
268	**Mary Ann** 1932 (956)
269	**Four Sisters Paper Dolls** 1943 (2358)
269	**Mickey Mouse and Minnie Mouse** 1933 (980)
271	**Happy Children** 1942 (2329)
272	**Four Playmates** 1941 (2126)
274	**Playtime Paper Dolls** 1942 (885)
275	**Betty Jane** 1934
278	**Jane Arden** 1942 (2408)
279	**The Paper Dolls Give A Party** 1943 This book (a jobber book) was copyrighted before the original (2410)
280	**Shirley Temple Dolls and Dresses** 1934 (2112)
280	**Six Shirley Temple Dolls** 1934/1935 (2112 & 1715)
280	**Daisy Mae and Li'l Abner** 1943 (2389)
282	**Just Like Mother** 1943 (2424)
283	**The New Shirley Temple** 1942 (2425)
284	**Joan Carroll** 1942 (2426)
287	**Daisy's Cut Out Dolls** 1922
287	**Mary Martin** 1943 (2427)
290	**Shirley Temple** 1936 (1715)
294	**Quiz Kids** 1942 (2430)
294	**Little Mary Mixup and Her Friend Peggy** 1922
295	**Paper Dolls** - Rose, Ice, Cherry, Cotton, May, & Harvest Queens 1944 (2431)
299	**Little Orphan Annie** 1943 (2436)
300	**Scootles and Kewpie Doll Book** (2131)
300	**Modern Miss** 1942 (2397)
301	**Ann Sothern** 1943 (2438)
303	**Polly and Molly in Fancy Dress** 1943 (1787 Shirley Temple)
303	**Shirley Temple** 1937 (1761)
304	**Kelly Sisters** 1944 (1782 Shirley Temple)
306	**Our Paper Dolls Go To School** 1947 (2550)
306	**Schoolmates** (2550)
313	**Air, Land and Sea Paper Dolls** 1943 (2445)
314	**Military Wedding** 1943 (2446)
315	**Paper Doll Cut-Outs of Gulliver's Travels** 1939 (1261)
321	**Red, White and Blue** 1943 (2450)
322	**Claudette Colbert** 1943 (2451)
322	**Pin Up Girl** 1945 (2489)
324	**Good Neighbor Paper Dolls** 1944 (2487)
325	**Carnival Paper Dolls** 1943. This book (a jobber book) was copyrighted before the original (2488)
329	**Little Miss America** 1941 (2358)
330	**Boots and Her Buddies** 1943 (2460)
332	**Betty Field** 1943 (2462)
338	**Shirley Temple** 1938 (1773)
338	**Lucille Ball** (2475)
345	**Paper Dolly Fun** 1944 (2478)
347	**Stage Door Canteen** 1943 (2468)
348	**Hour Of Charm** 1943 (2481)
349	**Paper Dolls We Love** 1940 (2295)
350	**School Girl Paper Dolls** 1942 (2400)
351	**14 Good Little Dolls** 1941 (2329)
355	**Pin-Up Girl** 1945 (2489)
362	**Twenty Paper Dolls** 1938 (885)
363	**Paper Dolls With Costumes Of 21 Nations** (2106)
367	**Mary Martin** 1942 (2427)
368	**Mary Martin** 1944 (2492)
369	**Fashion Shop Paper Dolls** 1938 (2193)
369	**Raggedy Ann Paper Dolls** 1944 (2497)
370	**Let's Play Wedding** (2194)
378	**Claudette Colbert** 1943 (2451)
379	**Vacation Days** 1947 (2518)
379	**The Princess Paper Doll Book** 1939 (2216)
380	**Ten Happy Paper Dolls** 1947 (2519)
381	**Playhouse Paper Dolls** 1947 (2520)
383	**Ten Paper Dolls**
387	**World's Fair Paper Dolls** (2106)
388	**Cowboy and Indian Cut-Outs** 1945 - coloring book/stand-ups (2150)
392	**Little Miss America** (2358)
397	**Hollywood Fashion Dolls** 1939 (2242)
399	**Shirley Temple** 1939 (1782)
423	**Lib and Mary** 1941 - Box (2358)

Saalfield

#	Title	#	Title	#	Title
429	**Standing Paper Dolls June and Marie** 1942 - Box (2410)	859	**Dainty Dollies** (2780)	1180	**Dollies to Paint, Cutout and Dress** 1918
447	**Joan Carroll** 1942 - Box (2426)	860	**Pert and Pretty** (2620 Hat Box)	1180	**Paper Dolls to Cut out and Paint** (1180 above)
448	**Mary Martin** 1942 - Box (2427)	861	**Bonnie Lassie** (2765 Petticoat)	1184	**The Happy Family** (listed in Saalfield catalogs of the 1920s)
449	**Ann Sothern** 1943 - Box (2438)	877	**Dolly Jean, Her Paper Doll House furniture & clothes** 1932	1211	**Goldilocks and The Three Bears** 1970 (4211)
450	**The New Shirley Temple Paper Dolls** 1943 - Box (2425)	881	**Many Things To Do** 1932 (1 paper doll included)	1212	**Sweet Sue** (6092)
451	**Raggedy Ann and Andy** (2497)	885	**Paper Dolls**, 10 dolls - 180 pieces to cut out 1932	1213	**Nanny and The Professor** 1970 (4213)
452	**Claudette Colbert** 1943 - Box (2451)	895	**A Happy Family Of Paper Dolls** 1932 (230)	1214	**Playmates** (4214)
453	**Really Truly Paper Dolls** 1943 - Box of 4 books (2358)	898	**Joan and Judy's Paper Doll Box** 1943 from the following books: Army and Navy Wedding Party #2446, Sweetheart #2458, and Stage Door Canteen #2468	1215	**Woody Woodpecker's House Party** (1344)
453	**Little Miss America** 1943 (2358)			1216	**Toodles A Walking Doll** (4416)
458	**Henry and Henrietta** 1938 (2189)			1217	**Shamrock Paper Dolls** (4217)
494	**A Boxful of Paper Dolls** - 5 books - 1943/44 catalog			1218	**Susan Dey As Laurie** 1972 (4218)
503	**Paper Dolls To Dress** 1951			1219	**Heather, Jill and Anne** - Mini Model Paper Dolls 1971 (6059)
552	**Five Activity Books for girls** 1939 The books could include any five of the following: Dolly Jean, Let's Play Doctor, The Trailer Family, Kitchen Play, Housekeeping With the Kuddle Kiddies, Sunny-Dale Farm or The Grocery Store.	900	**The Patchwork Poster Book Of Mother Goose** 1927 (cut-out & paste)	1220	**Through The Year With Three Paper Dolls** (1346 Pretty As A Rose)
		916	**The Cutting and Pasting Book Of Mother Goose** 1927	1221	**Wedding Paper Dolls** 1964/71 (4432)
		936	**My Book Of Paper Dolls** - Linentex book (1171)	1222	**Ballet Stars** 1964/71 (4431)
		956	**Sally Lou** 1931	1228	**Rock-A-Bye Baby** - Box makes a cradle (230)
567	**Kindergarten Paper Dolls** - Box 50 Dolls	963	**Stand-ups, The tale of Peter Rabbit** 1934	1243	**Mother and Daughter** 1963/70 (6078)
577	**Alice, Betty, Connie and Doris** 1941 - Box (2358)	964	**Stand-ups, Adventures of Alice In Wonderland** 1934	1244	**Teddy Bear Set** 1966/70 (1352 Quintuplets)
584	**Personality Paper Dolls** - Box (2400)	971	**Let's Play Store** 1933 - stand-ups	1245	**Best Friends** 1963/70 (1339 Bonnets and Bows)
592	**Paper Dolls In Uniforms Of The U.S.A.** 1943 - Box - (2445)	973	**Luna Park Panarama Book** 1933 - stand-ups	1246	**Wedding Day** 1967/70 (4420)
593	**Junior Volunteers** - Box (2450)	974	**Wild West Panarama Book** 1933 - stand-ups	1247	**Terri and Tonya** 1966/70 (4469 Jane Fonda)
609	**Keeping Busy** box set with 5 small activity books. One book "The Toymaker" has a paper doll page in black & white. Books are dated 1937.	975	**Hillside Farm** 1933 - stand-ups	1248	**Tricia** 1970 (4248)
		976	**Donny Double** 1933	1261	**Gulliver's Travels** 1939
		977	**Dotty Double** 1933	1270	**Gulliver's Travels** 1939 - Box (1261)
		980	**Mickey Mouse and Minnie Mouse** 1933	1279	**Three Paper Dolls - Pretty As A Picture** (6068 Bunny, Linda and Carol)
610	**Happy Hours For Girls** Box of five activity books that includes one paper doll book, "Five Paper Dolls" 1937 with dolls that come from book #230.	982	**Eight Autos To Build** 1933 - stand-ups	1280	**Sleepy Doll** 1971 (4280)
		989	**The Manger Scene to set-up** 1933 - stand-ups	1281	**Paper Dolls Around The World** 1964/71 (4433)
620	**A Book For Every Day In The Week** - Box (1 book is a reprint of 881)	994	**Ten Paper Dolls** 1933 (230)	1282	**Patchy Annie** (6058)
622	**Activity Box For Girls** 1942 (like #610 but later edition, same paper doll book.)	1003	**Junior Book Box For Girls** 1940 Similar to #552. Paper doll books of Dolly Jean and Housekeeping With The Kuddle Kiddies have been found inside. The books may vary from box to box.	1283	**Nanny and The Professor** 1971/72 (4213)
				1284	**Nursery Paper Dolls** 1963/64 (1341 Baby)
711	**Western Paper Dolls** (4448)			1306	**Champion Paper Dolls** 1960 (2757)
714	**Tuesday Weld** (4432)			1307	**Parade of Paper Dolls** (2760)
715	**Tammy Marihugh** (4433)	1010	**Pam and Her Dolly** (6092)	1308	**Star Bright** (4420 Sheree North)
716	**Carnival King and Queen** (4408)	1011	**Paper Dolls With Lace-On Costumes** 1969 (6068) Box (Michele & Carolyn)	1309	**Storyland Paper Dolls** (2798)
717	**Texas Rose** (4448)	1025	**Two Paper Dolls With Lace-On Costumes** - Box (6068) [Michele & Carolyn]	1310	**Kiddie Circus** (4430)
718	**Sue and Pam** (2766)	1026	**Toodles, a walking paper doll** - Box (4416)	1311	**Pretty As A Rose** (1346)
719	**College Chums** (4430 Campus Sweethearts)	1050	**Storybook Paper Doll** (4187)	1311	**Little Models** (4431 Bonnets and Bows)
720	**Baby Brother** (2783)	1051	**Mardi Gras** (4408)	1312	**Butterfly Ballet** (6093)
721	**Peggy Lou The Calendar Girl** 1961 (4449)	1052	**Western Paper Dolls** (4448)	1312	**Pageant Paper Dolls** (4438 Brenda Starr)
731	**Merry, Merry Painting & Crayoning** This set was listed in the 1929 Saalfield catalog. It is a box set which contained 6 paper dolls with 18 hats & dresses among other activities. The dolls may be from #1180 but can not be verified until a set of #731 is found.	1053	**Shirley Temple** 1959 (4435)	1313	**Pepe and The Senoritas** 1961 (2712 Carmen)
		1054	**Flower Girls** (4431)	1313	**Kewpie Kin** 1967 (4488)
		1055	**Campus Queens** (4430)	1314	**Once Upon A Time** (4444 Old Woman)
		1056	**Robin Hood** (2748)	1314	**Babyland** 1963/69 (1341 Baby)
		1057	**Little Miss Alice** (4410)	1315	**Little Women** (4445)
		1058	**Indian Paper Dolls** 1961 (4406)	1316	**Cotton Cuties** 1960 (6027 & 6079)
		1059	**Dainty Dollies** (2780)	1316	**Little Women** 1963 (1345)
735	**Indian Paper Dolls with Papoose Lace-up & Yarn** (4406)	1060	**Pert and Pretty** (2620) - [Hat Box]	1316	**Paper Dolls Of The Ballet** (4431)
		1061	**45 Toys I Can Make** 1934 (has 1 paper doll page, same as 881)	1316	**Once Upon A Time** (4444 Old Woman)
735	**Bonnie Lassie** - lace up doll°	1061	**Bonnie Lassie Paper Dolls** (2765) [Petticoat Dolls]	1317	**The Flying Nun** 1968/69 (5121)
804	**My Book Of Paper Dolls** (1171)	1062	**Little Honey Coloring Book** (w/paper doll)	1317	**Star Time** - From 4 books - 4420 Sheree North, 6093 Ballet, 2763 Ice Festival, 2757 Double Date
850	**Storybook Paper Dolls** (4187)	1073	**Robinson Crusoe's Island Home** 1934 - stand-ups		
851	**Mardi Gras** (4408)	1074	**Walking Paper Doll Family** 1934	1318	**Mother Goose** (2758)
852	**Western Paper Dolls** (4448)	1170	**The Four Little Dolls** 1920	1319	**Sugar 'N Spice** (2780)
853	**Shirley Temple** (4435)	1171	**My Book Of Paper Dolls**	1319	**The Four Gems** (4440 Hootenanny)
854	**Flower Girls** (4431)	1178	**Faye Emerson Paper Dolls** (2722)	1320	**Mini Moppets** 1969 (4440)
855	**Campus Queens** (4430)			1320	**Here Comes The Bride** (4420)
856	**Robin Hood** (2748)			1320	**Shirley Temple** 1959 - 18" Doll (5110)
857	**Little Miss Alice** (4410)			1321	**Mini Mods** 1969 (4441)
858	**Indian Paper Dolls** (4406)			1321	**Beauty Star** (2722 Faye Emerson)

Saalfield

79

1321 **Little Miss Alice and Her Dolly** (4410)	1351 **That Girl** (Marlo Thomas) 1967 (4479)	1407 **Parade of Paper Dolls** (2760)
1322 **Sugar 'N Spice** 1969 (4442)	1351 **Juliet Jones** 1964 (4326)	1408 **Star Bright** (4420 Sheree North)
1322 **Mother Goose Paper Dolls** (2758)	1352 **Sally Twinkletoes** 1966 (4415)	1409 **Storyland** (2798)
1322 **Romance** (2732 Diana Lynn)	1352 **The Quintuplets** 1964	1410 **Kiddie Circus** (4430)
1323 **Dolly and Me** 1969 (4443)	1353 **Colonial Paper Dolls** (1345 Little Women)	1411 **Little Models** 1962
1323 **At Our House** (1330)	1353 **Mother and Daughter** (1330)	(4431 Bonnets and Bows)
1323 **Charming Paper Dolls** (2753)	1354 **Six Stand-Up Dolls From Storyland** (2798)	1412 **Butterfly Ballet** (6093)
1324 **Tina** (6160)	1354 **Bridal Party** (1342)	1413 **Pepe and The Senoritas** 1961 (2712 Carmen)
1324 **Kiddie Circus** (4430)	1355 **Playtime Pals** (6020)	1414 **Once Upon A Time** (4444 Old Woman)
1324 **Tween Age** (6169)	1355 **Heidi and Peter** (4187)	1415 **Little Women** (4445)
1325 **Laugh-In** 1969 (6045)	1356 **Wiggie The Mod Model** 1967 (4486)	1417 **Star Time** - from 4 books -
1325 **Butterfly Ballet** (6093)	1356 **Carnival On Ice** (2763)	4420 Sheree North, 6093 Ballet,
1326 **King and Queen - Mardi Gras** (4408)	1357 **Charming Punch-Out Paper Dolls** - original from foreign company, new covers drawn	2763 Ice Festival, & 2757 Double Date
1326 **A Day With Debbie** (4446 Evelyn Rudie)		1418 **Mother Goose** (2758)
1327 **Surprise Package** (6189)		1419 **Sugar and Spice** (2780)
1328 **Mademoiselle Paper Dolls** (6128)	1357 **Karen** 1965	1420 **Shirley Temple** (5110)
1329 **Garden Party Paper Dolls** (2765 Petticoat)	1358 **Wedding Day** 1964/68 (4432)	1421 **Beauty Star** (2722 Faye Emerson)
1330 **Mother and Daughter** (resemble Jackie & Caroline) no date, but published in 1962	1358 **Colonial Paper Dolls** (1345 Little Women)	1422 **Romance** (2732 Diana Lynn)
	1358 **Melody Four** (4423 Martha Hyer)	1423 **Charming Paper Dolls** (2753)
	1359 **Around The World Paper Dolls, Take A Trip With Connie and Jean** (2767)	1424 **Kiddie Circus** (4430)
1330 **The Kewpies** (1332)		1425 **Butterfly Ballet** (6093)
1331 **Dutch Treat** (2717)		1426 **King and Queen** (4408)
1331 **Gina Gillespie** 1962	1359 **Paper Dolls Around The World** 1964 (4433)	1427 **Surprise Package** 1962 (6189)
1332 **The Kewpies** 1963		1428 **Mademoiselle Paper Dolls** (6128)
1332 **Mother and Daughter** 1963 (6078)	1360 **Betsy McCall** 1965/68 (5120)	1429 **Garden Party** (2765 Petticoat)
1333 **Tepee Paper Dolls** (4406)	1360 **Fiesta** 1965 (2487)	1430 **Mother and Daughter** (1330)
1333 **Sunshine Girl** (6041)	1361 **The Kewpies** 1963/67/68 (1332)	1431 **Gina Gillespie** (1331)
1334 **Winter Carnival** (2763)	1361 **Once Upon A Time** (4444 Old Woman)	1432 **Kewpie Paper Dolls** (1332)
1334 **Blondie** 1968 (4434)	1362 **Storyland Paper Dolls** (4444 Old Woman)	1433 **Tepee Paper Dolls** (4406)
1334 **Little Women** (1345)	1362 **Lilac Time** (2779)	1434 **Winter Carnival** (2763)
1335 **Betty and Her Play Pals**	1363 **Star Time** - from 4 books - 4420 Sheree North, 6093 Ballet, 2763 Ice Festival, & 2757 Double Date	1436 **The Brothers Grimm** (1336)
1335 **Julia** 1968 (4435)		1437 **Kissy** (1337)
1335 **Round The Clock** 1963 (2764)		1438 **American Beauties** (4308)
1336 **Finian's Rainbow** 1968 (4436)	1363 **Mother and Daughter** (6078)	1500 **Favorite Paper Dolls** 1947 (2486)
1336 **The Wonderful World Of The Brothers Grimm** 1963	1364 **Ballerina Paper Dolls** (6093)	1502 **Superman Cut-Outs** 1940 stand-ups (includes some outfits)
	1365 **10 Little Theater Paper Dolls** (4444 Old Woman)	
1336 **Pre Teen** (6169)		1503 **Mother, Dad and Us Kids** 1949 (2564)
1337 **Bonnets and Bows** (1339)	1366 **Pre Teen** (6169)	1504 **Top-Notch Paper Dolls** 1948 (2484 Paper Dolls and Wardrobe Box)
1337 **Kissy Paper Doll** 1963	1366 **Bonnets and Bows** (1339)	
1338 **American Beauties** 1953 (4308)	1367 **Indian Paper Dolls** (4406)	1505 **Hour Of Charm** 1943 (2481)
1338 **Baby Paper Doll** (2783)	1367 **Let's Pretend Circus** (4430)	1506 **Raggedy Ann and Andy** (2497)
1339 **Bonnets and Bows** 1963	1368 **Dainty Dolly** (4186)	1507 **Artist Models** (2489)
1339 **Paper Doll Playmates** (4451)	1368 **Nursery Paper Dolls** (1341 Baby)	1508 **Festival 1944** (2431)
1340 **Tiny Doll Parade** circa 1963 - assorted dolls from books 4444, 6189, 2780, 2608, 4186, & 2618	1369 **Four Campus Queens** (6128)	1509 **Paper Doll Party** (2410)
	1369 **Mod Fashions, Jane Fonda** 1966 (4469)	1510 **Baby Sparkle Plenty** 1948 (2500)
	1370 **Betsy McCall** 1965/66 (5120)	1511 **Paper Dolly Book** (2126)
1340 **Baby Brother** (2783)	1371 **Career Girls** (4438 Brenda Starr)	1512 **Juke Box** (2484 Paper Dolls and Wardrobe Box)
1340 **Here Comes The Bride** 1967 (4420)	1372 **Woody Woodpecker** (1344)	
1341 **Baby Paper Dolls** 1963	1376 **Tina** (6160)	1513 **Outdoor Paper Dolls** 1948 (2518)
1341 **Toodles The Toddler** 1966 (4416)	1377 **Little Women** (1345)	1514 **Modern Girls** 1943 (2397)
1342 **Woody Woodpecker** (1344)	1378 **Bubble Party** (6092)	1515 **Paper Doll Models** 1942 (2295)
1342 **Bridal Party** 1963	1379 **That Girl** 1967 (4479)	1516 **Style Shop** 1943 (2397)
1342 **Dutch Treat** 1961 (2717)	1380 **Six Stand-Up Dolls From Storyland** (2798)	1517 **Judy and Joyce** 1943 (2424)
1343 **Dutch Treat** (2717)		1518 **Four Cousins** 1941 (2216)
1343 **Sally Twinkletoes** 1966 (4415)	1381 **Gingham and Calico** (6020)	1519 **Henry and Henrietta** 1938 (2189)
1344 **Walter Lantz Cartoon Stars** 1963 - Woody Woodpecker, Andy Panda, etc.	1382 **Paper Doll Babies** (4414 Baby Dears)	1520 **Smart Paper Dolls** 1940 (2242)
	1383 **Heidi and Peter** (4187)	1521 **Model Paper Dolls** (2242)
1344 **Kewpies in Kewpieville** (6088)	1384 **Cinderella** (2590)	1522 **Eight Standing Dolls** 1948 (2583)
1345 **Little Women** 1963	1385 **Ballet Paper Dolls** (2616)	1523 **Four Plus Four Paper Dolls** 1948 (2583)
1345 **Tina** (6160)	1386 **Wiggie The Mod Model** 1967 (4486)	1524 **Fashion Paper Dolls** 1948 (2424)
1346 **Kindergarten** (6020)	1387 **The Happiest Millionaire** 1967 (4487)	1525 **Carol Sue and Her Friends** 1948 (2421)
1346 **Pretty As A Rose** 1963	1388 **Kewpie-Kin** 1967 (4488)	1526 **Cinderella** 1950 (2590)
1347 **Paper Doll Playmates** 1966/1968 (4451)	1389 **Wedding Party** (4432)	1527 **School Friends** 1949 (2313)
1347 **Gina Gillespie** 1963 (1331)	1390 **Ballet Stars** 1967 (4431)	1528 **Cover Girl** 1949 (2492 Mary Martin)
1348 **Midi-Mod** 1966 (4439 Judy Doll)	1391 **Woody Woodpecker and Andy Panda** (1344)	1529 **Carmen Paper Dolls** (Rita Hayworth) 1948 (2712)
1348 **Shirley Temple** 1959 - 18" doll (5110)		
1348 **Tricia** 1970 (4248)	1392 **Roommates** (4438 Brenda Starr)	1530 **Paper Dolls - Julia, Marie** 1948 (2426)
1349 **Tina** (4449)	1393 **Little Sweethearts** (1339 Bonnets and Bows)	1531 **High School Paper Dolls** 1948 (2425)
1349 **Storyland Paper Dolls** (2798)		1532 **Paper Dolls At Play** 1950 (2576)
1350 **Baby Brother** (2783)	1394 **Babes In Fairyland** (1341 Baby)	1533 **Mary and Jo** 1950 (2709 Deluxe)
1350 **Little Models** (6068 Bunny, Linda and Carol)	1406 **Champion Paper Dolls** (2757)	1534 **Five Baby Paper Dolls** 1950 (2348)

1535	**Hollywood Fashions** 1949 (2427 Mary Martin)
1536	**Jolly Juniors** 1950 (2713 Pasting Without Paste)
1537	**Lots Of Little Paper Dolls** 1949 (2313)
1538	**Hedy Lamarr** 1951 (2600)
1539	**Mary Martin** 1942 (2427)
1540	**Animal Paper Dolls To Dress** 1950 (2598)
1541	**Western Dolls** 1950 (2716 Riders of the West)
1542	**Gigi Perreau** 1951 (2605)
1543	**Choose Your Partners** 1951 (2717 Square Dance)
1544	**Vanity Paper Dolls** 1951 (2425)
1545	**Dora Paper Dolls** 1951 (2604)
1546	**Paper Dolls and Their Dollies** 1951 (2608 Sweetheart)
1547	**Paper Doll Cut-Outs and Costumes** 1951 (2715 Pasting Without Paste)
1548	**Lovely Lady** 1948 (2475)
1549	**Daisy Mae and Li'l Abner** 1951 (2360)
1550	**Here Comes The Bride** 1951 (2882)
1551	**Babs** 1951 (2883)
1552	**Peggy** 1951 (2884)
1553	**Sally** 1951 (2885)
1554	**Western Paper Dolls** 1950 (2716 Riders of the West)
1555	**Hedy Lamarr** 1951 (2600)
1556	**Wedding Party** 1951 (2721)
1557	**Faye Emerson** 1952 (2722)
1558	**Carmen Miranda** 1952 (2723)
1559	**Bonny Braids** 1951 (2724)
1562	**Circus Paper Dolls** (2610)
1563	**Winter Girl Wendy, Summer Girl Sue** 1952 (2611)
1564	**Pals and Pets** (2612)
1565	**Mother and Daughter** 1952 (2424)
1566	**Big Sister and Little Sister** 1952 (2424)
1567	**Best Friends** 1952 (2400)
1568	**Mary and Pat** 1952 (2400)
1569	**Nurse and Doctor** 1952 (2613)
1570	**Picnic Paper Dolls** 1952 (2614)
1571	**Happy Birthday Paper Dolls** 1952 (2615)
1573	**Summer Date** 1948 (2518)
1574	**The Well Dressed Girl** (2451)
1575	**Ballet Paper Dolls** 1953 (2616)
1575	**Southern Belles** 1953 (2618)
1576	**Merry Teens** 1953 (2617)
1577	**Calico Cut-Outs** 1953 (2730)
1578	**Joan Caulfield** 1953 (2725)
1579	**Diana Lynn** 1953 (2732)
1580	**Pretty Paper Dolls** 1953 (4309)
1581	**Laraine Day** (2731)
1582	**Southern Belles** 1953 (2618)
1583	**Best Friends** 1953 (2619)
1584	**Linda Darnell** 1953 (2733)
1585	**Eve Arden** 1953 (4310)
1586	**Marilyn Monroe** 1953 (4308)
1587	**Arlene Dahl** 1953 (4311)
1588	**Belle Of The Ball** 1948 (2492 Mary Martin)
1589	**Dolls You Love To Dress** 1949 (2438)
1590	**Pretty As A Picture** 1954 (2426)
1591	**Judy Holiday** 1954 (2734)
1592	**June and Stu Erwin** 1954 (2735)
1593	**Hat Box** 1954 (2620)
1594	**Pert and Pretty** 1954 (2621)
1595	**Little Toddlers** 1954 (2736)
1596	**Barbara Britton** 1954 (4318)
1597	**Ozzie and Harriet** 1954 (4319)
1598	**My Little Margie** 1943 (Gale Storm) (2737)
1599	**Town and Country** (2622)
1600	**Paper Doll Patsy and Her Pals** 1954 (2738)
1601	**Prince Valiant and Princess Aleta** 1954 (4321)
1602	**Style Show Paper Dolls** 1954 (2701 Teen Shop)
1603	**Paper Dolls With Glamour Gowns** (2739)
1604	**Rhonda Fleming** 1954 (4320)
1605	**Girl Friend - Boy Friend** 1955 (2740)
1606	**Beauty Queen** (2742)
1607	**Juliet Jones** 1955 (4326)
1608	**Paper Doll Playmates** 1955 (2743)
1609	**Jane Russell** 1955 (4328)
1610	**Cinderella** 1950 (2590)
1611	**Wedding Party** (2721)
1612	**Western Paper Dolls** (2716 Riders of the West)
1613	**Choose Your Partner** (2717 Square Dance)
1614	**Loretta Young** (4352)
1615	**Paper Dolls and Their Dollies** (2608 Sweetheart)
1616	**Six Pretty Paper Dolls** 1956 (2713 & 2715 Pasting Without Paste)
1632	**Tippy Teen - coloring book** w/black & white paper dolls 1967 (4612)
1661	**Gloria Jean** 1940
1664	**Gloria Jean** 1941
1666	**Gloria Jean** 1941
1680	**Gloria Jean** 1940 - Box (1661)
1682	**Gloria Jean** 1941 - Box (1664)
1683	**Gloria Jean** 1941 - Box (1666)
1706	**Eve Arden** 1956 (4310)
1707	**Baby Sitter** (2747)
1708	**Robin Hood and Maid Marian** 1956 (2748)
1709	**Nurse and Doctor** (2613)
1710	**Shirley**
1710	**Baby Brother** (2783)
1710	**Summer Girl Sue and Winter Girl Wendy** (2611)
1711	**Happy Birthday** (2615)
1711	**Molly**
1711	**Robin Hood and Maid Marian** (2748)
1712	**Merry Teens** (2617)
1712	**Melissa**
1712	**Wedding Party** (2721)
1713	**Pretty Paper Dolls** (4309)
1713	**Judy**
1713	**Indian Paper Dolls** (4406)
1713	**Mother Goose** (2758)
1714	**Little Toddlers** 1958 (2736)
1714	**Mother Goose** (2758)
1714	**Paper Doll Models - Sue and Pam** (2766)
1714	**Play Circus** (4430)
1715	**Baby Brother** (2783)
1715	**Indian Paper Dolls** (4406)
1715	**Shirley Temple Standing Dolls** 1935
1716	**Dainty Dolly** 1962 (4186)
1716	**Ballet Paper Dolls** (2616)
1716	**Judy** (1713)
1717	**Molly** (1711)
1717	**Polka Dot Darlings** (6027)
1717	**Indian Paper Dolls** (4406)
1717	**Playtime Pals** (6020)
1718	**Ballerina Paper Dolls** (6093)
1718	**Angel Paper Dolls** 1957 (2755)
1718	**Shirley** (1710)
1718	**Southern Belles** (2618)
1718	**Cinderella** 1950 (2590)
1719	**Melissa** (1712)
1719	**Shirley Temple Standing Doll** 1935 - Box
1719	**Southern Belles** (2618)
1719	**Charming Paper Dolls** 1957 (2753)
1719	**Mardi Gras** (4408)
1720	**Little Miss Alice** (4410)
1720	**Date Time** (2740)
1720	**A Day With Diane** (2764)
1720	**Kim Novak** 1957 (4409)
1721	**The Well Dressed Girl In Paper Dolls** (2451)
1721	**Party Play** (2718 Happy Birthday)
1721	**Pert and Pretty** (2620)
1721	**Little Miss Alice** 1957 (4410)
1722	**In Old New York** 1957 (4411)
1722	**Bonnie Lassie** (2765)
1723	**Fiesta Paper Dolls** (2487)
1723	**Double Date** 1957 (2757)
1723	**Rosita Paper Dolls** (2712 Carmen, Rita Hayworth)
1724	**Paper Dolls From Mother Goose** 1957 (2758)
1724	**Bonny Paper Dolls** (6079)-[Darling Doll Box]
1724	**Play Circus** (4430)
1725	**Style Show** (2701 Teen Shop)
1725	**Spanky and Darla** 1957 - Little Rascals - (2759)
1725	**Shirley Temple** 1960 (4435)
1726	**Leading Ladies** (2733)
1726	**Sandra Dee** (4413)
1726	**Majorette** 1957 (2760)
1727	**Shirley Temple** (4435)
1727	**My Very Own Paper Doll Dollies** (6189) Only the 2 small dolls are used.
1727	**Shirley Temple Standing Doll** - Box 1935
1727	**The Story Princess** 1957 - Alene Dalton (2761)
1728	**Shirley Temple Dolls** - Box 1939 catalog
1728	**Storybook Paper Dolls** (4187)
1728	**Sheree North** 1957 (4420)
1728	**Raggedy Ann** 1961 - Raggedy Andy is on back cover (2497)
1728	**Nanny and The Professor** 1970 (4213)
1729	**Paper Doll Cut-Outs and Costumes** (2715 - Pasting Without Paste)
1729	**Patty and Jeff** (2736-Little Toddlers)
1729	**Flower Girls** (4431)
1730	**Sugar 'N Spice** (4186)
1730	**Best Friends** (2619)
1730	**Cinderella** (2590)
1731	**Ice Festival** (2763)
1731	**Cinderella** (2590)
1731	**Rosita** (2712 Carmen)
1732	**Heidi and Peter** (4187)
1732	**Play Circus** (4430)
1732	**A Day With Diane** (2764)
1733	**My Twins**
1733	**Calypso Paper Dolls** (2723 Carmen Miranda)
1733	**Curtain Time** (2732 Diana Lynn)
1734	**Senorita Paper Dolls** (2712 Carmen)
1734	**Sally**
1734	**Campus Queens** (4430)
1735	**Anne**
1735	**Ballerina** (6093)
1735	**Petticoat Girls** (2765)
1736	**Fashions For The Modern Miss** (2766)
1736	**Helen**
1736	**Baby Brother** (2783)
1737	**Paper Doll Models - Sue and Pam** (2766)
1737	**Around The World With Connie and Jean** (2767)

Saalfield

#	Title	#	Title	#	Title
1737	My Very Own Paper Dollies (6189)	1780	Cinderella (2590)	1995	Evelyn Rudie 1958 (4425)
1738	Merry Teens 1954 (2717 Square Dance)	1780	Shirley Temple Playhouse 1935 - book (1739)	2002	Daisy Mae and Li'l Abner 1943 (2360)
1738	Sandra Dee (4413)	1781	Rosita (2712 - Carmen)	2003	Carol Sue and Her Friends 1943 (2421)
1738	Indian Paper Dolls (4406)	1782	Shirley Temple 1939	2004	Modern Girls 1943 (2397)
1739	Career Girls (2731 Laraine Day)	1782	Play Circus (4430)	2005	Skating Stars 1943 (2328)
1739	Shirley Temple 1959 (4435)	1783	My Twins (1733)	2006	Six Pretty Paper Dolls 1943 (2358)
1739	Mother Goose (2758)	1784	Sally (1734)	2051	The Book of Paper Doll Cut-Outs 1927 (includes story) (1180)
1739	Shirley Temple Playhouse 1935 - Box	1785	Anne (1735)	2051	Paper Cut-Out Dollies 1927 (includes story) (1180)
1740	Baby Talk (4414 Baby Dears)	1786	Helen (1736)	2077	Four Standing Dolls (230)
1740	Lovely Lady 1948 (2722 Faye Emerson)	1787	My Very Own Paper Doll Dollies (6189)	2093	Popeye Funny Films 1934 - Theater w/Popeye Characters
1740	Storybook Paper Dolls (4187)	1787	Shirley Temple in Masquerade Costumes 1940	2094	Paper Doll Family and Their House -1934
1741	Romance Paper Dolls (2732 Diana Lynn)	1788	Sandra Dee (4413)	2097	Comic Paper Dolls 1935
1741	Dainty Dollies (2780)	1789	My Very Own Paper Doll Dollies (6189)	2099	Stand-ups of Mother Goose 1934
1741	Teen Parade (2701 Teen Shop)	1789	Shirley Temple 1960 (4435)	2100	Mary Belle 1934 (275)
1742	Holiday Paper Dolls (2737 My Little Margie)	1790	Storybook Paper Dolls (4187)	2106	Paper Dolls Around The World 1935
1742	Colonial Paper Dolls (4411 in Old N.Y.)	1791	Dainty Dollies (2780)	2109	Paper Doll Family 1935
1742	Western Paper Dolls (4448)	1791	Romance Paper Dolls (2732)	2111	Toy Soldiers - stand-ups - Box
1743	Little Ballet Dancers (6093)	1792	Western (4448)	2112	Shirley Temple Dolls and Dresses 1934
1743	My Twins (1733)	1792	Holiday Paper Dolls (2737 - My Little Margie)	2125	Marionettes - A Toy Theater 1936 - stand-ups
1743	Campus Queens (4430)	1793	Campus Queen (4430)	2126	Polly Pepper Paper Dolls 1936
1744	Sally (1734)	1793	Ballet (6093)	2128	Peter Rabbit - stand-ups 1936
1744	Pretty As A Picture (2739 Glamour Gowns)	1794	Pretty As A Picture (2739 - Glamour Gowns)	2131	Scootles and Kewpie Doll Book 1936
1744	Flower Girls (4431)	1794	Flower Girls (4431)	2139	Grandfather's Farm 1936 - stand-ups
1745	Evelyn Rudie 1958 (4425)	1795	Evelyn Rudie 1958 (4425)	2140	Housekeeping with the Kuddle Kiddies 1936
1745	Anne (1735)	1796	Little Friends (2736)	2141	Grocery Store To Set Up 1937 (971)
1746	Little Friends (2736 Little Toddlers)	H1851	Scooby Doo 1975 Coloring book/stand-ups	2142	The Three Bears 1937 catalog - stand-ups
1746	Little Miss Alice (4410)	H1852	Hong Kong Phooey 1975 - Coloring book/stand-ups	2150	Cowboys and Indians 1937 - stand-ups
1747	Bonnie Lassie - Lynette and Maureen (2765)	H1853	Korg 1975 - Coloring book/stand-ups	2158	Sunny-Dale Farm 1937 - stand-ups
1748	Play Circus (4430)	C1854	The New Zoo Revue 1975 - Coloring book/stand-ups	2160	Petunia and Patches 1937
1749	My Very Own Paper Doll Dollies (6189) -The 2 small dolls are used.	H1854	Delvin 1975 - Coloring book/stand-ups	2164	Dresses Worn By The "First Ladies" Of The White House 1937
1750	Helen (1736)	H1855	Valley Of The Dinosaurs 1975 - Coloring book/stand-ups	2169	The Trailer Family 1938 - has 4 stand-up dolls but no outfits
1751	Flower Girls (4431)	C1855	Animal World 1975 - Coloring book/stand-ups	2171	Caps to Put Together - Fire Chief, Police Captain, etc.
1752	Sugar 'N' Spice (4186)	H1856	Speed Buggy 1975 - Coloring book/stand-ups	2172	Twenty Paper Dolls 1938 (885)
1753	Ring Around The Rosy (1346 Pretty As A Rose)	C1861	Run Joe Run 1975 - Coloring book/stand-ups	2173	Dolly Jean 1938 (877)
1754	Date Time 1965 (2740 Girl Friend, Boy Friend)	1863	Space 1999 - stand-ups	2175	American Soldiers 1937 - stand-ups
1755	Jo and Sue 1970 (2764)	1902	Fashion Paper Dolls 1943 (2424)	2176	Let's Play Doctor 1938
1756	Party Play (2718 Happy Birthday)	1916	Style Shop 1943 (2397)	2179	Paper Dolls With Costumes of 21 Nations 1938 (2106)
1757	Schoolmates (2759)	1925	Seven Paper Dolls 1939 (885)	2183	Kitchen Play 1938 (w/paper dolls)
1758	Paper Dolls From Mother Goose 1957 (2758)	1934	Paper Doll Dress Shop 1940 (2193)	2185	Baby Dear 1938
1760	Baby Brother (2783)	1935	Smart Paper Dolls 1940 - 3 books #1, #2, #3 (2242)	2188	Fire Fighters in Action - stand-ups 1938
1761	Robin Hood and Maid Marian (2748)	1940	Ten Paper Dolls (2313)	2189	Henry and Henrietta 1938
1761	Shirley Temple - Dolls and Dresses 1937	1945	Claudette Colbert (2503)	2193	Fashion Shop 1938
1762	Wedding Party (2721)	1945	A Dozen Paper Dolls 1941 (885)	2194	Let's Play Wedding 1938
1763	Indian Paper Dolls (4406)	1948	Rita Hayworth (Carmen) (2712)	2197	Jolly Pirates 1938 - stand-ups
1765	Shirley Temple 1936 - 34" tall	1953	Four Cousins 1941 (2216)	2205	Twenty Four Cut Out Boats 1938 - stand-ups
1767	Playtime Pals (6020)	1954	Baby Dolls 1941	2216	The Princess Paper Doll Book 1939
1768	Cinderella 1961 (2590)	1958	Outdoor Paper Dolls 1941 (2361)	2224	Ten Paper Dolls (230)
1769	Nurse and Doctor Paper Dolls 1952 (2613)	1958	My Little Margie 1954 (2737)	2226	Mary and Sue 1939 (275) & (956)
1769	Southern Belles 1961 (2618)	1968	Paper Dolly Coloring Book 1942 (2335)	2227	Paper Dolls Of All Nations 1939 - Worlds Fair Edition (2106)
1770	A Day With Diane (2764)	1970	Big Sister Paper Dolls 1942 (2329)	C2231	The New Zoo Revue 1974
1770	Shirley Temple Christmas Book 1937 (1 paper doll from #1739 - Playhouse)	1971	Brother and Sister Paper Dolls 1942 (2329)	2232	Punch-Out Drag Racing 1974 - stand-ups
1771	The Well Dressed Girl (2451)	1972	Toddler Paper Dolls 1942 (2329)	C2232	Planet Of The Apes - stand-ups
1772	In Old New York Colonial Paper Dolls (4411)	1973	Popular Paper Dolls 1943 (2358)	2241	Peter Rabbit Stand-Up Story Book 1974
1773	Fiesta (2487)	1975	Let's Play Paper Dolls 1942 - This is Polly, This is Marie (2126)	2242	Hollywood Fashion Dolls 1939
1773	Shirley Temple (Movie Wardrobe) 1938	1976	Paper Doll Models 1942 (2295)	2242	Easter Fun 1974 w/1 paper doll in black & white.
1774	Bonny Paper Dolls (6079 Darling Doll Box)	1992	My Doll Sue, My Doll Lou 1942 (2126)	2245	Goldilocks and The Three Bears 1939
1775	Style Show (2701 Teen Shop)	1993	My Paper Dolls - This Is Patsy, This Is Winnie 1942 (2126)	X2271	Santa's Punchouts - stand-ups
1776	Leading Ladies (2733)	1993	Paper Doll Models (2295)	C2272	Star Trek - Punch-out and Play Book 1975
1777	Shirley Temple (4435)			2280	The Kewpies - A Coloring & cut-out book 1962 (9553)
1778	Storybook Paper Dolls (4187)				
1779	Flower Girls (4431)				

2284	Ruth E. Newton's Paper Doll Cut-Outs 1940	
2295	Paper Dolls On Parade 1940	
2296	Paper Dolls 1940 (230)	
2298	Paper Doll Playmates 1940 catalog (885)	
2299	Paper Dolls Around The World (2106)	
2313	50 Paper Dolls 1940	
2321	Tiptop Paper Dolls 1940	
2328	Skating Party Paper Dolls 1941	
2329	14 Good Little Dolls 1941	
2335	Children Of America - Coloring/paper doll book 1941	
2348	The Badgett Quadruplets 1941	
2349	Four Playmates (2126)	
2356	Charlie Chaplin and Paulette Goddard 1941	
2358	Little Miss America 1941	
2360	Daisy Mae and Li'l Abner 1941	
2361	Debs and Sub Debs 1941	
2389	Daisy Mae and Li'l Abner 1942	
2397	The Modern Miss In Paper Dolls 1942	
2400	School Girl 1942	
2408	Jane Arden 1942	
2410	Paper Doll Party 1944	
2411	Paper Dolls - Anna, Bess, Cherry, and Dee 1943 (2358)	
2421	3 Paper Doll Books 1942 (in a partial box)	
2424	Mommy and Me 1943	
2425	The New Shirley Temple 1942	
2426	Joan Carroll 1942	
2427	Mary Martin 1942	
2430	Quiz Kids 1942	
C2431	Little Orphan Annie Activity Book 1974 (paper doll in black & white)	
2431	Festival Paper Dolls 1944	
C2432	New Zoo Revue Activity Book 1974 (paper doll in black & white)	
2434	Planet Of The Apes - cut & color book 1967/1974	
2436	Little Orphan Annie 1943	
2438	Ann Sothern 1943	
2440	Wild West Cut-Outs - stand-ups	
2445	Victory Paper Dolls 1943	
2446	Army and Navy Wedding Party 1943	
2450	Uncle Sam's Little Helpers 1943	
2451	Claudette Colbert 1943	
2458	Sweetheart Paper Dolls 1943	
2460	Boots and Her Buddies 1943	
2462	Betty Field 1943	
2466	Kelly Sisters 1944 - (1782 Shirley Temple)	
2467	Polly and Molly In Fancy Dress 1943 (1787 Shirley Temple)	
2468	Stage Door Canteen 1943	
2471	The Six Million Dollar Man - stand-ups 1975	
2475	Lucille Ball 1944	
2478	Nancy and Her Dolls 1944	
2481	Hour Of Charm 1943	
2483	Juniors Paper Dolls 1945 (2400)	
2484	Paper Dolls and Wardrobe Box 1944	
2484	Space 1999 - coloring book w/paper doll in black & white 1976	
2485	Rock-A-Bye Baby 1945	
2486	Bob and Betty 1945	
2487	Good Neighbor 1944	
2488	Carnival 1944	
2489	Artist Models 1945	
2492	Mary Martin 1944	
2497	Raggedy Ann and Andy 1944	
2500	Baby Sparkle Plenty 1948	
2503	Claudette Colbert 1945	
2510	The Wonderful World of The Brothers Grimm 1963 (1336)	
2511	Nursery Paper Dolls (1341 Baby)	
2512	Kindergarten Fashions (1339 Bonnets and Bows)	
2513	Woody Woodpecker and His Friends 1968 (1344)	
2514	Circus Paper Dolls 1964 (4430)	
2515	Junior Vogue (6128)	
2518	Romance Paper Dolls 1945	
2519	Dainty Dolls For Tiny Tots 1946	
2520	Push Out Paper Dolls 1946	
2545	Circus Coloring Book w/stand-ups	
2546	Air Hostess 1947	
2550	Schoolmates 1947	
2550	Circus Coloring Book w/stand-ups	
2551	Circus Coloring Book w/stand-ups	
2564	Family Of Paper Dolls 1947	
2573	United Nations Paper Dolls (2106)	
2576	Honey Kitten 1948	
2583	Stand Together Paper Dolls 1947	
2584	16 Paper Dolls 1948	
2585	Big Moment 1948 (2410)	
2586	Juke Box 1948 (2484 Paper Dolls and Wardrobe Box)	
2587	Summer Date 1948 (2518)	
2589	Lovely Lady 1948 (2475)	
2590	Cinderella 1950	
2591	Five Baby Paper Dolls 1948 (2348)	
2592	Lots Of Little Paper Dolls 1949 (2313)	
2593	Hollywood Fashions 1949 (2427 Mary Martin)	
2594	Senior Prom 1949 (2425)	
2595	Dolls You Love To Dress 1949 (2438)	
2596	The Well Dressed Girl 1949 (2451)	
2597	Vanity Paper Dolls (2425)	
2598	Animal Paper Dolls 1950	
2599	Doll House 1948 (2700)	
2600	Hedy Lamarr 1951	
2601	Mary Martin 1952 (2427)	
2602	Little Dressmakers 1949 (2713)	
2603	Prince and Princess 1949 (2706)	
2604	Dora Grows Up 1951	
2605	Gigi Perreau 1951	
2606	Belle Of The Ball 1948 (2492)	
2606	Sweetheart Paper Dolls (2608)	
2606	Mary & Jo (2709 - Deluxe Mounted Dolls)	
2607	The Well Dressed Girl In Paper Dolls (2451)	
2607	Pretty As A Picture (2426)	
2607	Brand New Baby (2718)	
2608	Sweetheart Paper Dolls 1951	
2608	Dora Grows Up (2604)	
2608	Circus (2610)	
2609	Daisy Mae and Li'l Abner 1951 (2360)	
2609	Fashions For The Modern Miss (2766)	
2609	Southern Belles (2618)	
2610	Circus 1952	
2610	Hat Box 1954 (2620)	
2610	Ballet Paper Dolls (2616)	
2610	Fairytale Paper Dolls 1963 (1336) (Brothers Grimm)	
2611	Diana Lynn 1953 (2732)	
2611	Winter Girl Wendy, Summer Girl Sue 1952	
2611	Ice Festival (2763)	
2611	Jane Russell 1955 (4328)	
2611	Nursery Paper Dolls (1341 Baby)	
2612	Pals and Pets 1952	
2612	Nancy Takes A Trip (2767)	
2612	Kindergarten Fashions 1964 (1339 Bonnets and Bows)	
2613	Nurse and Doctor 1952	
2613	Brand New Baby (2718)	
2613	Woody Woodpecker and His Friends (1344)	
2613	Prince and Princess (2706)	
2613	Style Show (2701 Teen Shop)	
2614	Picnic 1952	
2614	Circus Paper Dolls 1964 (4430)	
2614	Donna Reed (4412)	
2614	Paper Dolls With Glamour Gowns (2739)	
2615	Happy Birthday 1952	
2615	Girl Friend, Boy Friend (2740)	
2615	Raggedy Ann and Andy (2497)	
2615	Junior Vogue 1963 (6128)	
2616	Ballet Paper Dolls 1953	
2616	Prince Valiant and Princess Aleta 1954 (4321)	
2616	School Chums (2759)	
2617	Merry Teens 1953	
2617	Dutch Treat 1961 (2717)	
2617	Juliet Jones (4326)	
2618	Southern Belles 1953	
2618	Happy Birthday 1961 - outfits from #4431Bonnets and Bows, #2616 Ballet, #4449 Cindy, and #2760 Majorette. Dolls redrawn from #2743 Playmates.	
2619	Best Friends 1953	
2619	The Queen Of Dance (2739 Glamour Gowns)	
2620	Hat Box 1954	
2620	Wee Friends (2736 Little Toddlers)	
2621	Pert and Pretty 1954	
2621	Fashions (2779)	
2622	Town and Country 1954	
2622	Happy Holiday (2723 Carmen Miranda)	
2623	Style Show 1954 (2701 Teen Shop)	
2623	Posy Pals (6041)	
2624	Honeymoon Paper Dolls (2740 Girl Friend-Boy Friend)	
2625	Little Ballerina (2616)	
2626	Square Dance Party 1961 (2717)	
2627	Wedding Day (2721)	
2628	Girls Of The West 1961 (2716 Riders of the West)	
2629	Pre-Teen Paper Dolls 1961 (6116)	
2630	Cha-Cha-Cha (2487)	
2631	Musical Majorettes 1962 (2760)	
2632	Candy Queens 1962 (2737 My Little Margie)	
2633	Designer 1962 (2730 Calico)	
2634	Penny and Her Pets 1962 (2734)	
2635	Sandy 1962 (2735)	
2646	Eve Arden 1956 (4310)	
2647	Baby Sitter (2747)	
2648	Robin Hood and Maid Marian 1956 (2748)	
2649	Wedding Party (2749)	
2650	Polka Dot Darlings (6027)	
2651	Jane Russell 1955 (4328)	
2652	Ballet Paper Dolls (2616)	
2653	Charming Paper Dolls (2753)	
2654	Raggedy Ann and Andy 1957 (2497)	
2655	Angel Paper Doll (2755)	
2657	Double Date (2757)	
2658	Paper Dolls From Mother Goose (2758)	
2659	Little Rascals (2759)	
2660	Majorette Paper Dolls (2760)	
2661	The Story Princess (2761)	
2662	Junior Models (4309)	
2663	Ice Festival (2763)	

Saalfield

2664	**A Day With Diane** (2764)	2715	**Pasting Without Paste Paper Dolls For Little Dressmakers** 1950
2665	**The Petticoat Girls** (2765)	2716	**Riders of The West** 1950
2666	**Belle Of The Ball** 1948 (2492)	2716	**School Chums** (2759)
2666	**Fashions For The Modern Miss** 1957 (2766)	2717	**Square Dance** 1950
2667	**Around The World With Connie and Jean** (2767)	2717	**Dutch Treat** 1961
2668	**Juliet Jones** (4326)	2718	**Brand New Baby Paper Dolls** 1951
2669	**Merry Teens** (2717 Square Dance)	2718	**Happy Birthday** - Outfits from #4431 Bonnets and Bows, #2616 Ballet, #4449 Cindy, & #2760 Majorette. Dolls redrawn from #2743 Playmates
2670	**Career Girls** (2731 Laraine Day)		
2671	**Fiesta** (2487)		
2672	**Happy Birthday** (2615)	2719	**Raggedy Ann and Andy** 1950 (2497)
2673	**Lovely Lady** (2722 Faye Emerson)	2719	**The Queen Of Dance** (2739 Glamour Gowns)
2674	**Holiday** (2737 My Little Margie)		
2675	**Pretty As A Picture** (2739 Glamour Gowns)	2720	**Wee Friends** (2736 Little Toddlers)
		2721	**Wedding Party** 1951
2676	**Romance** (2732 Diana Lynn)	2721	**Fashions - A Paper Doll Book** (2779)
2677	**Nurse and Doctor** (2613)	2722	**Happy Holiday** (2723 Carmen Miranda)
2678	**Little Ballet Dancers** (6093)	2722	**Faye Emerson** 1952
2679	**Lilac Time** (2779)	2723	**Carmen Miranda** 1952
2680	**Sugar 'N Spice** (2780)	2723	**Posy Pals** (6041)
2681	**Bonny** (6079 Darling Dolls)	2724	**Honeymoon Paper Dolls** 1961 (2740 Boy Friend-Girl Friend)
2682	**Leading Ladies** (2733 Linda Darnell)		
2683	**Baby Brother** (2783)	2724	**Bonny Braids** 1951
2684	**Robin Hood** (2748)	2724	**Baby Sitter** 1956 (2747)
2685	**Bride and Groom** (2721)	2725	**Joan Caulfield** 1953
2686	**Indian Princess** (4406)	2725	**Little Ballerina** (2616)
2689	**Playtime Pals** (6020)	2726	**Square Dance Party** (2717)
2690	**Cinderella** (2590)	2727	**Wedding Day** (2721)
2691	**Mother and Daughter** (2618 Southern Belles)	2728	**Girls Of The West** (2716 Riders of the West)
2692	**Round The Clock** (2764)	2729	**Pre-Teen** 1961 (6116)
2693	**Lucky Paper Dolls** (2607 Well Dressed) which originated from (2451)	2730	**Calico Cut-Outs** 1953
		2730	**Cha-Cha-Cha Paper Dolls** (2487)
2694	**Paper Dolls With Early American Costumes** (4411)	2731	**Laraine Day** 1953
		2731	**Musical Majorettes** (2760)
2695	**Champion Paper Dolls** (2757)	2732	**Diana Lynn** 1953
2696	**Parade Of Paper Dolls** (2760)	2732	**Candy Queens** (2737 My Little Margie)
2697	**Star Bright** (4420 - Sheree North)	2733	**Linda Darnell** 1953
2698	**Storyland** (2798)	2733	**Designer Paper Dolls** (2730 Calico)
2699	**Fashions For The Modern Miss** (2766)	2734	**Penny and Her Pets**
2700	**Doll House Paper Dolls** 1948	2734	**Judy Holliday** 1954
2701	**Teen Shop Paper Dolls** 1948	2735	**June and Stu Erwin** 1954
2701	**Beauty Queen** 1955 (2742)	2735	**Sandy**
2702	**Belle Of The Ball** 1948 (2492)	2736	**The Old Woman Who Lived In A Shoe** (4444)
2702	**Paper Doll Playmates** (2743)		
2703	**Pretty As A Picture** 1948 (2426)	2736	**Little Toddlers** 1954
2703	**Brand New Baby** (2718)	2737	**My Little Margie** (Gale Storm) 1954
2704	**Fashion Plate** 1948 (2462)	2737	**Sweetheart Paper Dolls** (6160)
2704	**Dude Ranch** (2716 Riders of the West)	2738	**Paper Doll Patsy and Her Pals** 1954
2705	**Pasting Without Paste Paper Dolls** 1950 (2715)	2738	**Nancy Takes A Trip** (2767)
		2739	**Paper Dolls With Glamour Gowns** 1954
2705	**Classmates** 1948 (1664)	2739	**Raggedy Ann and Andy** (2497)
2706	**Prince and Princess** 1949	2740	**Girl Friend-Boy Friend** 1954
2706	**Sweetheart Paper Dolls** (2608)	2740	**Happy Birthday** - Outfits from #4431 Bonnets and Bows, #2616 Ballet, #4449 Cindy, & #2760 Majorette. Dolls redrawn from #2743 Playmates.
2707	**Brand New Baby** (2718)		
2707	**Ten Of Us** (2519)		
2708	**Circus** (2610)		
2708	**Four Great Big Paper Dolls** 1949	2741	**Raggedy Ann and Andy** 1944 (2497)
2709	**Deluxe Mounted Dolls With Dresses** 1949	2741	**Fashions** (2779)
2709	**Fashions For The Modern Miss** (2766)	2742	**Posy Pals** (6041)
2710	**Girl Friend - Boy Friend** 1954 (2740)	2742	**Beauty Queen**
2710	**Ballet Paper Dolls** (2616)	2743	**Donna Reed** 1961 (4412)
2711	**Ice Festival** (2763)	2743	**Paper Doll Playmates** 1955
2712	**Carmen Paper Dolls - Rita Hayworth** 1948	2744	**The Queen Of Dance** (2739)
		2744	**Brand New Baby** (2718)
2712	**Nancy Takes A Trip** (2767)	2745	**Happy Holiday** (2723-Carmen Miranda)
2713	**Prince and Princess** (2706)	2745	**Dude Ranch** (2716-Riders of the West)
2713	**Pasting Without Paste Little Dressmakers** 1949	2746	**Eve Arden** 1956 (4310)
		2746	**Prince and Princess** (2706)
2714	**Donna Reed** 1961 (4412)	2747	**Baby Sitter** 1956
2715	**Raggedy Ann and Andy** 1961 (2497)	2747	**Square Dance Party** (2717)

2748	**Robin Hood and Maid Marian** 1956	2782	**Leading Ladies** (2733 Linda Darnell)
2749	**Bridal Party** 1956	2783	**Baby Brother** 1959
2750	**Polka Dot Darlings** 1957 (6027)	2784	**Robin Hood and Maid Marian** (2748)
2751	**Jane Russell** 1955 (4328)	2785	**Bride and Groom** 1959 (2721)
2752	**Ballet Paper Dolls** (2616)	2786	**Indian Princess** (4406)
2753	**Charming Paper Dolls** 1957	2788	**Storyland Paper Dolls** 1960 (2798)
2754	**Raggedy Ann and Raggedy Andy** 1957 (2497)	2789	**Playtime Pals** (6020)
2755	**Angel Paper Dolls** 1957	2790	**Cinderella** (2590)
2757	**Double Date** 1957	2791	**Mother and Daughter** (2618 Southern Belles)
2758	**Paper Dolls From Mother Goose** 1957	2792	**Round The Clock** (2764)
2759	**Little Rascals - Spanky and Darla** 1957	2793	**Lucky Paper Dolls** (2607 Well Dressed Girl) which originated from #2451
2760	**Majorette Paper Dolls** 1957		
2761	**The Story Princess** (Alene Dalton) 1957	2794	**Paper Dolls With Early American Costumes** (4411 In Old New York)
2762	**Junior Models** (4309)		
2763	**Ice Festival** 1957	2795	**Champion Paper Dolls** (2757)
2764	**A Day With Diane** 1957	2796	**Parade Of Paper Dolls** 1960 (2760)
2765	**The Petticoat Girls and Their Party Dresses** 1957	2797	**Star Bright** (4420 Sheree North)
		2798	**Storyland Paper Dolls** 1960
2766	**Fashions For The Modern Miss** 1957	2882	**Here Comes The Bride** 1949 - Box
2767	**Around The World With Connie and Jean** 1958	2883	**Babs** 1949 - Box
		2884	**Peggy** 1949 - Box
2768	**Juliet Jones** 1955 (4326)	2885	**Sally** 1949 - Box
2769	**Merry Teens** (2717-Square Dance)	2888	**Western Push-Outs** 1950 stand-ups
2770	**Career Girls** (2731-Laraine Day)	3401A	**Funorama With Woody Woodpecker and His Friends** 1976, Has paper doll in color, clothes to be colored (1344)
2771	**Fiesta Paper Dolls** (2487)		
2772	**Faye Emerson** 1952 (2722)		
2772	**Happy Birthday** (2615)	3403A	**Patchwork Paper Dolls** 1971/72 - Has pages in color and to be colored. (6059)
2773	**Lovely Lady** (2722-Faye Emerson)		
2774	**Holiday Paper Dolls** (2737-My Little Margie)	3404A	**Favorite Fairy Tales** - stand-ups
		3407A	**Harveyland Safety First** 1972 - Coloring/punch-out toys (5116)
2775	**Pretty as a Picture** (2739 Glamour Gowns)		
2776	**Romance** (2732 Diana Lynn)	3408A	**Early America Activity Album** (Frontier Village-stand-ups) (5118)
2777	**Nurse and Doctor** 1952 (2613)		
2778	**Little Ballet Dancers** (6093)		
2779	**Lilac Time** 1959		
2780	**Sugar 'N Spice** 1959		
2781	**Bonny Paper Dolls** 1959 (6079)		

Saalfield

3642A	**Wedding Paper Dolls** 1964/71 (4432)
3643A	**Six Stand-Up Dolls From Storyland** (2798)
3644A	**Sugar and Spice** 1969 (4442)
3716	**Fess Parker Activity Book** (w/paper doll in black and white) 1964
3731	**The Addams Family Activity Book** (w/cut-outs)
3739	**Merry Christmas Fun** ornaments, stand-ups etc.
3754	**Ship To Shore** - War stand-ups
3816	**Project Go** - Space stand-ups
3827	**My Three Sons** coloring book w/ black & white paper dolls (3927)
3843	**Wedding Day** coloring /paper doll book (9619)
3927	**My Three Sons** 1971 coloring book w/black & white paper dolls.
N3941	**Pre-Teen Paper Dolls** (6169)
N3942	**Dainty Dolly Paper Dolls** (4186)
N3943	**Paper Doll Playmates** 1966/68 (4451)
N3944	**Kindergarten Paper Dolls** (6020)
3954	**Wedding Day** (9619) coloring/paper doll book
N3961	**Sugar and Spice** 1969 (4442)
N3962	**Toodles** - The Doll That Walks (4416)
N3963	**Randy and Cher** 1966 (4439 Judy Doll)
N3964	**Babyland** (1341 Baby)
N3965	**Mitzi and Sissy** (4446)
N3966	**Three Young Gals** (6169)
4009	**Really Truly Dolls** - Box - (2358)
N4041	**Dinah-Mite** 1974 - punch-out figures -stand-ups
P4041	**Daddy's Girl** 1974
N4042	**For Miss America - Henrietta Hippo** 1974
P4042	**Carnaby Street Dolls** 1973 (4260)
N4043	**Colonial America** 1974
P4043	**Teen Set** 1973 (4262)
P4044	**The Models** 1973 (4263)
N4061	**Colonial America** 1974 (N4043)
D4111	**For Miss America - Henrietta Hippo** 1974 - Box (N4042)
R4111	**Three Standing Dolls With Lace-On Costumes** 1975 - Box (6068 Michelle, Elaine, etc.)
R4112	**Short Stop Sue and Her Wardrobe** 1975 - Box
R4113	**Five Little Belles** - Box
4128	**Susan Dey** (4218)
R4131	**Sleepy Doll** - Box (4280)
4157	**Pretty Pam** 1948 - box Doll from #2467 which had re-drawn dolls of Shirley Temple #1787. In this set the clothes are also re-drawn.
4158	**Nancy Lou** 1948 box Same information as #4157
4170	**Rose** - Box (6028)
4171	**Violet** - Box (6028)
4172	**Susan** - Box (6028)
4177	**Wendy** 1953 - Box (2611)
4178	**Sue** 1953 - Box (2611)
4182	**Rose** 1952 - cloth dresses - Box (6028)
4182	**Violet** 1952 - cloth dresses - Box (6028)
4182	**Susan** 1952 - cloth dresses - Box (6028)
4186	**My Bonnie Lassie** 1957
4187	**Heidi and Peter** 1957 - Box
4211	**Goldilocks and The Three Bears** 1970
4212	**Sweet Sue and Her Dolly Ellen** (6092)
4213	**Nanny and The Professor** 1970
4214	**Playmates** - Original from foreign company, new covers by Saalfield
4215	**Woody Woodpeckers House Party** 1966/68 (1344)
4216	**Toodles A Walking Doll** (4416)
4217	**Shamrock Paper Dolls** - original from foreign company, new covers by Saalfield.
4218	**Susan Dey** 1972
4219	**Heather, Jill and Anne** 1971 (6059 Patchwork)
4220	**Through The Year With 3 Paper Dolls** (1346 Pretty As A Rose)
4221	**Wedding Paper Dolls** 1964/71 (4432)
4222	**Ballet Stars** 1964/71 (4431)
4230	**Mary, Mary Quite Contrary** 1972
4231	**Amy Jo** 1972
4232	**Holly** 1972
4233	**Ballet Paper Doll** 1972
4234	**Wee Three** 1969/73 (4440 Mini Moppets)
4235	**Sunbeam** 1974
4236	**Prints and Polka Dots** 1973
4237	**Suzanne's Wow Wardrobe** 1967/73 (4486 Wiggie)
4238	**Nanny and The Professor** 1970 (4213)
4240	**Flower Girl** 1966/69 (4452 Sugar Plum)
4241	**Terri and Tonya** 1966/70 (4469 Jane Fonda)
4242	**The Teddy Bear Set** 1966 (1352 Quintuplets)
4243	**Mother and Daughter** 1963/70 (6078)
4244	**The Teddy Bear Set** 1966/70 (1352 Quintuplets)
4245	**Best Friends** 1963/70 (1339 Bonnets and Bows)
4246	**Wedding Day** 1967/70 (4420)
4247	**Terri and Tonya** 1966/70 (4469 Jane Fonda)
4248	**Tricia** 1970
4249	**Sleepy Doll** 1971 (4280)
4250	**Tina** (6160)
4251	**Toodles The Toddler** 1966 (4416)
4252	**Woody Woodpecker and Andy Panda** (1344)
4253	**Six Stand-up Dolls from Storyland** (2798)
4254	**Dolly and Me** 1969 (4443)
4260	**Teen Boutique** 1973
4261	**Susan Dey** 1972/73 (4218) dolls redrawn wearing different clothes
4262	**Fave Teens** 1973
4263	**Girlfriends** 1973
4279	**3 Paper Dolls "Pretty As A Picture"** (6068 Bunny, Linda and Carol)
4280	**Sleepy Doll** 1971
4281	**Paper Dolls Around The World** 1964/71 (4433)
4282	**Patchy Annie** (6058)
4283	**Nanny and The Professor** 1970/71 (4213)
4284	**Nursery Paper Dolls** 1963/64 (1341 Baby)
4286	**A Day With Debbie** (4446)
4300	**Old West Stand-Ups** 1952
4304	**Tom Corbett Space Cadet Push-Outs** 1952 stand-ups
4305	**Circus Push-Outs** 1953 stand-ups
4308	**Marilyn Monroe** 1953
4309	**Bonnie Bows** 1953
4310	**Eve Arden** 1953
4311	**Arlene Dahl** 1953
4312	**Coronation Paper Dolls and Coloring Book** 1953
4316	**Project Go! Big Space Punchouts** (stand-ups) no date
4317	**Meadow Brook Farm** - A Punch-out Panorama Book
4318	**Barbara Britton** 1954
4319	**Ozzie and Harriet** 1954
4320	**Rhonda Fleming Paper Dolls & Coloring book** 1954
4321	**Prince Valiant and Princess Aleta** 1954
4322	**Play Train** 1954 - stand-ups & coloring book
4323	**Marilyn Monroe** 1954 (4308)
4326	**Juliet Jones Paper Dolls & Coloring book** 1955
4327	**Paper Doll Parade** (12 dolls from 3 books - Southern Belles #2618, Dora #2604, & Square Dance #2717)
4328	**Jane Russell Paper Dolls & Coloring book** 1955
4329	**Finian's Rainbow** 1968 (4436)
4329	**17 Paper Dolls** (from 3 books #2608 Sweetheart, #2616 Ballet, & #2615 Happy Birthday)
4330	**Four Great Big Paper Dolls** (2708)
4331	**The Addams Family** 1965 Activity book with cut-outs
4343	**Curiosity Shop** 1971
4344	**The Teddy Bear Set** 1966/70 (1352 Quintuplets)
4351	**Beautiful Models** (from 2 books - #2739 Glamour Gowns & #2712 Carmen)
4352	**Loretta Young Paper Dolls & Coloring Book** 1956
4356	**Fess Parker** 1964 - stand-ups
4406	**Indian Paper Dolls With Pictures to Color** 1956
4406	**Julie Andrews** (4424)
4407	**Circus Paper Dolls** (2610)
4407	**Ann Sothern** 1956
4407	**Butterfly Ballet** (6093)
4408	**Sunshine Girl** (6041)
4408	**Pepe and The Senoritas** 1961 (2712) Pepe doll added
4408	**Mardi Gras - King & Queen Statuette Dolls** 1956
4409	**Raggedy Ann and Andy Paper Dolls and Coloring Book** 1944 (2497)
4409	**Kim Novak Paper Dolls With Pictures To Color** 1957
4409	**Mother Goose** (2758)
4410	**Little Women** 1963 (1345)
4410	**Little Miss Alice Paper Dolls, Pictures to Color** 1957
4410	**Martha Hyer** 1958 (4423)
4410	**Donna Reed** (4412)
4411	**Pretty As A Rose** (1346)
4411	**In Old New York - Colonial Paper Dolls With Pictures To Color** 1957
4411	**Hatbox** (6068 Janie, Sue and Nancy)
4411	**Six Stand-Up Dolls From Storybook Land** (2798)
4412	**Donna Reed** 1959
4412	**Pageant Paper Dolls** (4438 Brenda Starr)
4412	**Gingham and Calico Cut-Outs** (6020)
4413	**Sandra Dee** 1959
4413	**Kewpie Kin** 1967 (4488)
4413	**Tina** 1969 (4449)
4414	**Babyland** 1963/69 (1341 Baby)
4414	**Baby Dears** 1959
4415	**Ann Sothern** 1959 (4407)
4415	**Sally Twinkletoes and Peggy Twirl** 1966
4416	**Paper Dolls Of The Ballet** 1964/69 (4431)
4416	**Toodles The Toddler - A Walking Paper Doll** 1966
4416	**Donna Reed** 1959 (4412)
4417	**Sandra Dee** 1959 (4413)

Saalfield

4417 **Mod Paper Dolls** 1966 (4439 Judy Doll)	4440 **Hootenanny** 1964	4466 **Donna Reed** 1959 (4412)
4417 **The Flying Nun** 1969 (5121)	4440 **Mini Moppets** 1969	4466 **Bonnets and Bows** (1339)
4418 **Happiness Is Babyland** 1966 (1352 Quintuplets)	4441 **Joanne Woodward** 1958 (4436)	4467 **Let's Play Pretend Circus Paper Dolls** (4430)
4418 **Baby Dears** (4414)	4441 **Kewpies in Kewpieville** 1966 (6088)	4467 **Sandra Dee** 1959 (4413)
4419 **The Four Gems** (4440 Hootenanny)	4441 **Mini Mods** 1969	4467 **Paper Doll Patsy and Her Pals** (from Paper Doll Patsy 2738 & Best Friends 2619)
4419 **Tuesday Weld** 1961 (4432)	4441 **Six Stand-Up Dolls From Storyland** (2798)	
4419 **Polly Bergen** 1959 (4434)	4442 **Sugar 'N Spice** 1969	4468 **12 Paper Dolls At Play** (from Playmates 2743 & Picnic 2614)
4419 **Ann Sothern** (4407)	4442 **Polly Bergen** 1958 (4434)	
4420 **Shirley Temple** 1959 - 18" doll (5110)	4442 **Fashion Land** (4407)-[Ann Sothern]	4468 **Nursery Paper Dolls and Punch-Outs** 1963/64 (Baby 1341)
4420 **Sheree North** 1957	4443 **Dainty Dolly** (4186)	
4420 **Here Comes The Bride** 1967	4443 **Dolly and Me** 1969	4468 **Baby Dears** 1959 (4414)
4420 **6 Stand-up Dolls From Storybookland** (2798)	4443 **A Day With Debbie** (4446)	4469 **Jane Fonda - Mod Fashions** 1966
	4443 **Jeannie Stand-Up and Her Kitty** (4449)	4469 **Ann Sothern** 1956 (4407)
4421 **Little Miss Alice and Her Dolly** (4410)	4444 **The Old Woman Who Lived In A Shoe** 1960	4469 **Little Friends** (Town and Country 2622 & 2736 Little Toddlers)
4421 **Bridal Party** (2749)		
4421 **Giselle MacKenzie** 1957	4444 **Ballet** 1966 (2616)	4470 **Betsy McCall** 1965/66 (5120)
4421 **Gingham and Calico Cut-Outs** (6020)	4445 **Little Women** 1960	4470 **Shirley Temple** 1959 - 18" Doll (5110)
4422 **Paper Doll Babies** (4414 Baby Dears)	4446 **Evelyn Rudie** 1958	4470 **Sheree North** (4420)
4422 **Mother Goose Paper Dolls** (2758)	4447 **Shari Lewis** 1958	4471 **Bridal Party** (2749)
4422 **Dude Ranch** (2716 Riders of the West)	4448 **Texas Rose** no date, circa 1959	4471 **Career Girls** (4438 Brenda Starr)
4422 **Virginia Mayo** 1957	4449 **Through The Year With Cindy** 1959	4471 **Marlo Thomas as "That Girl"** 1969 (4479)
4423 **At Our House** (1330 Mother and Daughter)	4450 **Coronation Paper Dolls and Coloring Book** 1953 (4312)	4471 **Gisele MacKenzie** (4421)
4423 **Martha Hyer** 1958		4472 **Julia** 1968/69 (4435)
4423 **Marilyn Monroe** (4308)	4451 **Paper Doll Playmates** 1966	4472 **Dude Ranch** (2716 Riders of the West)
4423 **Mardi Gras** (4408)	4451 **Jane Russell Paper Dolls and Coloring Book** 1955 (4328)	4472 **Virginia Mayo** 1957 (4422)
4424 **Heidi and Peter** 1961 (4187)		4472 **Costume Party With Woody Woodpecker and Friends** 1966 (1344)
4424 **Tween-Age** 1966 (6169)	4452 **Toodles** 1970 (4416)	
4424 **Julie Andrews** 1958	4452 **Sugar Plum Pals** 1966	4473 **Martha Hyer** (4423)
4425 **Heidi and Peter** (4187)	4452 **17 Paper Dolls** - from 3 books - Ballet 2616, Sweetheart 2608, & Happy Birthday 2615	4473 **Mardi Gras** (4408)
4425 **Gisele MacKenzie** 1958 (4428)		4473 **Flower Girl Paper Dolls** 1966/69 (4452 Sugar Plum)
4425 **Evelyn Rudie** 1958		
4426 **Wedding Paper Dolls** (4420)	4453 **Flower Girls** (1346-Pretty as a Rose)	4474 **Petite Paper Dolls** (6068 Bunny, Linda and Carol)
4426 **Double Date** 1963 (2757)	4453 **Four Great Big Paper Dolls** (2708)	
4426 **Dainty Dolly** 1958 (4186)	4454 **Bright Eyes** 1966 (6068)- [Carol, Bunny, and Linda]	4474 **Julie Andrews** 1958 (4424)
4427 **Heidi and Peter** 1958 (4187)		4474 **Heidi and Peter** (4187)
4427 **Cinderella** (2590)	4454 **Beautiful Models** - from 2 books - Carmen 2712 & Glamour Gowns 2739	4475 **White House** 1969
4428 **Giselle MacKenzie** 1958		4475 **Giselle MacKenzie** 1958 (4428)
4428 **Ballet** (2616)	4455 **Loretta Young Paper Doll and Coloring Book** 1956 (4352)	4475 **Evelyn Rudie** 1958 (4425)
4429 **Kim Novak** 1958		4475 **Baby Brother** 1959 (2783)
4430 **Campus Sweethearts** 1957 (A Carry Doll Kit)	4456 **Julie Andrews** (4424)	4476 **Dainty Dolly** 1958 (4186)
	4456 **Indian Paper Dolls with pictures to color** 1956 (4406)	4476 **Tina** (6160)
4430 **Kiddie Circus**		4476 **Kindergarten** 1969 (6020)
4431 **Ballet Paper Dolls** 1964 (Double Doll Book)	4457 **Circus Paper Dolls** (2610)	4477 **Heidi and Peter** (4187)
	4457 **Ann Sothern** 1956 (4407)	4477 **Little Women** (1345)
4431 **Flower Girls** (A Carry Doll Kit) 1957	4457 **Butterfly Ballet** (6093)	4478 **Giselle MacKenzie** 1958 (4428)
4431 **Bonnets and Bows** no date, circa 1960	4458 **Sunshine Girl** (6041)	4478 **Bubble Party** (6092)
	4458 **Pepe** (2712 Carmen)	4479 **Kim Novak** 1958 (4429)
4432 **Tuesday Weld** 1960	4458 **Wedding Day Paper Dolls** 1964/68 (4432)	4479 **Marlo Thomas as "That Girl"** 1967
4432 **Martha Hyer** 1958 (4423)		4479 **Through The Year With Cindy** (4449)
4432 **Double Wedding** 1964 - (Double Doll Book)	4458 **Mardi Gras** (4408)	4480 **Campus Sweethearts - A Carry Doll Kit** (4430)
	4459 **Paper Dolls Around The World** 1964 (4433)	
4433 **United Nations** 1964 - (Double Doll Book)		4480 **Kiddie Circus** (4430)
4433 **Tammy Marihugh** 1960	4459 **Kim Novak Paper Dolls and Coloring Book** 1957 (4409)	4481 **Bonnets and Bows** (4431)
4434 **Polly Bergen** 1958		4481 **Flower Girls** (4431)
4434 **Tuesday Weld** 1960/61 (4432)	4459 **Mother Goose** (2758)	4484 **Polly Bergen** 1958 (4434)
4434 **Blondie** 1968	4460 **Betsy McCall** 1965/68 (5120)	4485 **Shirley Temple** (4435)
4435 **Shirley Temple** 1958	4460 **Martha Hyer** 1958 (4423)	4486 **Wiggie, The Mod Model** 1967
4435 **Sandra Dee** (4413)	4460 **Little Miss Alice Paper Dolls** 1957 (4410)	4486 **Joanne Woodward** 1958 (4441)
4435 **Julia** 1968	4461 **Hat Box** (6068 Janie, Sue and Nancy)	4487 **Happiest Millionaire** 1967
4436 **Joanne Woodward** 1958	4461 **The Kewpies** 1963/67/68 (1332)	4487 **Shirley Temple** (4435)
4436 **Finian's Rainbow** 1968	4461 **In Old New York Paper Dolls and Coloring Book** 1957 (4411)	4488 **Kewpie Kin** 1967
4436 **Donna Reed** 1959/64 (4412)		4488 **3 Baby Dolls** (4414 Baby Dears)
4437 **Shirley Temple** (4435)	4462 **Storyland** (4444 Old Woman)	4489 **Wedding Party** 1964/1967 (4432)
4437 **Bonnets and Bows** (1339)	4463 **Mother and Daughter** 1963/68 (6078)	4489 **Little Charmers** 1960 (4186)
4437 **Tina** (4449)	4463 **Circus Paper Dolls w/pictures to color** (2610)	4490 **Shirley Temple** (4435)
4438 **Three Baby Dolls** (4414)-[Baby Dears]		4490 **Ballet Stars** 1967 (4431)
4438 **Brenda Starr** 1964	4464 **Prince and Princess Paper Dolls and Coloring Book** 1949 (2706)	4491 **Joanne Woodward** (4441)
4438 **Baby Paper Doll** (2783)		4491 **Flower Girls** 1957 - A Carry Doll Kit (4431)
4439 **Judy Doll - Miss Teen Age America** 1964	4465 **Raggedy Ann and Andy Paper Dolls and Coloring Book** 1944 (2497)	
4439 **Little Charmers** 1960 (4186)		
4439 **Paper Doll Playmates** 1966/68 (4451)	4466 **Let's Play Paper Dolls and Color The Pictures** (2612 Pals and Pets)	
4440 **Shirley Temple** 1959 (4435)		

Saalfield

4491	**Woody Woodpecker and Andy Panda** 1966/1968 (1344)
4492	**Roommates** (4438 Brenda Starr)
4492	**Polly Bergen** 1958 (4434)
4493	**Little Sweethearts** 1963/68 (1339 Bonnets and Bows)
4493	**Jeannie - A Stand-up Paper Doll and Her Kitty** (4449)
4493	**Dainty Dolly** (4186)
4494	**Babes In Fairyland** 1963/68 (1341 Baby)
4494	**The Old Woman Who Lived in a Shoe** (4444)
4495	**Tricia** 1970 (4248)
4495	**Little Women** 1960 (4445)
4512	**Tippy Teen** 1967 - Coloring Book w/black & white paper dolls (4612)
4513	**Shirley Temple's Busy Book** 1959 Black & white paper doll of Shirley's doll (5326)
4515	**Story of the Ballet** 1964 - Paper Doll/Coloring Book (9568)
4517	**Ballet Coloring Book** 1963/64 Paper Doll/Coloring Book (9568)
4580	**Once Upon A Wedding Day - Paper Doll/Coloring Book** (9619)
4585	**Betsy McCall Year' Round coloring book** 1964 w/black & white paper dolls
4586	**Once Upon A Wedding Day - Paper Doll/Coloring Book** (9619)
4612	**Tippy Teen** 1967 - Coloring book w/black & white paper dolls.
4615	**Ballet Coloring Book** 1963/64 (9568)
4695	**The Addams Family** 1965 - Coloring book/stand-ups
5017	**Modern Girls** 1950 (2216)
5033	**Paper Dolls To Dress** 1951 - Box w/4 books from 2882, 2883, 2884, & 2885
5110	**Shirley Temple** 1958
5111	**Candy Stripers** 1973
5111	**Sandra Dee** 1959 - Box (4413)
5112	**Lost Horizon** 1973
5112	**Tuesday Weld** 1960 - Box (4432)
5113	**Classic Boutique** (originated from 2 foreign books)
5114	**Nanny and the Professor** 1970/71 (4213)
5115	**Dodie from "My Three Sons"** 1971
5116	**Harveyland Safety First** 1972 - Play book
5118	**Early American Activity Album - Frontier Village** - stand-ups
5119	**Funorama - Woody Woodpecker and Andy Panda** 1972 (1344)
5120	**Betsy McCall** 1965
5121	**The Flying Nun** 1968
5122	**Models of Today** (4439 Judy Doll)
5123	**The Happy Bride** (6054)
5124	**The Flying Nun** 1968/69 (5121)
5125	**Boutique Paper Dolls** 1968 (4439 Judy Doll)
5126	**Mother Goose Paper Dolls** (2758)
5127	**Little Women** (1345)
5128	**Wedding Day** (6054)
5129	**Little Girls Are Everything Nice** (5229)
5130	**Betsy McCall** 1965 (5120)
5131	**The Flying Nun** 1968 (5121)
5132	**Models of Today** (4439 Judy Doll)
5133	**Happy Bride** (6054)
5134	**The Flying Nun** 1968 (5121)
5135	**Boutique Paper Dolls** 1968 (4439 Judy Doll)
5136	**Mother Goose** (2758)
5137	**The Partridge Family** 1971
5137	**The Partridge Family** 1971 (5137 above) Chris is redrawn as a blonde in this edition.
5138	**Patchwork Paper Dolls** 1971 (6059)
5139	**Hee Haw** 1971
5140	**Julia** 1968/71 (4435)
5141	**The Partridge Family** 1971 (5137)
5141	**Darling Paper Dolls** 1969 (4452 Sugar Plum)
5142	**Circus Stars** (4430)
5143	**The Partridge Family** 1971/72 (5137)
5144	**Darling Paper Dolls** 1966/69/72 (4452 Sugar Plum Pals)
5145	**Patchwork Paper Dolls** 1971/72 (6059)
5151	**Six Standing Dolls** 1942 - Box (Copyrighted before the original 2410)
5153	**Tony** 1949 - Box (2425)
5154	**Marcella** 1949 - Box (2425)
5160	**Baby Sparkle Plenty** 1948 (pictured w/#2500)
5160	**Shirley Temple** 1958 (5110)
5161	**Debbie Darling** - Box (6027)
5161	**Carmen Paper Dolls - Rita Hayworth** 1948 - Box (2712)
5162	**Betty Darling** (6027)
5163	**Harmony Street Activity Book** 1971
5163	**Ranchland** 1952 - Box (2716 Riders of the West)
5164	**Pets to Dress** 1952 - Box (2598)
5165	**Fashion Fun** 1952 - Box (2715 Pasting Without Paste)
5166	**Bride and Groom** 1952 - Box (2721)
5167	**Bonny Braids** 1951 - Box (2724)
5169	**Debbie Darling** 1952 - Box (6027)
5170	**Diane Darling** - Box (6079)
5171	**The Partridge Family - Pictorial Activity Album** 1973 includes stand-ups
5171	**Dottie Darling** - Box (6079)
5172	**Debbie Darling** - Box (6027)
5173	**Betty Darling** 1952 - Box (6027)
5176	**Nurse and Doctor** - Box (2613)
5177	**Birthday Party** - Box 1953 (2615)
5178	**Paper Dolls From 6 to 16** - Box (2604)
5180	**Jeanette** - Box 1954
5181	**Corinne** - Box 1954
5183	**Diana Lynn** - Box 1953 (2732)
5184	**Linda Darnell** - Box 1953 (2733)
5187	**Diane Darling** 1957 - Box (6079)
5188	**Dottie Darling** 1957 - Box (6079)
5190	**Barbara Britton** 1954 - Box (4318)
5191	**Rhonda Fleming** 1954 - Box (4320)
5194	**Colonial Paper Dolls with Magic Stay-On Costumes** - Box (4411)
5195	**Little Miss Alice** - Box (4410)
5196	**Evelyn Rudie** 1958 - Box (4446)
5197	**Donna Reed** 1960 - Box (4412)
5214	**Cradle Baby** 1948
5215	**Papoosie** 1949 - doll & story, no outfits
5219	**Ride Em Cowboy** - stand-ups
5219	**Funorama With Woody Woodpecker and His Friends** 1964 (1344)
5221	**Santa Claus Push-Outs** (tree ornaments)
5224	**The Manger scene** - stand-ups
5225	**Marie Osmond** 1973
5229	**Little Girls Are Everything Nice** - from foreign set with new covers
5230	**Mary, Mary Quite Contrary** 1972 (4230)
5231	**Amy Jo** 1972 (4231)
5232	**Holly** 1972 (4232)
5233	**Ballet Paper Doll** 1972 (4233)
5234	**Wee Three** 1969/73 (4440 Mini Moppets)
5235	**Sunbeam** 1974 (4235)
5236	**Prints and Polka Dots** 1973 (4236)
5237	**Suzanne's Wow Wardrobe** 1967/73 (4486 Wiggie)
5242	**Circus Stars, 7 Little Performers** (4430)
5243	**The Partridge Family** 1971/72 (5137)
5246	**Summertime Sue, Wintertime Wendy** 1974
5261	**Favorite Family** - stand-ups
5291	**Santa's Punch-Outs** - stand-ups
5292	**Merry Christmas Busy Book** - things to make, etc. no paper dolls
5326	**Shirley Temple's Busy Book** 1959 With black & white paper doll of Shirley's doll.
5526	**Shirley Temple's Busy Book** (5326)
5968	**Christmastime Portfolio ornaments**, stand-ups etc.
6005	**Personality Paper Dolls** (2400)
6020	**Preschool Paper Dolls** 1958 - Box
6021	**Kissy - A Paper Doll** 1965 - Box (1337)
6024	**The Happy Bride** - Box (2749)
6024	**Susan Dey** 1972 - Box (4218)
6025	**Sue, A "Just Like Me" Doll** 1958 - Box (6117)
6027	**Darling Dolls With Wavy Hair** 1952 - Box
6027	**Sleepy Doll** 1971/73 (4280)
6028	**Lovely Dolls With Real Cloth Dresses** 1952 - Box
6029	**Darling Dolls With Wavy Hair** 1961 - Box (6194)
6030	**Shirley Temple Play Kit** 1958 (9859)
6032	**Shirley Temple Play Kit** 1958 (9859)
6033	**Darling Dolls** - Box (6027)
6039	**Darling Dolls With Wavy Hair** - Box (6194)
6040	**Kathy, A "Just Like Me" Doll** - Box (6117)
6040	**Preschool Paper Dolls** - Box (6020)
6041	**Mary Lou - A Darling Doll With Wavy Hair** 1958 - Box
6042	**Little Audrey's Dress Designer Kit** 1962
6043	**Sheri Lewis and Her Puppets** 1963 - Box (6060)
6044	**Lovely Dolls W/Real Cloth Dresses** - box (6028)
6044	**Dodie** 1971 - Box (5115)
6045	**Laugh-In Party** 1969 - Box
6048	**Candy Stripers** 1973 - Box (5111)
6049	**Curiosity Shop Activity** (finger puppets) - Box
6050	**Sheri Lewis and Her Puppets** (activity box)
6050	**The Partridge Family** - Box (5137)
6052	**Sweetheart Dolls** 1954 - Box
6053	**Blondie** 1968 - Box (4434)
6054	**Happiness Is Learning How** (w/weatherman paper doll) 1973 - Box
6054	**Elizabeth the Beautiful Bride** 1966
6055	**Daisy A Darling Doll With Wavy Hair** - Box (6169)
6055	**Julia** 1968 - Box (4435)
6055	**Julia** 1970 Box (4435) Inside pages are dated 1968
6056	**Little Audrey's Dress-Up Play Doll** - standing doll (6042)
6056	**Dolly and Me** 1969 - Box (4443)
6057	**Fashion Whirl Paper Dolls** 1968/70 - Boxed game
6058	**The Holiday Twins - Betty and Bobby** 1970 - Box

Saalfield

6058	**Patchy Annie "The Rockaway Doll"** 1962 - Box
6059	**Here Comes The Bride** - Box (2749) 1956
6059	**Patchwork** 1971 - Box
6060	**Shari Lewis and Her Puppets** 1960 - Box
6060	**Sugar 'N Spice** 1971 (4442)
6061	**Make Believe and Play Stewardess** 1970 - Box
6062	**Marlo Thomas as "That Girl"** 1969 - Box (4479)
6063	**Pre-School Paper Dolls** - Box (6020)
6064	**Kindergarten Paper Dolls** 1966 - Box (6020)
6066	**Marlo Thomas as "That Girl"** - Box (4479)
6067	**Kewpie-Kins in Kewpieville** 1968 - Box (6088)
6068	**Paper Dolls with Lace-on Costumes** (Janie, Sue & Nancy) 1955
6068	**Paper Dolls With Lace-On Costumes** (Bunny, Linda & Carol) 1964
6068	**Paper Dolls With Lace-On Costumes** (Elaine, Michele and Carolyn) 1969
6069	**The Flying Nun** 1968 - Box (5121)
6071	**Party Paper Dolls** 1973, date on box, 1969 on inside pages (4442)
6072	**Mini Moppets** 1969/73 (4440)
6076	**Wedding Party Dolls** Dolls and costumes 1956 - Box (2749)
6078	**Mother and Daughter** 1963 - Box
6078	**Teen Boutique** 1973 - Box (4260)
6079	**Darling Dolls with Wavy Hair** 1957 - Box
6079	**Susan Dey** 1973 - Box (4218)
6081	**Penny** (6091)
6082	**Kissy** - 24" tall 1963 (1337)
6084	**Sandra Dee Play Kit** 1960 (4413) One doll from #4413 w/new clothes that lace on plus coloring clothes.
6088	**Kewpie Dolls** 1963 - Box
6091	**Penny "The Personality Doll"** 1964 - Box
6092	**Connie Darling and Her Dolly** 1964 - Box
6093	**Paper Doll Ballet** 1957 - Box
6093	**Connie Darling and Her Dolly** - Box (6092)
6097	**Sweetheart Dolls With Cloth Dresses** 1957
6112	**Story Princess Dolls** (Alene Dalton) 1957 - Box (2761)
6116	**Polly and Molly and Their Dollies** - Box (some boxes have 6 sheets of clothes, others have 9 sheets of clothes)
6117	**Kathy and Sue Two "Just Like Me" Dolls** 1958 (2' high)
6128	**Four Hi-Heel Standing Dolls** 1959
6128	**Beauty Queens** (6128 Four Hi-Heel standing dolls)
6143	**Kathy and Sue, 2 "Just Like Me" dolls** (6117)
6155	**Julia** - Box (4435)
6157	**The Partridge Family** 1972 - Box (5137)
6158	**Blue Belle Paper Dolls** - Box (6128)
6159	**Patchwork Paper Dolls** 1974 - Box (6059)
6160	**You Are A Doll** 1962 - has blank face for child's picture - Box
6160	**You Are A Beautiful Doll** 1963 (6160 above)
6168	**Standing Dolls with Lace-On Costumes** 1969/74 (6068)
6169	**3 Darling Dolls** 1964 - Box
6180	**TV Fun Time - Starring Woody Woodpecker** - Box (1344)
6181	**Anne, Judy and Carol, Darling Dolls with Wavy Hair** 1955 - Box (5180 & 5181 plus 1 new doll)
6189	**Six Standing Dolls with Lace-On Costumes** 1956 - Box
6194	**Darling Dolls with Wavy Hair** 1957 - Box
6212	**Preschool Paper Dolls** (6020) - Box
6312	**Preschool Paper Dolls** (6020) - Box
6631	**Ballet Paper Dolls** 1964 (4431)
6632	**Double Wedding** 1964 (4432)
6633	**United Nations Paper Dolls** 1964 (4433)
6714	**Emergency + 4** - Box - Stand-ups
6840	**Preschool Paper Dolls** (6020) - Box
6843	**Shari Lewis** (6060) - Box
6868	**Paper Dolls with Lace-On Costumes** (6068 Carol, Bunny & Linda)
7890	**Project Go - Space stand-ups** (3816)
7990	**Project Go - Space stand-ups** (3816)
8006	**Mardi Gras** (4408)
9514	**Ballet Coloring Book** Coloring/paper doll book 1963/64 (9568)
9515	**Once Upon A Wedding Day** (9619)
9518	**Tippy Teen** 1967/72 Coloring book with black & white paper dolls (4612)
9546	**Christmas in Kewpieville** 1962/66 Coloring book with one paper doll from #9553 & one new doll added. Both in black & white to be colored.
9553	**The Kewpies** - A coloring & cut-out book 1962
9558	**Kissy** 1963 paper doll/coloring book (doll from #1337)
9568	**The Story of the Ballet** - Coloring/paper doll book 1963/64
9591	**Once Upon A Wedding Day** paper doll/coloring book (9619)
9619	**Once Upon A Wedding Day** - Coloring/paper doll book
9632	**Tressy Fashion Model** - Coloring/paper doll book
9646	**Christmas in Kewpieville** 1962/66 - See description for #9546.
9652	**The Kewpies** - Coloring & cut-out book (9553)
9653	**The Kewpies** - Coloring & cut-out book (9553)
9658	**Kissy** - Box (1337)
9658	**Kissy** 1963 paper doll/coloring book (9558)
9668	**Ballet Coloring Book and Paper Doll** (9568)
9691	**Wedding Day** paper doll/coloring book (9619)
9856	**Kathy "Just Like Me"** - 2' tall 1958 (6117) - Box
9857	**Six Lace-On Dolls** - Box (6189)
9859	**Shirley Temple Play Kit** 1958
9860	**Darling Dolls with Real Hair** - Box (6079)
9861	**Paper Doll Sisters** - Box (6189)
9868	**Paper Dolls with Lace-On Costumes** (6068)
9869	**Shirley Temple Play Kit** 1961 (9859)

Books without numbers:

Gary and Beth 1939 (2242)
Don and Jack 1939 (2242)
Vicky and Marge 1939 (2242)
Peter and Suzanne 1939 (2242)
Babs and Mac 1939 (2242)

The above five 7¼ x 8½" books can be found in a small box entitled 5 Paper Doll Books #257. Ten of the Twelve dolls from #2242 Hollywood Fashion Dolls are represented in these small books.

Miss Diane (2358)
Ann, Olive and Gladys (2358)
Hattie and Kathie (2358)
Connie, Ida-Mae (2358)

The above four 7¼ x 8½" books can be found in a small box entitled Really Truly Paper Dolls #453. All 15 dolls from #2358 Little Miss America 1941 are represented. (Another box #4009 Really Truly Dolls is a re-make of box #453. Size and titles of the books are not known but are thought to be the same.)

Five Paper Dolls 1937 (230) small book, probably from an activity box.

Many Things To Do 1935 has 1 paper doll in black and white. The original book #881 was in color.

Paper Dolls, Bob and Judy small book 6½ x 7½", probably from an activity box.

Polly Dolly

Saalfield

The Merrill Publishing Company

The Merrill Publishing Company was formed in 1934 by Miss Marion Merrill. Miss Merrill graduated from high school in Chicago in 1920. Later she went on to graduate from Northwestern University with a Bachelor of Arts degree in 1933.

Miss Merrill had worked for the Western Printing and Lithographing Company in the late 1920s and up to 1933. By 1933, Miss Merrill had rough-drafted some children's books which she wanted to publish. She set out to find a reliable printer in Chicago who had the equipment and experience to produce top quality books. She was directed to the Regensteiner Corporation, developer of three and four color process printing.

In a book published in 1943 by Theodore Regensteiner*, an account is given of Miss Merrill's first visit to their office. During her interview, an agreement was worked out that Miss Merrill would submit six of her books in dummy form to a few head buyers for chain stores in New York, and, if she were able to get the buyers' approval, the Regensteiner Corporation would immediately proceed with the printing of a limited edition of each book. Needless to say Miss Merrill's books met with instant approval, and a 10-year contract was drawn up with the Regensteiner Corporation.

Right from the start, The Merrill Publishing Company produced paper dolls, story books, coloring books and other books for children. The first paper doll book was Quintuplets, The Dionne Babies #3488, 1935. This was followed by the Wedding of the Paper Dolls #3497, 1935. In 1940 The Merrill Co. published two different sets of Gone With The Wind, #3404 and #3405, and in 1941 the Ziegfeld Girl, #3466. All of these books are rare collectors items now. Through the years The Merrill Company produced over 160 paper doll books of which a small fraction are reprints.

When the contract agreement with the Regensteiner Corporation ended in December 1944, Miss Merrill had the company name changed from The Merrill Publishing Company to The Merrill Company Publishers. She found a new printer and went on to publish books for another twenty some years. Miss Marion Merrill died in 1978, and in April 1979, the company was sold to Jean Woodcock, a paper doll collector and author who now owns all of the company records and archives.

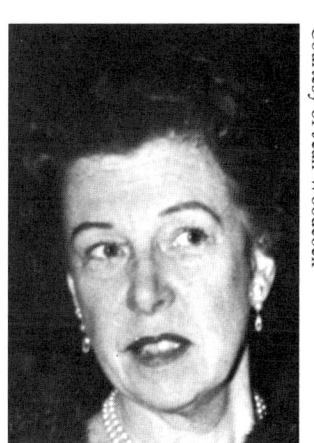

Marion Merrill

*Theodore Regensteiner, My First Seventy-five Years. Chicago. Regensteiner Corporation. 1943

Stationery used by the Merrill Publishing Co. at the time they were publishing their books on Gone with the Wind.

1542 Little Ballerina 1953 $35 - 45

Courtesy of Virginia Crossley

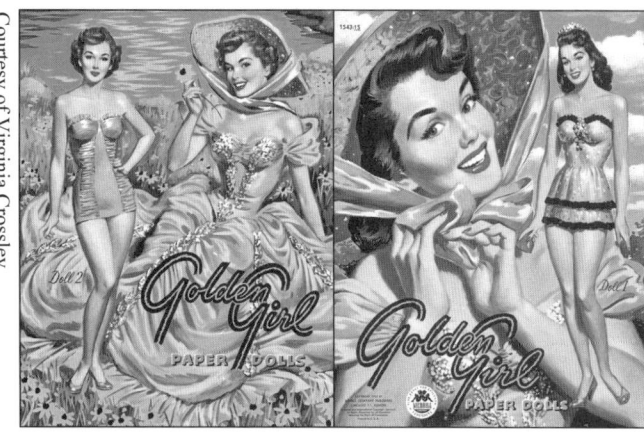

1543 Golden Girl 1953 $75 - 90   **1544 Johnny, Janey and Judy in Storybook Land** 1952 $30 - 40

1546 Around the Clock with Sue and Dot 1952 $30 - 40   **1547 The Little Fairy** 1951 $35 - 50

1548 American Beauty Paper Dolls 1951 $45 - 55   **1548 Kitty goes to Kindergarten** 1956 $35 - 45

1549 Big 'N' Little Sister 1951 $40 - 50   **1549 Sally's Silver Skates** 1956 $45 - 55

Merrill

1550 Let's Play with the Baby 1948 $40 - 60

1551 High School Dolls 1948 $65 - 90

1552 Pert and Pretty 1948 $75 - 125

1553 The Heavenly Twins and Their Guardian Angels 1948 $75 - 100

1554 Dolls From Storyland 1948 $35 - 55

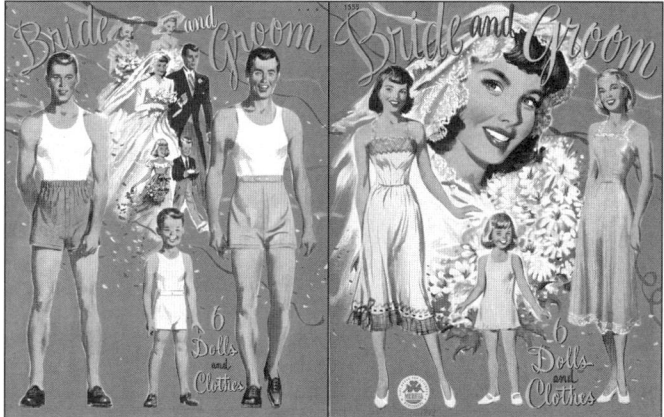
1555 Bride and Groom 1949, 8 page $30 - 40, 6 page $25 - 35

1556 Polly and her Playmates 1951, 8 pages $45 - 55, 6 pages $35 - 40

1557 The Judy Paper Dolls 1951 $35 - 40

Courtesy of Virginia Crossley

Merrill

1558 Betty Grable 1951, 8 pages $175 - 250, 6 pages $135 - 150   **1559 The Pink Wedding** 1952, 8 pages $50 - 75, 6 pages $40 - 50

1560 Betty Blue and Patty Pink 1949 $50 - 75   **1560** Inside front cover

1560 Airliner Pilot and Stewardess 1953 $60 - 75

1561 The Little Family and Their Little House 1949 $85 - 110   **1561** Inside front and back cover

Merrill

92

1561 B is for Betsy 1954 40 - 50

1562 Children in the Shoe 1949 $50 - 75

1562 Inside front and back cover

1562 Cathy goes to Camp 1954 $35 - 45

1563 Esther Williams 1950 $100 - 175

1563 Inside front cover

Merrill

1563 In Peter Pumpkin's House 1955 $25 - 35

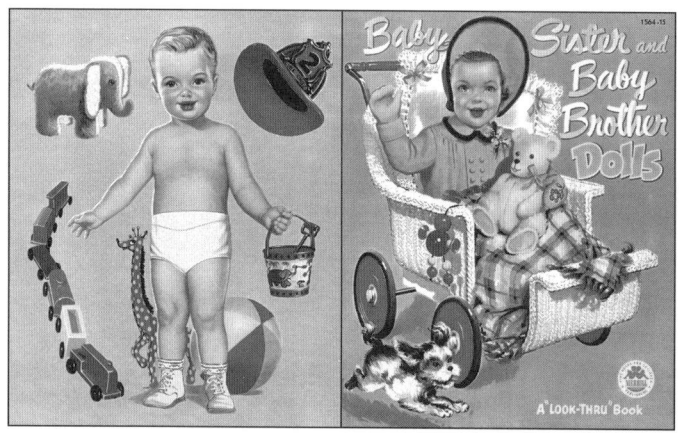 

1564 Baby Sister and Baby Brother Dolls 1950 $30 - 40   **1564** Inside front cover

Courtesy of Virginia Crossley

1564 Karen goes to College 1955 $35 - 50

2550 Ann Blyth 1952, 8 pages $100 - 175, 6 pages $90 - 125   **2550** Inside front cover

Merrill

2551 Piper Laurie 1953 $100 - 175 **2551** Inside front cover

2552 Betty Grable 1953 $175 - 250 **2552** Inside front cover

2553 Esther Williams 1953 $100 - 175 (paper doll/coloring book) **2554 Janet Leigh** 1953 $100 - 175 (paper doll/coloring book)

2562 Umbrella Girls 1956 $50 - 75 **2562** Inside front and back cover

Merrill

95

2564 Lindy-Lou 'n' Cindy-Sue 1954 $65 - 90   2564 Inside front and back cover

2565 Children 'Round the World 1955 $35 - 45   2565 Inside front and back cover

2580 Heavenly Blue Wedding 1955 $45 - 65   2580 Inside cardboard sheets of dolls

2582   6 and Sweet 16 1955 $45 - 65   2582 Inside cardboard sheets of dolls

Merrill

    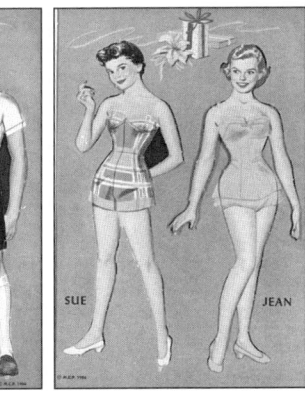

2583 Pink Prom Twins 1956 $45 - 65   **2583** Inside cardboard sheets of dolls

2584 The Ranch Family 1957 $45 - 65   **2584** Inside cardboard sheets of dolls

2968 Little Miss Christmas and Holly-Belle 1965 $50 - 75   **2968** Inside front cover   **3400 College Style** 1941 $75 - 100

Courtesy of Virginia Crossley

M3403 Stand-Up Dolls – Honey and Bunny 1936 $100 - 140

Courtesy of Virginia Crossley

Merrill

M3404 New Quintuplet Dolls 1936 $125 - 150

3404 Gone With the Wind 1940 $300 - 500

Courtesy of Virginia Crossley

3405 Little Princess 1936 $95 - 125

3405 Gone With the Wind 1940 $300 - 500

3408 Grown-Up Paper Dolls 1936 $80 - 125

3408 Sub-Deb Paper Dolls 1941 $80 - 100

Merrill

3411 Bride and Groom Military Wedding Party 1941 $100 - 150   **3411** Inside covers

3415 Drum Major and Majorette 1941 $90 - 120

3416 Dolls We Love 1936 $90 - 125   **3416** Last page of clothes, showing the nurse

3418 Sonja Henie 1941 $125 - 200   **3423 Airliner Paper Dolls** 1941 $100 - 150

Merrill

Courtesy of Emma Terry

3424 Victory Volunteers 1942 $100 - 150

3425 Army Nurse and Doctor 1942 $100 - 125

3426 Baby Sandy 1941 $100 - 140

3426 Twin Babies 1942 $70 - 90

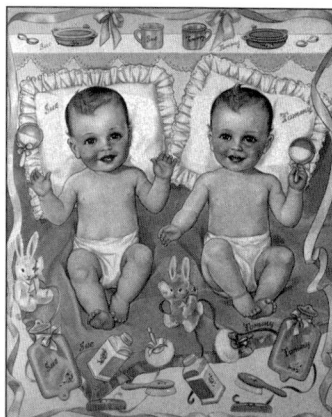
3426 Inside front cover

3428 Our New Baby 1937 $70 - 90

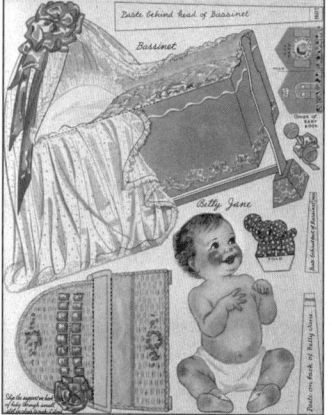
3428 Inside front and back cover

3428 Navy Scouts 1942 $100 - 150

Merrill

3436 Paper Doll Family and Their Trailer 1938 $100 - 150

3438 Tyrone Power and Linda Darnell 1941 $185 - 300   **3440 Star Babies** 1945, 8 page $65 - 90, 6 page $50 - 65

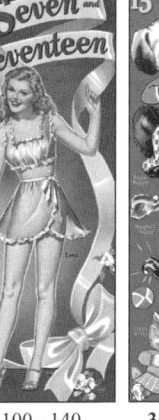

3441 Seven and Seventeen 1945, 8 page $80 - 125, 6 page $100 - 140   **3442 15 Puppy-Kitty Cut-Outs** 1938 $125 - 150

3442 Big 'N' Easy 1949 $50 - 80   **3443 Teen Town** 1946 $80 - 100

Merrill

101

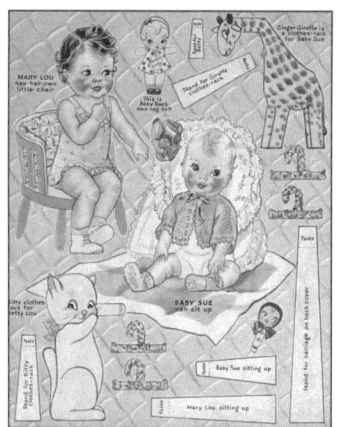

3444 Baby Sisters 1938 $90 - 125   3444 Inside front and back cover

3444 Blue Bonnet Paper Dolls 1942 $90 - 125   3444 Inside front and back cover

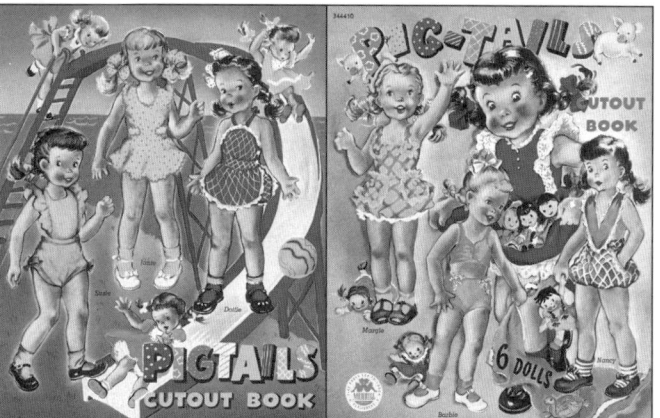

3444 Pig-Tails 1949 $35 - 40   **3445 Coke Crowd** 1946 $100 - 150

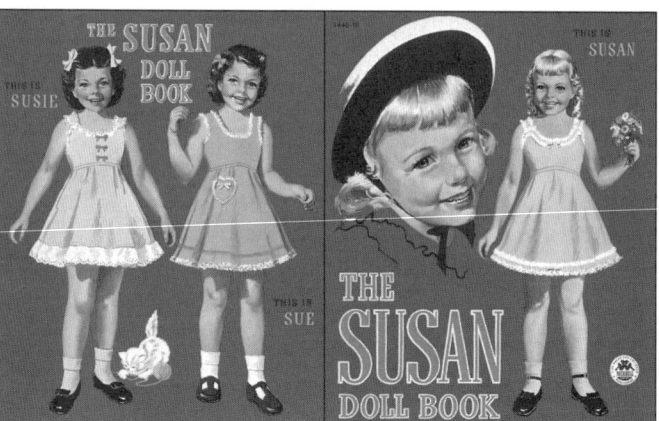

3446 27 Dancing School Paper Dolls 1938 $100 - 150   **3446 The Susan Doll Book** 1950 $35 - 40

Merrill

3447 Ballet Dancers 1947, 8 page $50 - 65, 6 page $35 - 45   **3448 Dream Girl** 1947 $70 - 90

3449 Cowboy and Cowgirl 1950 $40 - 60   **3450 The Two Marys** 1950 $45 - 65

3453 The Six Little Steppers 1953 $40 - 55   **3455 Cradle Tots** 1945, 8 page $75 - 90, 6 page $65 - 80

This book (3453) is from #1562.
The back cover dolls are re-drawn.

3459 6 Grown-up Paper Dolls 1941 $75 - 90

Merrill

3459A A Party of 6 Paper Dolls 1941 $75 - 90

3460 Jeanette MacDonald 1941 $175 - 300

Courtesy of Virginia Crossley

3466 Happy Birthday 1939 $100 - 135

3466 Ziegfeld Girl 1941 $300 - 500

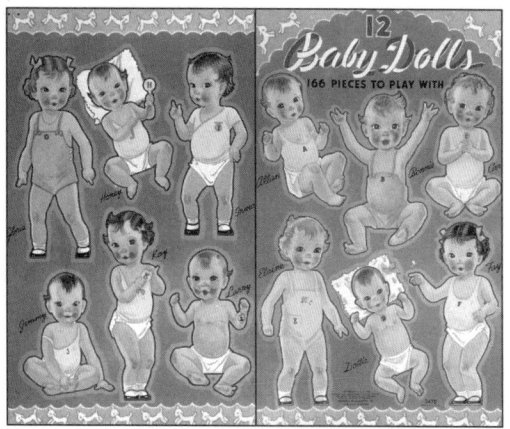

3470 12 Baby Dolls 1939 $85 - 110

3472 Make Clothes for Patsy 1941 $75 - 95

3472 Double Wedding 1939 $100 - 175

3472 Inside front and back cover

Merrill

Saalfield

The next three color pages picture original paper doll books published by the Saalfield Publishing Company. Each is identified by its title and book number.

1661 Gloria Jean

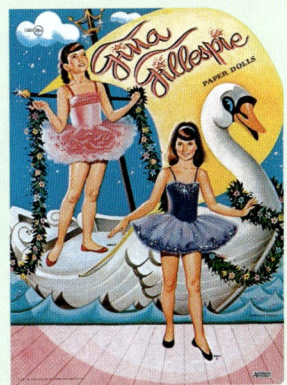
1331 Gina Gillespie

4446 Evelyn Rudie

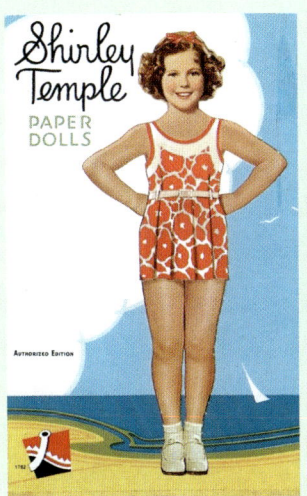
1782 Shirley Temple

2389 Daisy Mae

2735 June and Stu Erwin

2723 Carmen Miranda

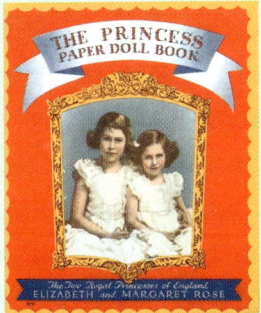
2216 Princess Paper Doll

2356 Charlie Chaplin

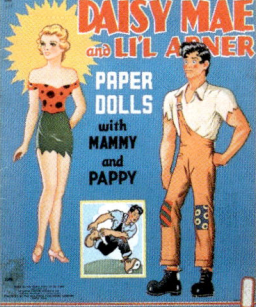
2360 Daisy Mae

2451 Claudette Colbert

2475 Lucille Ball

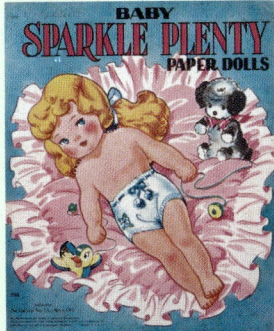
2500 Baby Sparkle Plenty

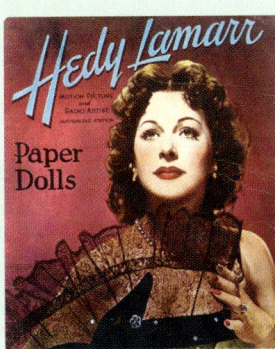
2600 Hedy Lamarr

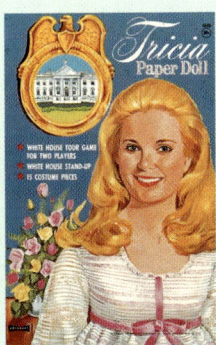
4248 Tricia

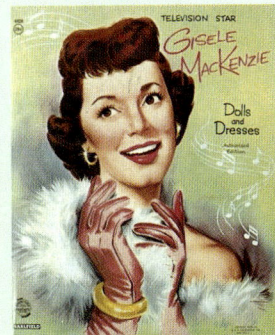
4428 Gisele MacKenzie

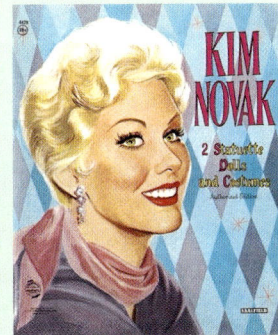
4429 Kim Novak

1074 Walking Paper Doll Family

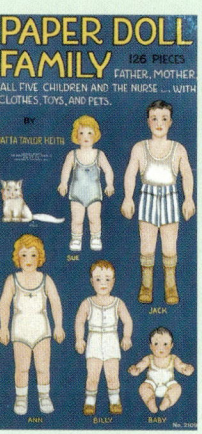
2109 Paper Doll Family

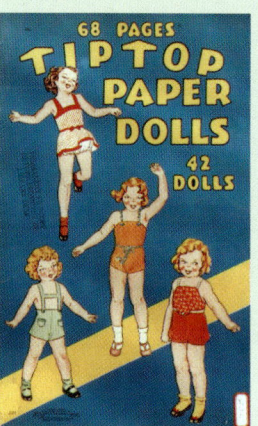
2321 Tiptop

2445 Victory

2358 Little Miss America

1332 Kewpies

1336 Brothers Grimm

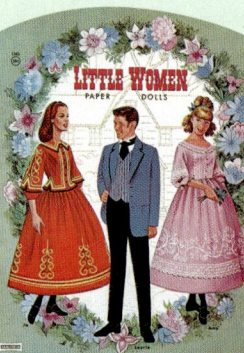
1345 Little Women

1352 Quintuplets

5139 Hee Haw

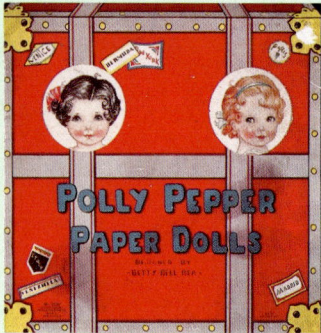
2126 Polly Pepper

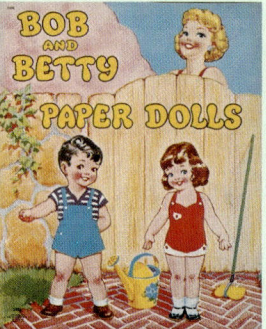
2486 Bob and Betty

4440 Hootenanny

4479 That Girl

2425 Shirley Temple

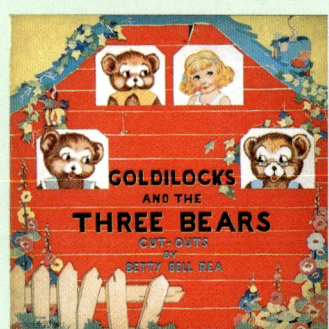
2245 Goldilocks

113 United We Stand

2497 Raggedy Ann and Andy

4444 Old Woman In the Shoe

4448 Texas Rose

Saalfield

2748 Robin Hood

2759 Spanky and Darla

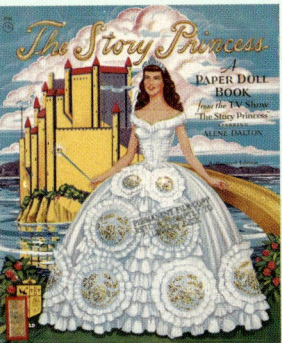
2761 Story Princess

4434 Blondie

4310 Eve Arden

4438 Brenda Starr

4435 Julia

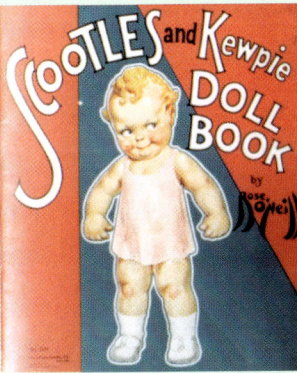
2131 Scootles and Kewpie

4447 Shari Lewis

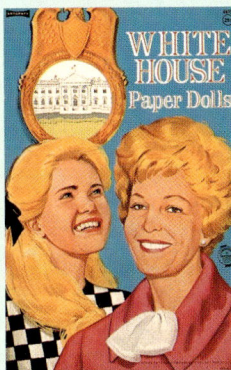
4475 White House

2176 Let's Play Doctor

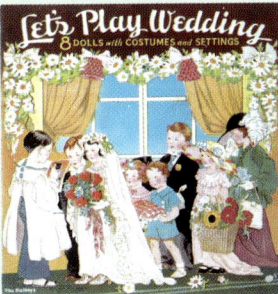
2194 Let's Play Wedding

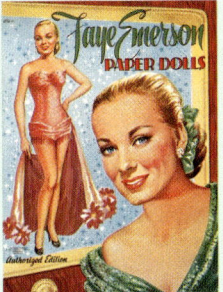
2722 Faye Emerson

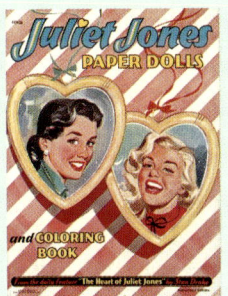
4326 Juliet Jones

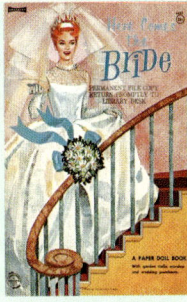
4420 Here Comes the Bride

2408 Jane Arden

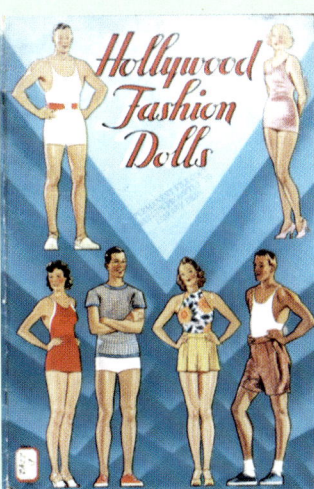
2242 Hollywood Fashion Dolls

2329 14 Good Little Dolls

2708 4 Great Big Paper Dolls

Saalfield

107

Merrill

These two color pages picture original paper doll books published by the Merrill Publishing Company. Each is identified by its title and book number.

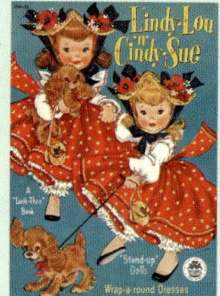
2564 Lindy-Lou 'n' Cindy Sue

4853 Angel Baby Dolls

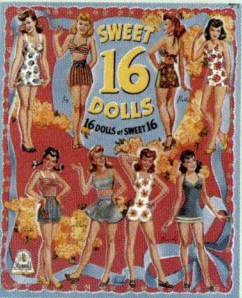
4862 Sweet 16 Dolls

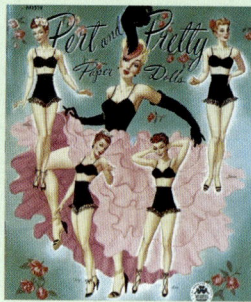
1552 Pert and Pretty

3428 Navy Scouts

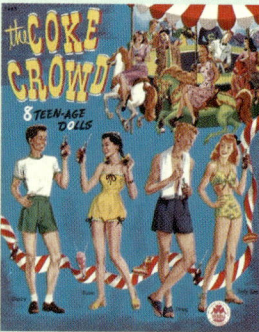
3445 Coke Crowd

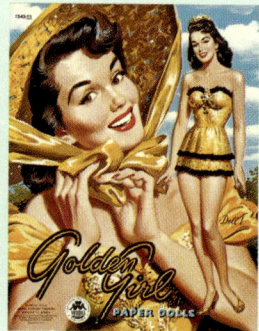
1543 Golden Girl

2968 Little Miss Christmas

4856 Magazine Cover Girls

1561 Little Family

4855 Navy Girls and Marines

3424 Victory Volunteers

4863 Baby's First Year

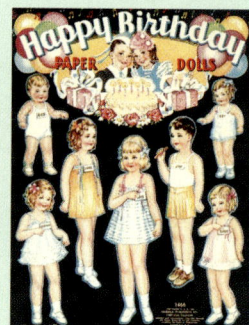
3466 Happy Birthday

3477 High School

3403 Stand-up Dolls

3446 27 Dancing School Dolls

3442 15 Puppy-Kitty

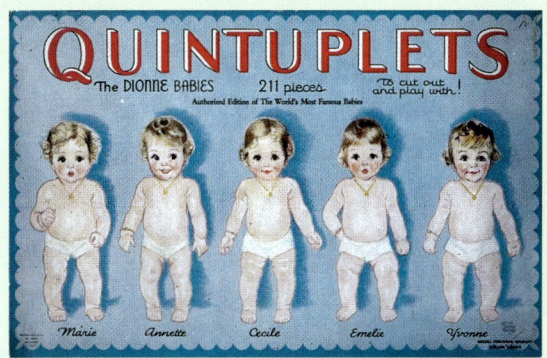
3488 Quintuplets, The Dionne Babies

3488 Dionne Quints

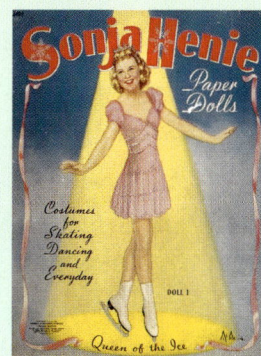
3492 Sonja Henie

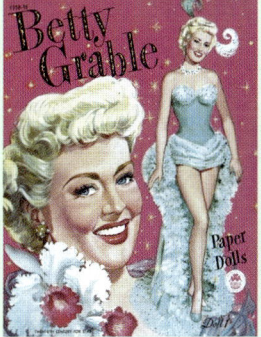
1558 Betty Grable

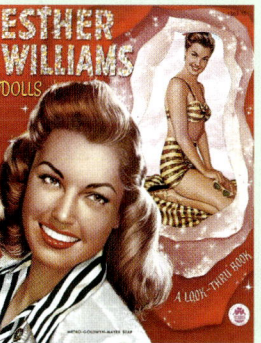
1563 Esther Williams

3405 Gone With The Wind

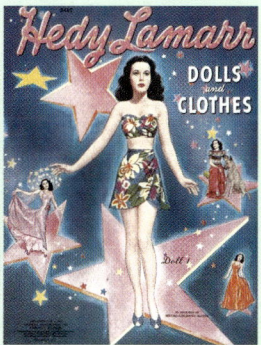
3482 Hedy Lamarr

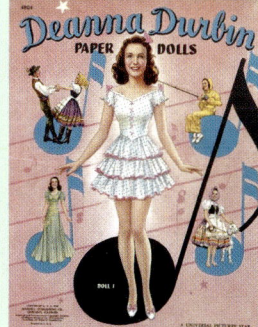
4804 Deanna Durbin

4816 Bette Davis

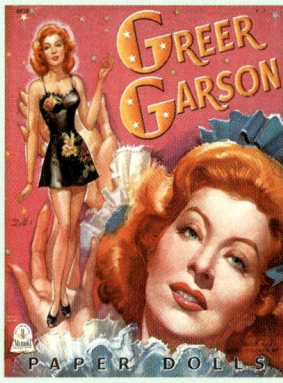
4858 Greer Garson

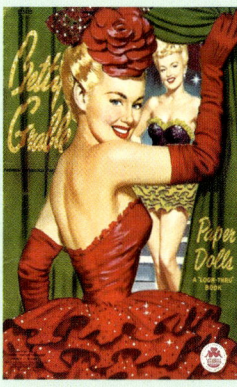
2552 Betty Grable

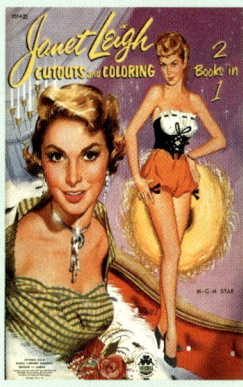
2554 Janet Leigh

2551 Piper Laurie

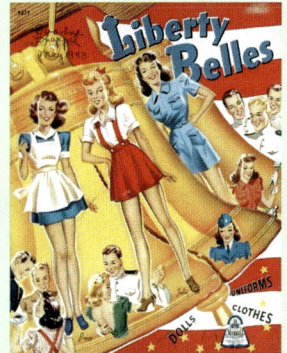
3477 °Liberty Belles

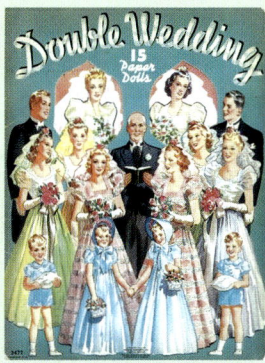
3472 Double Wedding

2550 Ann Blyth

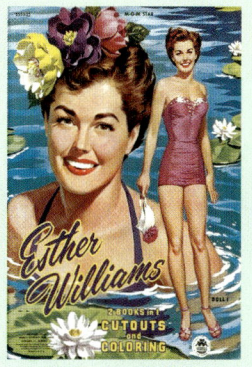
2553 Esther Williams

4800 Alice Faye

Merrill

Watkins-Strathmore

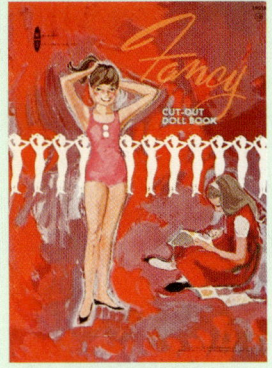
1805-B Fancy

1805-C Baby Doll

1820-5 Bridal Doll

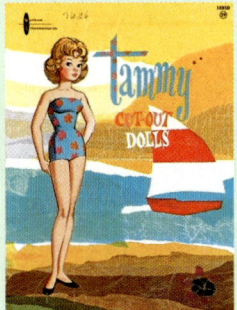
1885-D Tammy

1885-E Tiny Thumbelina

1892-6 Jane and Michael

4976 Peggy

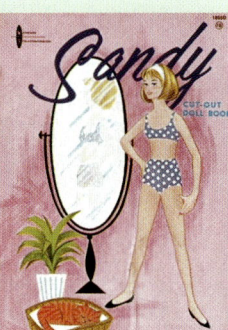
1805-D Sandy

1820-7 Twins, Lance and Lorie

Coloring books by various companies

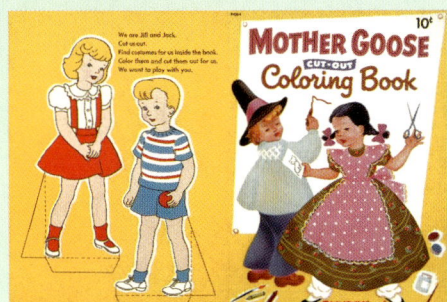
P4304 Mother Goose (Playday Books)

2508 Pam and Her Pram (Lowe)

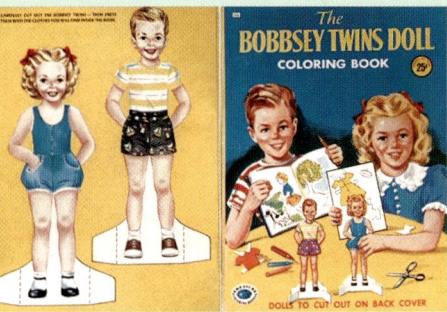
326 Bobbsey Twins (Treasure Books)

370 Sing Along with Peggy Lee (Treasure Books)

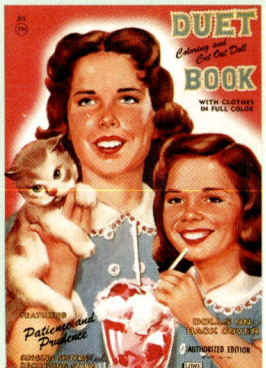
2873 Duet Book (Lowe)

2595 Rosemary Clooney (Lowe)

Dell

 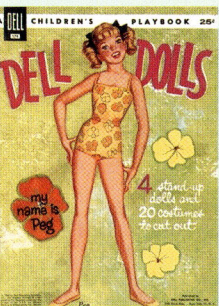 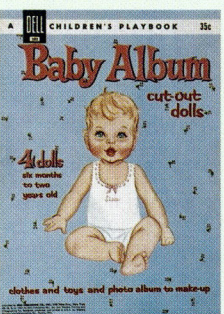 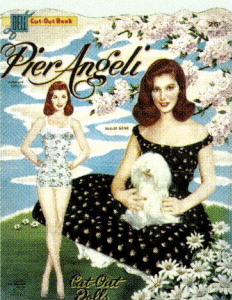 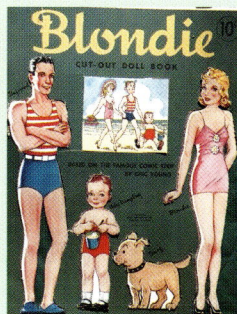 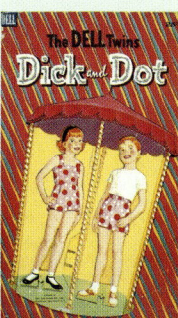

No. 2 Dell Twins   174 Dell Dolls   202 Baby Album   Pier Angeli   Blondie   Dell Twins

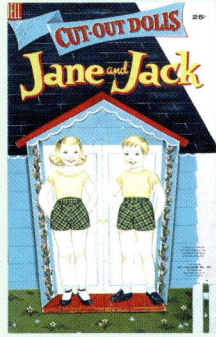 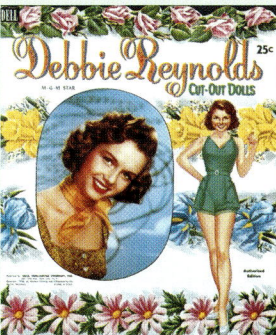 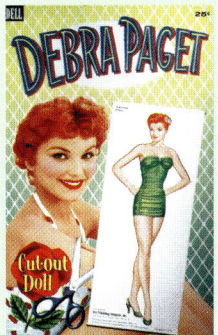 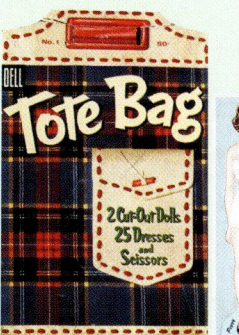 

Jane and Jack   Debbie Reynolds   Debra Paget   No. 1 Tote Bag   Pete and Peg

Pocket Books/Golden Press

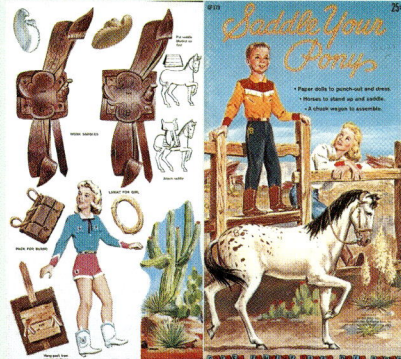  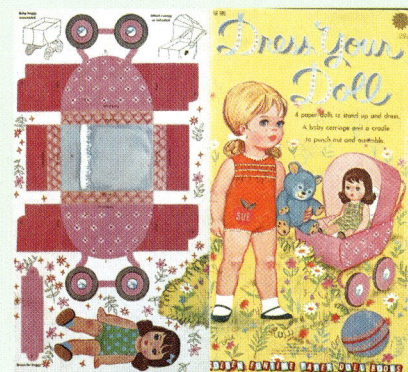

GF179 Saddle Your Pony   GF164 Career Girls   GF180 Dress Your Doll

 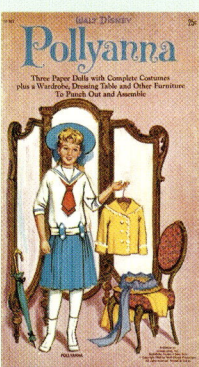   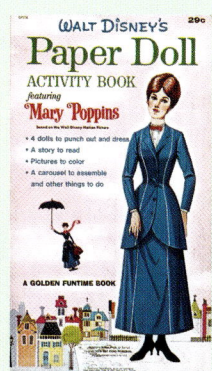 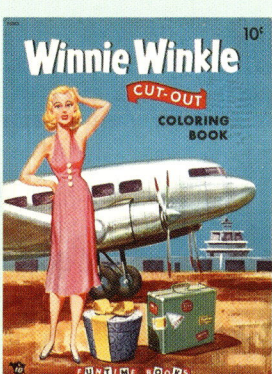

GF148 Paper Dolls   GF163 Pollyanna   GF221 Tammy and Pepper   GF237 Charmin' Chatty   GF238 Mary Poppins   F5053 Winnie Winkle

Dell • Pocket Books • Golden Press

111

Simon & Schuster, Inc.

Judy and Jim

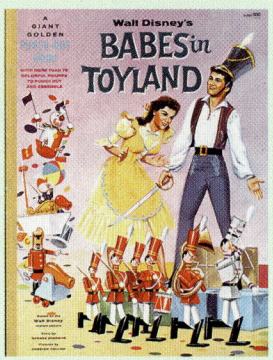
10363 Babes in Toyland

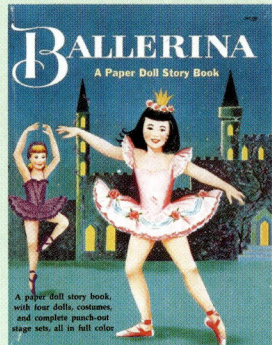
383 Ballerina

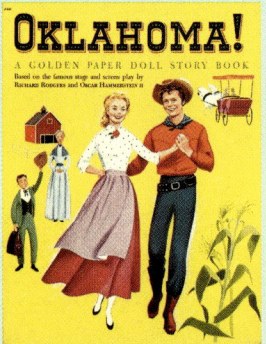
438 Oklahoma!

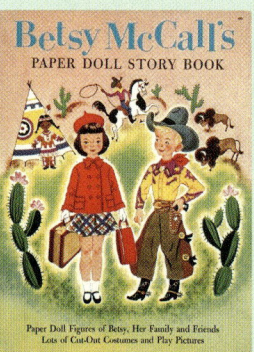
483 Betsy McCall

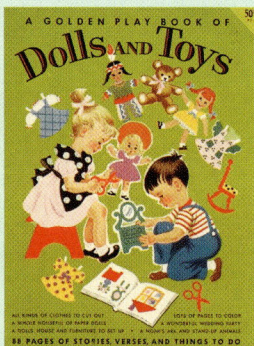
P-3 Dolls and Toys

113 Little Golden Paper Dolls

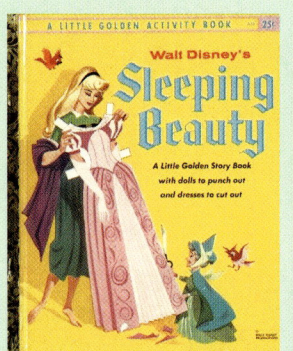
A-33 Sleeping Beauty

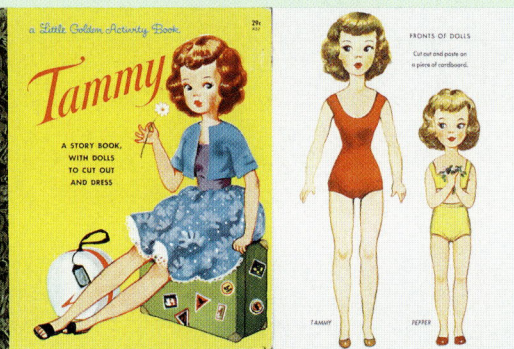
A-52 Tammy

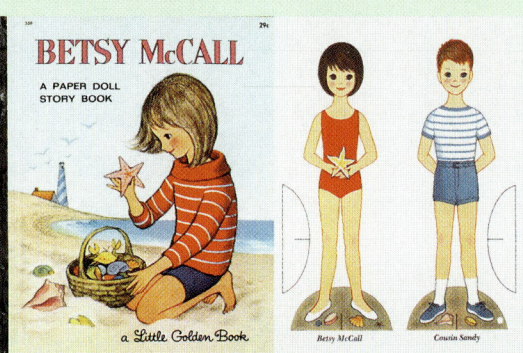
559 Betsy McCall

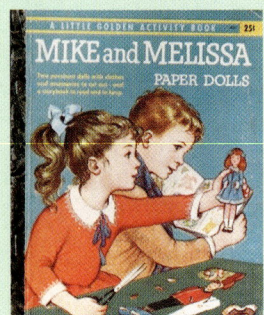
A-31 Mike and Melissa

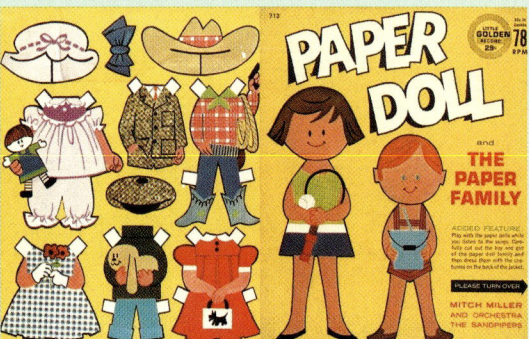
713 Paper Doll-Little Golden Record

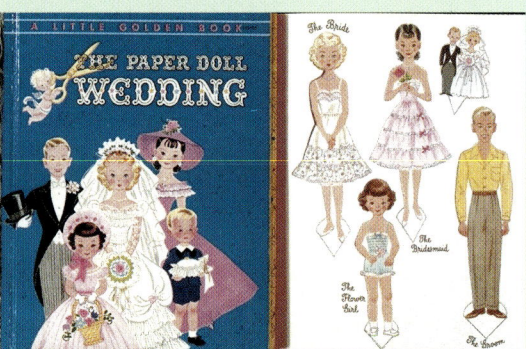
193 The Paper Doll Wedding

3475 Sonja Henie 1939 $175 - 300 **3477 High School** 1940 $90 - 125

3477 Liberty Belles 1943 $90 - 125 **3477** Inside front cover

3478 Rita Hayworth 1942 $200 - 350 **3480 Deanna Durbin** 1940 $135 - 185

3481 Real Baby Paper Dolls 1940 $75 - 95

Courtesy of Virginia Crossley

Merrill

3481 Soldiers and Sailors House Party 1943 $100 - 175   **3481** Inside front cover

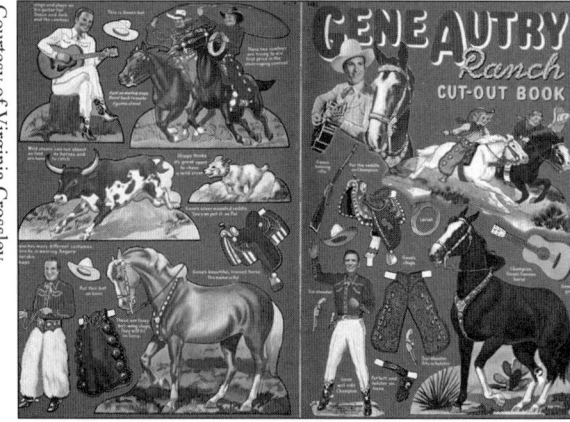

Courtesy of Virginia Crossley

3482 Gene Autry Ranch Cut-Out Book 1940 $75 - 125   **3482 Hedy Lamarr** 1942 $175 - 300

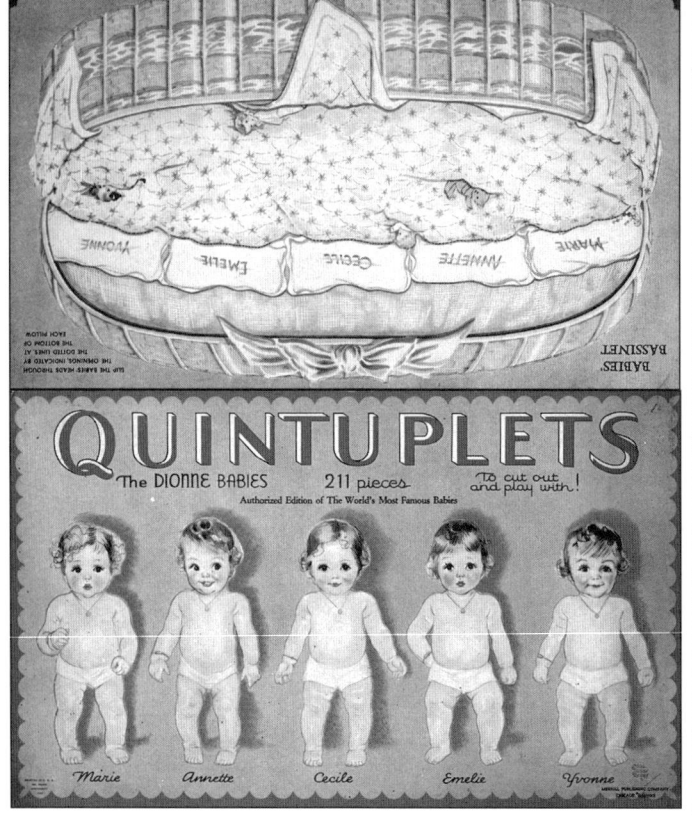
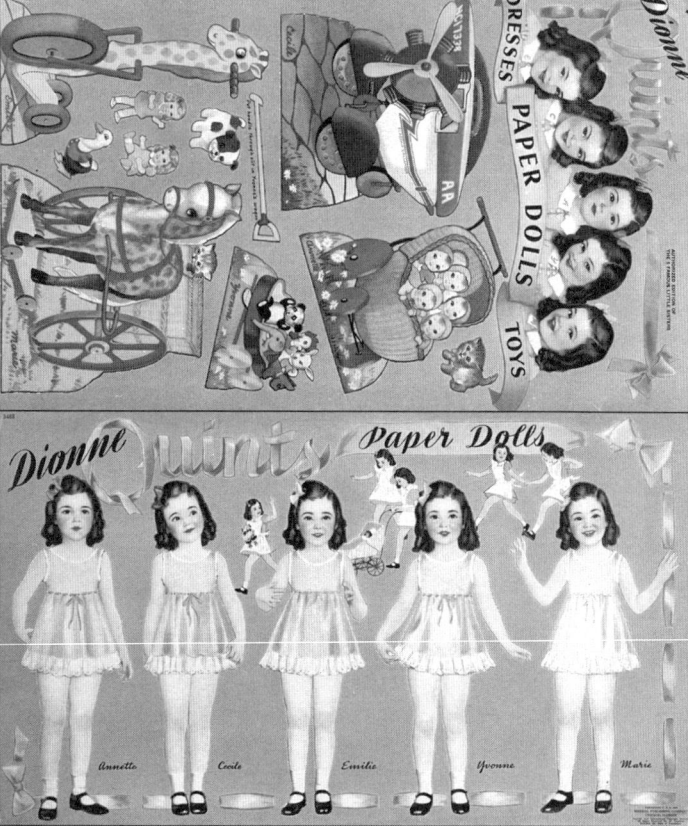

M3488 Quintuplets, The Dionne Babies 1935 $150 - 200   **3488 Dionne Quints Paper Dolls** 1940 $150 - 225

Merrill

114

Courtesy of Virginia Crossley

3492 Sonja Henie 1940 $200 - 350

3492 Boarding School 1942 $90 - 125

3492 Inside page

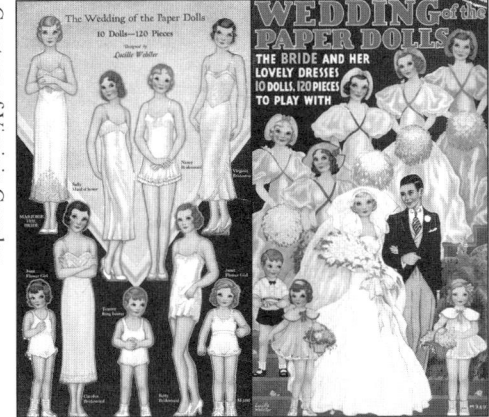

M3497 Wedding of the Paper Dolls 1935 $100 - 150

3500-A Let's Play House with the Dionne Quints, Cecile 1940 $80 - 110

3500-B Let's Play House with the Dionne Quints, Annette 1940 $80 - 110

Merrill

3500-C Let's Play House with the Dionne Quints, Emilie 1940 $80 - 110

3500-D Let's Play House with the Dionne Quints, Yvonne 1940 $80 - 110

3500-E Let's Play House with the Dionne Quints, Marie 1940 $80 - 110

4800 Alice Faye 1941 $200 - 350

4804 Deanna Durbin 1941 $175 - 300

4816 Bette Davis 1942 $175 - 300

Courtesy of Virginia Crossley

Merrill

116

right: 4829 Trudy in Her Teens 1943 $35 - 50

left: 4828 Jill and Her Trunk Full of Clothes 1943 $35 - 50

4827 New Baby 1943 45 - 60   **4827** Inside front cover

4851 Paper Doll Wedding 1943 (dated 1944 on the inside) $95 - 125   **4852 Girl Pilots of the Ferry Command** 1943 $100 - 150

4853 Angel Baby Dolls 1943 $95 - 125   **4854 Slumber Party** 1943 $65 - 90

4855 Navy Girls and Marines 1943 $100 - 175   **4856 Magazine Cover Girls** 1944 $95 - 125

Merrill

117

4857 Watch Me Grow 1944 $100 - 125   **4858 Greer Garson** 1944 $185 - 300

4859 First Date 1944 $75 - 100   **4860 Baby Mine** 1944 $125 - 150

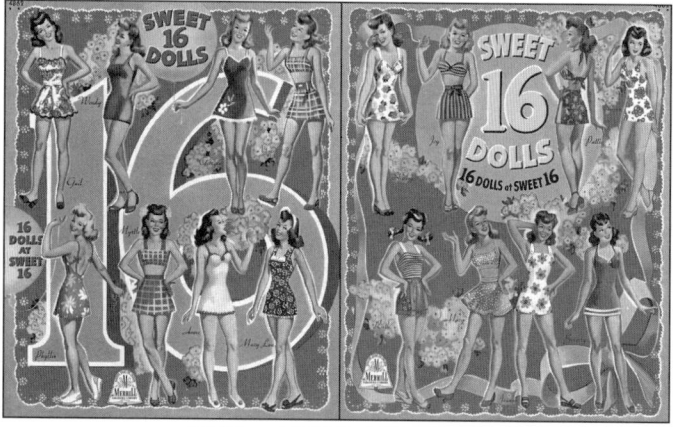

4862 Sweet 16 Dolls 1944 $85 - 100   **4863 Baby's First Year** 1945 $125 - 150

4865 Roller Rhythm 1944 $75 - 100   **4866 Ride a Pony** 1944 $75 - 100

Merrill

Paper Dolls Published by the Merrill Publishing Company:

This list contains all original and reprint books of paper dolls and related books published by the Merrill Company. If a book is a reprint it will have the number of the original book it is derived from in parenthesis following the title. If there should be more than one title for that number the book will be indicated unless it is obvious. All original paper doll books are pictured in the Merrill picture section.

1500	**Our Cowboy** 1950 coloring book w/stand-ups on back cover.
1542	**Little Ballerina** 1953
1543	**Golden Girl** 1953
1544	**Johnny, Janey and Judy in Storybook Land** 1952
1545	**Six Little Steppers** 1953 (1562 - Children in the Shoe)
1546	**Around The Clock With Sue and Dot** 1952
1546	**Four Little Girls From School** 1951/1957 (1556 - Polly)
1547	**The Little Fairy Paper Dolls** 1951
1547	**Cinderella, Jack and Jill Story Favorites** 1952/1957 (1544)
1548	**American Beauty Paper Dolls with Dresses Worn By White House Ladies** 1951
1548	**Kitty Goes To Kindergarten** 1956
1548	**Fairy Princess** 1951/1958 (1547 - Little Fairy)
1549	**Big 'N' Little Sister** 1951
1549	**Sally's Silver Skates** 1956
1550	**Let's Play With The Baby** 1948
1550	**White House Party Dresses** 1961 (1548)
1551	**High School Dolls** 1948
1551	**Sky Babies** 1959 (3440)
1552	**Pert and Pretty** 1948
1552	**Three Ice Skating Dolls** 1956/1960 (1549)
1553	**Heavenly Twins and Their Guardian Angels** 1948
1553	**Jane, Jean and Joan** 1950/1959 (3446-Susan)
1554	**Dolls From Storyland** 1948
1554	**Ballerina Dolls** 1953/1960 (1542)
1555	**Bride and Groom** 1949
1556	**Polly and Her Playmates** 1951
1556	**School Friends** 1956/1960 (1548-Kitty)
1557	**The Judy Paper Dolls** 1951
1557	**Gay and Gail** 1953/1958 (1543)
1557	**Airline Hostess and Pilot** 1962 (1560)
1558	**Betty Grable** 1951
1558	**Pink Cloud Bride & Her Pink Wedding** 1952/1961 (1559)
1559	**Pink Wedding** 1952
1559	**Jackie, Jeff and Julie** 1961 (1564 Karen)
1560	**Betty Blue and Patty Pink** 1949
1560	**Airliner Pilot and Stewardess** 1953
1560	**This is Suzie, Here is Jo-Ann** 1962 (1561-B is for Betsy)
1561	**The Little Family and Their Little House** 1949
1561	**B is for Betsy** 1954
1561	**Jack and Jill** 1962 (1563-Peter)
1562	**Children in the Shoe** 1949
1562	**Cathy Goes to Camp** 1954
1562	**Dolls from Storyland** 1963 (1554)
1563	**Esther Williams** 1950
1563	**In Peter Pumpkin's House** 1955
1564	**Baby Sister and Brother Dolls** 1950
1564	**Karen Goes to College** 1955
1565	**This is Lucy Locket Who Lost Her Pocket** 1949/1956 (3442-Big and Easy)
1566	**Midge 'N' Marge and Linda 'N' Lee** 1951/1956 (1549-Big and Little)
2550	**Ann Blyth** 1952
2551	**Piper Laurie** 1953
2552	**Betty Grable** 1953
2553	**Esther Williams** 1953 Coloring book & paper dolls
2554	**Janet Leigh** 1953 Coloring book & paper dolls
2562	**Umbrella Girls** 1956
2564	**Lindy-Lou 'N' Cindy-Sue** 1954
2565	**Children 'Round the World** 1955
2570	**Betty Blue and Patty Pink** 1949/1958 (1560)
2571	**Let's Play Paper Dolls - Baby Sister & Baby Brother Dolls** 1950/1958 (1564)
2571	**Twins, Baby Sister and Baby Brother** 1950/1960 (1564)
2572	**Seven Children Live In A Shoe** 1949/1958 (1562) Back cover dolls re-drawn like reprints "6 Little Steppers" #3453 (pictured) & #1545.
2580	**Heavenly Blue Wedding** 1955
2581	**Candy and Her Cousins** 1961 (2564)
2582	**Six and Sweet Sixteen** 1955
2582	**Big 'N' Little Six Sisters - Six & Sweet Sixteen** 1955/1960 (2582 above)
2583	**Pink Prom Twins** 1956
2584	**The Ranch Family** 1957
2968	**Little Miss Christmas and Holly Belle** 1965
3400	**College Style** 1941
3402	**Mickey Rooney Punchout** 1941 stand-ups
M3403	**Stand-Up Dolls, Honey and Bunny** 1936
M3404	**New Quintuplet Dolls** 1936
3404	**Gone With The Wind** 1940
3405	**The Little Princess** 1936
3405	**Gone With The Wind** 1940
3408	**Grown-Up Paper Dolls** 1936
3408	**Sub Deb** 1941
3411	**Bride and Groom Military Wedding Party** 1941
3415	**Drum Major and Majorette** 1941
3415	**Drum Majorette and Major** 1942 Has different front cover, otherwise same as the 1941 book above.
3416	**Dolls We Love** 1936
3418	**Sonja Henie** 1941
3423	**Airliner Paper Dolls - Pilot & Stewardess** 1941
3424	**Victory Volunteers** 1942
3425	**Army Nurse and Doctor** 1942
3426	**Baby Sandy** 1941
3426	**Twin Babies** 1942
3428	**Our New Baby** 1937
3428	**Navy Scouts** 1942
3430	**American Defense Battles - stand-ups** 1940
3436	**Paper Doll Family and Their Trailer** 1938
3438	**Tyrone Power and Linda Darnell** 1941
3440	**Star Babies** 1945
3441	**Seven and Seventeen** 1945
3442	**15 Puppy-Kitty Cut-Outs** 1938
3442	**Big 'N' Easy** 1949
3443	**Teen Town** 1946
3443	**Bride and Groom** 1949 (1555)
3444	**Baby Sisters** 1938
3444	**Blue Bonnet** 1942
3444	**Pig-Tails** 1949
3445	**Coke Crowd** 1946
3445	**Bonnie and Billy** 1954 (1550 Let's Play With the Baby)
3446	**27 Dancing School Paper Dolls** 1938
3446	**The Susan Doll Book** 1950
3447	**Ballet Dancers** 1947
3447	**Trudy In Her Teens** 1954 (1551 High School)
3448	**Dream Girl** 1947
3448	**Dancing Dolls With Famous Costumes** 1954 (3447)
3449	**Cowboy and Cowgirl** 1950
3450	**The Two Marys** 1950
3451	**My First Cut-Out Book** 1952 (1564 Baby Sister & Brother)
3452	**Becky and Betsy** 1952 (1560 Betty Blue)
3453	**Six Little Steppers** 1953 (1562 Children in the Shoe) w/dolls on back cover re-drawn. (This book is pictured on page 103)
3454	**The Jones Family** 1953 (1561 Little Family)
3455	**Cradle Tots** 1945
3456	**Glamour Girls, 9 Dancing Dolls** 1953 (1552 Pert &Pretty)
3457	**Angel Babies** 1953 (1553 Heavenly Twins)
3458	**Sherry & Adele, Diane & Lynn** 1953 (3448 Dream Girl)
3459	**6 Grown-Up Paper Dolls** 1941
3459	**Cowgirl Jill and Cowboy Joe** 1950/1955 (3449)
3459A	**A Party of 6 Paper Dolls** 1941
3460	**Jeanette MacDonald** 1941
3460	**Sally, Sandra and Sue** 1950/1955 (1557 Judy)
3461	**Story Book Dolls** 1948/1955 (1554)
3462	**Babyland** 1945/1950/1955 (3455)
3463	**Judy and Jan** 1950/1956 (3450)
3464	**Patty's Playtime Dolls** 1949/1956 (3444 Pig Tails)
3466	**Happy Birthday** 1939
3466	**Ziegfeld Girl** 1941
3470	**12 Baby Dolls** 1939
3472	**Double Wedding** 1939
3472	**Make Clothes for Patsy** 1941
3475	**Sonja Henie** 1939
3477	**High School** 1940
3477	**Liberty Belles** 1943
3478	**Rita Hayworth** 1942
3480	**Deanna Durbin** 1940
3481	**Real Baby Paper Dolls** 1940
3481	**Soldiers and Sailors House Party** 1943

3482	**Gene Autry Ranch Cut-Out Book** 1940 stand-ups & a few outfits	
3482	**Hedy Lamarr** 1942	
M3488	**Quintuplets, The Dionne Babies** 1935	
3488	**Dionne Quints Paper Dolls** 1940	
3492	**Sonja Henie** 1940	
3492	**Boarding School** 1942	
3495	**Big Farm Punch-Out Book** 1940 stand-ups	
M3497	**Wedding of the Paper Dolls** 1935	
3500A	**Let's Play House With The Dionne Quintuplets** 1940 - Cecile	
3500B	**Let's Play House With The Dionne Quintuplets** 1940 - Annette	
3500C	**Let's Play House With The Dionne Quintuplets** 1940 - Emilie	
3500D	**Let's Play House With The Dionne Quintuplets** 1940 - Yvonne	
3500E	**Let's Play House With The Dionne Quintuplets** 1940 - Marie	
4800	**Alice Faye** 1941	
4802	**Gene Autry Cowboy Punch-Out Book** 1941 stand-ups	
4804	**Deanna Durbin** 1941	
4816	**Bette Davis** 1942	
4827	**New Baby** 1943	
4828	**Jill and Her Trunk full of Clothes** 1943	
4829	**Trudy in Her Teens** 1943	
4851	**Paper Doll Wedding** 1943	
4852	**Girl Pilots of the Ferry Command** 1943	
4853	**Angel Baby Dolls** 1943	
4854	**Slumber Party** 1943	
4855	**Navy Girls and Marines** 1943	
4856	**Magazine Cover Girls** 1944	
4857	**Watch Me Grow** 1944	
4858	**Greer Garson** 1944	
4859	**First Date** 1944	
4860	**Baby Mine** 1944	
4862	**Sweet 16** 1944	
4863	**Baby's First Year** 1945	
4865	**Roller Rhythm** 1944	
4866	**Ride A Pony Judy and Jill** 1944	

Merrill Publishing Company Coloring Books with Paper Dolls Inside in Black and White

The following is a list of coloring books published by the Merrill Publishing Company that includes some pages of paper dolls inside the book in black and white to be colored. Some of the books contain the same paper dolls while others may have the same paper dolls with additional paper dolls that are different.

1574	**Rainy Day Fun** 1951	
1574	**Fun On A Rainy Day** 1956	
1583	**Giggle Book** 1960	
2500	**Children of Other Lands** 1954	
2500	**Boys and Girls from Far Away Lands** 1956	
2500	**Children Round The World** 1959	
2502	**My First Book of Bible Stories** 1953	
2502	**First Bible Stories** 1954	
2503	**The Happy Book** 1952	
2503	**Jolly Fun Book** 1954	
2505	**The Champ** 1954	
2510	**Giant Size Busy Book** 1951	
2510	**Sunny Hours on a Rainy Day** 1955	
2511	**Smiles** 1952	
2516	**Happy Hours on a Rainy Day** 1954	
2518	**Playmates in Their Native Costumes** 1962	
2526	**Easy Coloring** 1955	
M3401	**Read, Color, Cut and Paste** 1936	
3431	**Playtime Reading** 1937	
3454	**Read and Color** 1939	
3461	**Jeanette MacDonald Costume Parade** 1942	
3478	**Rainy Day Fun** 1940	
4837	**210 Things To Do** 1942	
4942	**Great Big Playtime Busy Book** 1958	
4942	**Great Big Playtime Busy Book** 1962	

The Dell Publishing Company

The Dell Publishing Company was founded by George Delacorte in the 1920s. Most of the paper dolls the company published were printed by the Western Printing and Lithographing Company (Western Publishing Co.) Some of the paper dolls are reprints of Whitman paper dolls and one is reprinted from a Saalfield book.

Dell Paper Doll Books With Numbers:

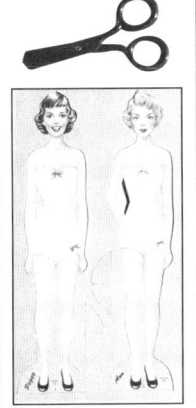

No. 2 The Dell Twins, Dick and Dot 1956 $25 - 35

No. 1 Tote Bag 1956 $25 - 35 (from Whitman 2627)

106 Bride Doll Book 1957 $35 - 50 (from Whitman 5340)

106 Inside front cover

169 4 Ballerina Cut-Out Dolls 1960 $30 - 45

169 Inside front and back cover

Dell

121

117 Gale Storm 1957 $85 - 125

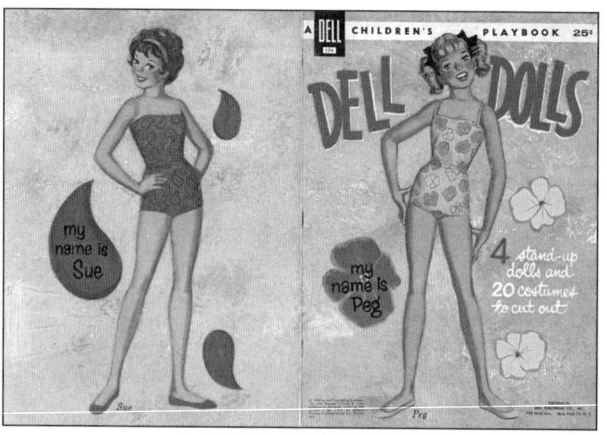  

174 Dell Dolls 1960 $20 - 35   **174** Inside front and back cover

187 Dick and Dot 1961 $25 - 35   **187** Inside front cover

195 Pretty Bride Wedding Party 1961 $30 - 45   **195** Inside front and back cover

Dell

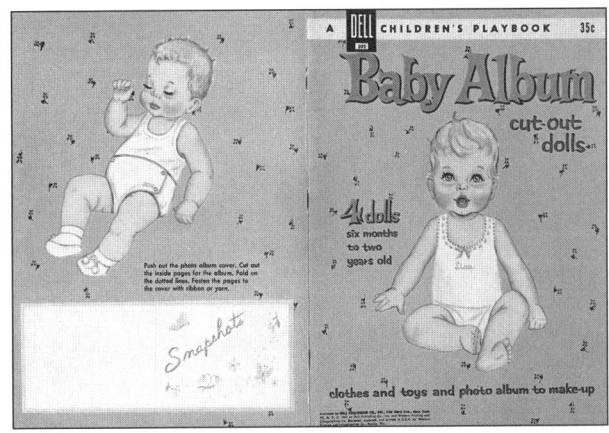  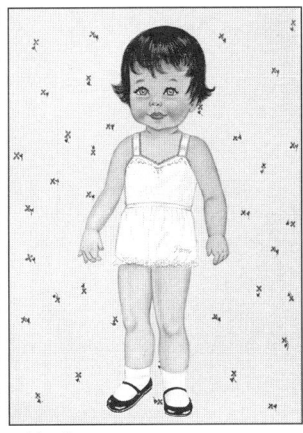

202 Baby Album 1961 $30 - 40   **202** Inside front and back cover

 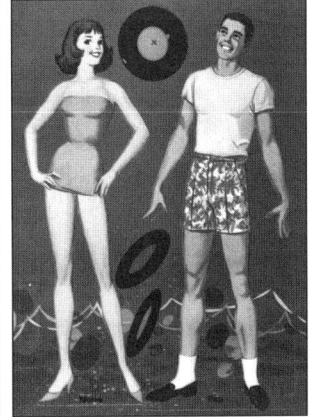

207 Platter Party 1961 $30 - 40   **207** Inside front cover

  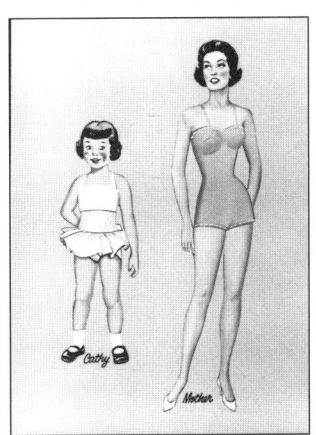

213 Family of Dolls 1961 $35 - 50   **213** Inside front and back cover

09286-303 Fashion Show 1962 $35 - 50   **09286-303** Inside front cover

Dell

Dell Paper Doll Books Without Numbers:

Pier Angeli 1955 $90 - 150

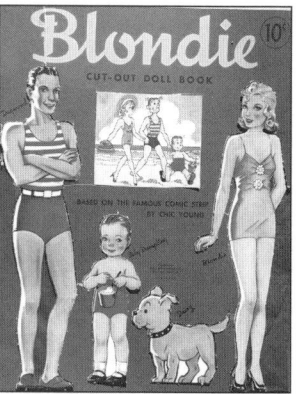
Blondie 1940 $90 - 150
(from Whitman 982)

Bride Doll Book 1953/55 $25 - 45
(from Whitman 2109)

The Dell Twins, Dick and Dot 1955 $25 - 35

Five Dionne Quintuplets 1937 $100 - 175 (from Whitman books 1055. The dolls have been re-drawn) Courtesy of Emma Terry

Gulliver's Travels 1939 $95 - 150 (from Saalfield 1261)

Jane and Jack 1956 $25 - 35

Our Soldiers 1941 $60 - 90

Debra Paget 1954 $100 - 150

Pete and Peg 1950 $25 - 35
(from Whitman 1182)

Dell

Debbie Reynolds 1953 $100 - 150

Snow White and the Seven Dwarfs
1938 $150 - 250
In this Dell set, the dwarfs average about 6" tall and Snow White is 12" tall. The doll of Snow White is reprinted from the Whitman set 2185 and the dwarfs are reprinted from the Whitman sets 970 and 2185. Courtesy of Madalaine Selfridge

Elaine Stewart 1954 $100 - 150

Shirley Temple's Birthday Book no date, circa 1930s $70 - 95

Jane Withers
1938 $85 - 140 for an un-cut book. This doll of Jane Withers is from the front cover of the Dell paper doll book and is re-drawn from the original Whitman book 996. The doll on the back cover and the clothes inside are from the original Whitman 996 and are not re-drawn.

Dell published the comic book **Tillie The Toiler** with a paper doll on the back cover during the 1940's and quite possibly the 1950's. An example of a 1949 comic book is shown here. Courtesy of Peggy Ell

Comic Book 237 Tillie The Toiler 1949 $10 - 12

Comic Book 215 Sparkle's Plenty 1947 $10 - 12
(Back cover)

Comic Book Vol. 1, No. 6 Marge's Little Lulu
1948 $10 - 12 (Back cover)

Comic Book 647 Bugs Bunny Album
1955 $10 - 12

Dell

In the 1980s Dell Published Two More Paper Doll Books:

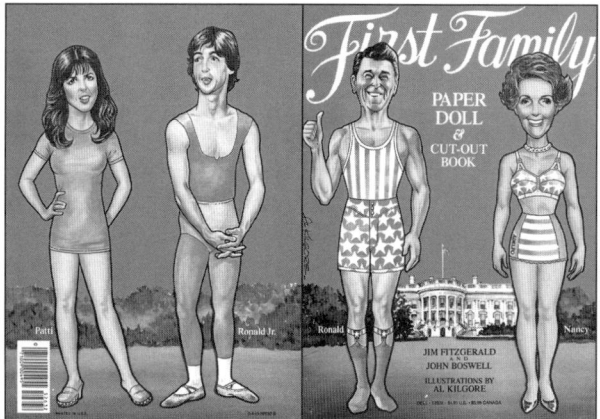

52632 **First Family** 1981 $10 - 12

41627 **Cutting Up with Ramona!** 1983 $8 - 10

The following list contains all the known paper doll and paper toy books published by the Dell Publishing Co., Inc.

Any reprints were usually of Whitman paper dolls and when this is the case the number of the original book or box will be in parentheses with the word "Whitman."

No. 1 **Tote Bag** 1956 (2627 Whitman)	175 **Disneyland Park** 1960 stand-ups	215 **A Doll's Birthday Party** 1961 stand-ups
No. 2 **The Dell Twins, Dick and Dot** 1956	176 **Trucks and Trailers** 1960 stand-ups	41627 **Cutting Up With Ramona!** 1983
No. 2 **The Manger Scene** 1954 stand-ups (reprint of no# book of same title)	181 **Jet Planes** 1960 stand-ups	52632 **First Family** 1981
103 **Pete and Peg** 1950 (1182 Whitman)	182 **Washington D.C.** 1960 stand-ups	06-230 **Let's Play Doctor and Nurse** 1962 stand-ups
106 **Bride Doll Book** 1957 (5340 Whitman)	183 **The Three Little Pigs** 1960 stand-ups	06-530 **A Dell Children's Punch-Out Mother Goose** 1962 stand-ups
110 **My Doll Kit** 1957 picture not available	187 **Dick and Dot** 1961	06-555 **National Velvet** 1962 stand-ups
117 **Gale Storm** 1957	189 **Yogi Bear** 1959 stand-ups (150)	06-620 **Peter Rabbit** 1962 stand-ups
149 **Satellite Rocket Launcher** 1959 stand-ups	195 **Pretty Bride Wedding Party** 1961	06-850 **Top Cat** 1962 stand-ups
150 **Yogi Bear** 1959 stand-ups	202 **Baby Album** 1961	09286-303 **Fashion Show** 1962
151 **Solar System** 1959 mobile to assemble	204 **A Farm** 1961 stand-ups	
152 **Farmyard Punchout** 1959 stand-ups	207 **Platter Party** 1961	
169 **4 Ballerina Cut-Out Dolls** 1960	208 **The Manger Scene** 1954 stand-ups (reprint of no# book of same title)	
174 **Dell Dolls** 1960	213 **Family of Dolls** 1961	

The Following Dell Books Have No Number

Pier Angeli 1955
Blondie 1940 (982 Whitman)
Bride Doll Book 1953/1955 (2109 Whitman)
The Dell Twins, Dick and Dot 1955
Five Dionne Quintuplets 1937
  (1055 Whitman, dolls redrawn)
Gulliver's Travels 1939
  of Saalfield book #1261)
Halloween Party Book 1955
  party favors, masks etc.
Jane and Jack 1956

Manger Scene 1954 stand-ups
Our Soldiers, Cut Out Army Uniforms 1941
Debra Paget 1954
Pete and Peg 1950 (1182 Whitman)
Debbie Reynolds 1953
Snow White and the Seven Dwarfs 1938
  (in this book Snow White is reprinted from 2185 Whitman and is 12" tall. The dwarfs average 6" tall and are re-printed from 2185 and 970 Whitman)

Elaine Stewart 1954
Shirley Temple's Birthday Book
  no date, circa 1930s
Jane Withers 1938
  (996 Whitman, with the front cover doll re-drawn)

Simon and Schuster, Inc.
Pocket Books, Inc.
Golden Press, Inc.

Little Golden Books

Western Publishing Company began printing Little Golden Books in 1942 when the first series of Little Golden Books was created for Simon and Schuster, Inc. The Little Golden Book series was designed and produced by The Artists and Writers Press division of Western and later by the subsidiary Artists and Writers Press, Inc. In 1958 Western and Pocket Books, Inc. teamed up to purchase the interests in Golden Book properties from Simon and Schuster, Inc. and a new company was established. The new company was given the name of Golden Press, Inc. In 1964 Western became the sole owner of Golden Press, Inc. by purchasing Pocket Books' share of the enterprise.

In 1951 The Little Golden Paper Dolls #113 was published by Simon and Schuster. This was the first paper doll book in the popular small size Little Golden Books and included a story about the paper dolls. In 1954 The Paper Doll Wedding #193 was published and was of the same size format.

The Little Golden Activity Books were published after 1954 for approximately nine years. These books were also in the small format of the regular Little Golden Books and were devoted to paper dolls and stamp books primarily. A few other types of activities were used also. These activity books all have the letter "A" in front of their number.

Paper Doll Story Books

The Paper Doll Story Books published by Simon and Schuster were of a larger format than the Little Golden Books. The first of these, Judy and Jim, was published in 1947 and had no number. It was reprinted in 1948 with a new cover and the number 430. A companion book Mother Goose Land With Judy and Jim followed in 1949 with the number 431. Four inside pages of cardboard contained the dolls and many toys. The colorful story pages have slots and the dolls can be placed directly in the different scenes. Many pages of outfits are also included in these exceptionally nice books. Three other books of this type are Betsy McCall #483, Oklahoma #438 and Ballerina #383.

Funtime Books, Giant Funtime Books, Golden Funtime and Golden Play Books

In the early 1950s, Pocket Books, Inc. produced a series of coloring books called Funtime Books and some contained paper dolls. The stock numbers of these books are preceded with the letter F. The dolls and clothes are inside the book and are to be colored. One exception is Winnie Winkle #F5053. This book has a doll in color on the front and back cover (both dolls identical) and another doll inside to be colored. Clothes for all dolls are inside the book to be colored.

During this same time period, Pocket Books, Inc. also produced activity books called Giant Funtime Books. Later, when Golden Press, Inc. was formed, the books were called Golden Funtime Books. The stock number of these books is preceded with the letters GF. Many of these activity books contained paper dolls.

Only one Golden Play Book has been found to contain paper dolls on the back cover. This book has 88 pages and is called Dolls and Toys #P-3. There are six dolls on the back cover. Inside are outfits, a doll house and furniture to assemble and other cut-outs. There are doll-related stories throughout the book and many of the pages are in color.

Simon and Schuster, Inc.

Judy and Jim, A Paper Doll Story Book 1947 $75 - 100 (no number on book)

113 The Little Golden Paper Dolls 1951 $75 - 100
The first edition of 113 is pictured here. This edition has 30 pages and is the only edition that has a bed and a closet. The book cover is white and is edition "A."

This is a list of reprints in the order that they appeared through the years.
113   "B" edition, 28 pages and new cover picture
113.25 "C" edition, 28 pages, same new cover as "B" edition
A-3   The cover art comes from "B" and "C" editions above. 20 pages and dolls are glued to the covers.
280   Has the original first cover but in light blue instead of white. 24 pages.
A-47   Has same cover as 280 in blue. 20 pages.

113.25 The Little Golden Paper Dolls
$50 - 75
("C" edition)

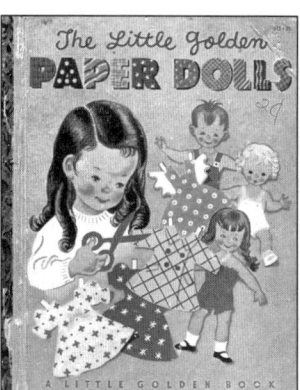

193 The Paper Doll Wedding
1954 $75 - 100
("A" edition)
28 pages.

Reprinted A-22 ("B" edition) has 24 pages and A-22 ("C" edition) has 20 pages. All have the same front cover picture.

438 Oklahoma! A Golden Paper Doll Story Book 1956 $75 - 100

Simon & Schuster • Pocket Books • Golden Press

431 Mother Goose Land with Judy and Jim 1949 $75 - 100

P-3 Dolls and Toys 1953 $60 - 85

483 Betsy McCall's Paper Doll Story Book 1954 $75 - 100

483 Inside pages

483 Inside pages

Golden Press, Inc.

A-14 Ginger Paper Doll 1957 $50 - 75

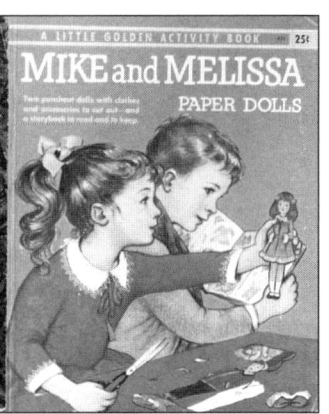
A-31 Mike and Melissa 1959 $50 - 75

A-31 Inside page

Simon & Schuster • Pocket Books • Golden Press

  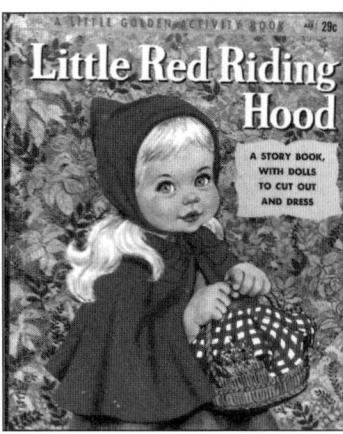 

A-33 Walt Disney's Sleeping Beauty 1959 $75 - 100   **A-34 Little Red Riding Hood** 1959 $75 - 100

A-36 Cinderella 1960 $75 - 100   **A-41 Hansel and Gretel** 1961 $60 - 85

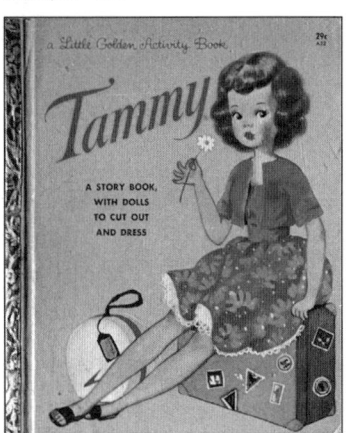 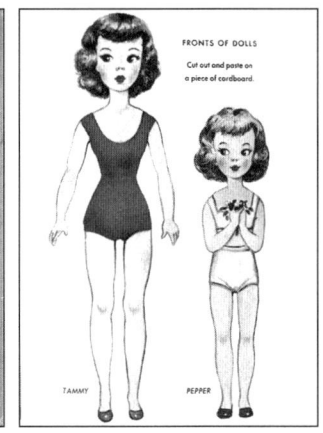

A-52 Tammy 1963 $50 - 75

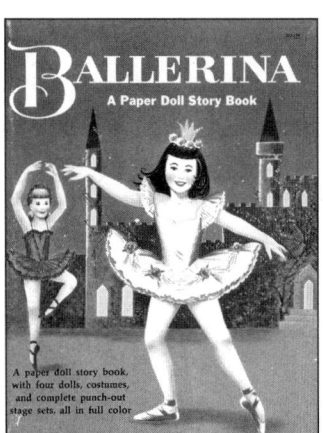 

383 Ballerina, A Paper Doll Story Book 1960 $45 - 60   **383** Inside pages

Simon & Schuster • Pocket Books • Golden Press

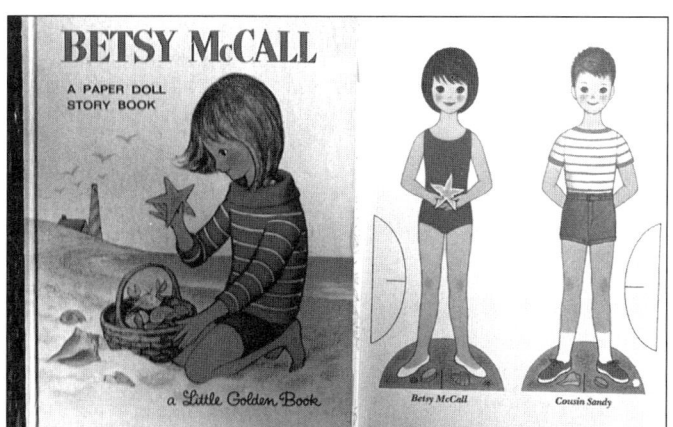

559 Betsy McCall 1965 $50 - 75

10363 Walt Disney's Babes in Toyland
1961 $50 - 75
A Giant Golden Punch-Out Book. Includes many stand-up figures but only 2 outfits. One is a cloak for Barnaby and the other is a cloak for Mary who is wearing a wedding gown. (Reprint book GF196 has less pages and does not have the figures of Mary and Tom in their wedding attire or the cloak for Mary.

713 Paper Doll-Little Golden Record
$20 - 35
Pictured are the front and back covers of the record sleeve for the Little Golden Record of *Paper Doll*. The sleeve measures 6½" x 7¾" and is printed in full color. The 78 rpm yellow record was performed by the Sandpipers, Mitch Miller and Orchestra. It sold for 29¢.

Pocket Books, Inc.

Giant Funtime Books

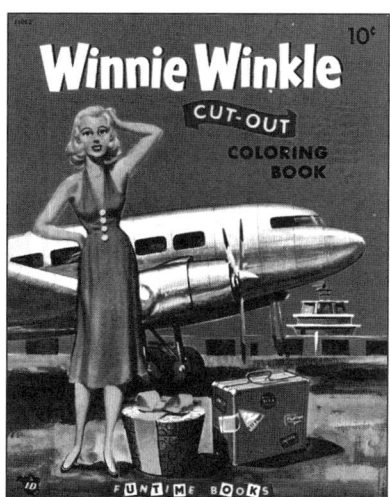

F5053
Winnie Winkle 1953 $25 - 35
This is a coloring cut-out book. The clothes are in black and white to be colored. This is the only Funtime book known to have paper dolls on the outside covers. (Back cover same as the front cover) For other Funtime books that have paper dolls inside the book in black and white, see the list of Funtime Books.

GF106 Career Girls 1955 $20 - 30

The Funtime and Giant Funtime books were published by Pocket Books, Inc. until 1958. After that, by Golden Press.

Simon & Schuster • Pocket Books • Golden Press

Golden Funtime Books

GF148 Paper Dolls 1960 $20 - 30   **GF148** Inside pages   **GF163 Pollyanna** 1960 $25 - 40   **GF163** Inside front cover

GF164 Career Girls 1960 $20 - 30   **GF164** Inside front and back cover   **GF179 Saddle Your Pony** 1961 $20 - 30

GF180 Dress Your Doll 1961 $20 - 30   **GF180** Inside front and back cover   **GF221 Tammy** 1963 $25 - 40

 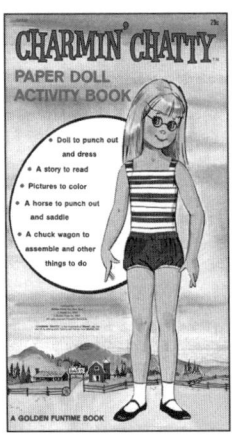 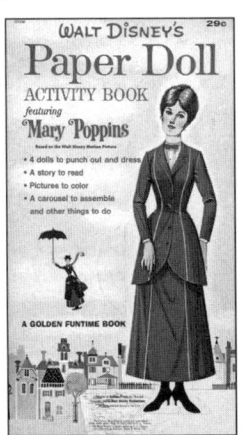 

GF221 Tammy and Pepper 1963/1964 $25 - 40   **GF237 Charmin' Chatty** 1964 $25 - 40   **GF238 Walt Disney's Mary Poppins** 1964 $25 - 40   **GF238** Inside back cover

Simon & Schuster • Pocket Books • Golden Press

Simon and Schuster, Inc.

- No# **Judy and Jim, A Paper Doll Story Book** 1947 (reprints of this book will have letter editions of B, C, D, E & F found on the inside front cover. Edition "F" also has the number 430 on the front cover.)
- 113 **The Little Golden Paper Dolls** 1951
- 123 **Happy Birthday** 1952 party favors to make.
- 129 **Tex and His Toys** 1952 paper toys
- 176 **Christmas Manger** 1953 stand-ups
- 193 **The Paper Doll Wedding** 1954
- 280 **The Little Golden Paper Dolls** 1951 (113)
- 430 **Judy and Jim, A Paper Doll Story Book** 1947/1948 edition "F" (reprint of no# book)
- 431 **Mother Goose Land With Judy and Jim** 1949 Paper Doll Story Book
- 438 **Oklahoma! A Golden Paper Doll Story Book** 1956
- 483 **Betsy McCall's Paper Doll Story Book** 1954
- 707 **McCall's Giant Golden Make-It Book** 1953 Includes "Connie" paper doll in color
- P-3 **A Golden Play Book of Dolls and Toys** 1953
- P-9 **Golden Fun Book** 1953 Three paper dolls inside book
- A-100 **Cinderella Puppet Show** 1949 Includes puppets
- A-100 **Mother Goose Land With Judy and Jim** 1949 (431)

Little Golden Activity Books

- A-3 **Paper Dolls** 1951 (113)
- A-14 **Ginger Paper** Doll 1957
- A-15 **Trim The Christmas Tree** 1957 tree decorations
- A-22 **The Paper Doll Wedding** 1954 (193)
- A-31 **Mike and Melissa Paper Dolls** 1959
- A-32 **Ginger Paper Doll** 1957 (A-14)
- A-33 **Walt Disney's Sleeping Beauty Paper Dolls** 1959
- A-34 **Little Red Riding Hood Paper Dolls** 1959
- A-36 **Cinderella Paper Dolls** 1960
- A-41 **Hansel and Gretel Paper Dolls** 1961
- A-47 **Paper Dolls** 1951 (113)
- A-48 **Gordon's Jet Flight** 1961 Jet airplane to assemble
- A-50 **Trim the Christmas Tree** 1957 (A-15)
- A-52 **Tammy** 1963 Paper doll story book

NOTE: #A36 Cinderella is also in the Read & Hear record series #00172. The back & front clothes are printed on separate pages instead of back to back on the same page.

Golden Press, Inc.

- 310 **Dennis The Menace, Giant Golden Punch-Out Book** 1960 stand-ups
- 362 **The Huckleberry Hound Giant Punch-Out Book** 1960 stand-ups
- 383 **Ballerina, A Paper Doll Story Book** 1960
- 385 **Giant Golden Punch-Out Book Of Animals** 1960 stand-ups
- 386 **Giant Golden Punch-Out Book of Birds** 1961 stand-ups
- 388 **The Giant Golden Punch-Out** 1955/56/57/58/59 stand-ups
- 389 **The Giant Golden Punch-Out Book #2** 1956/58/59/60 stand-ups
- 559 **Betsy McCall 1965 Paper doll story book, A Little Golden Book**
- 697 **McCall's Golden Do-It Book** 1960 Includes "Perky" paper doll in color. (2 pages)
- 10363 **Walt Disney's Babes In Toyland** 1961 stand-ups, including one outfit.
- 10364 **Walt Disney's Pinocchio, A Giant Golden Punch-Out Book** 1961 stand-ups
- 15803 **Raggedy Ann and Andy's Dandy Do-It Book!** 1978 Includes paper dolls inside in color and black & white, with outfits to be colored.

Pocket Books, Inc.

- #40 **Cut-Out Coloring Book** no date (two black & white paper dolls inside)

The following lists of Funtime Books contain paper dolls or stand-up figures. A few are just coloring books. All known books are listed. If the books contain paper dolls on the outside covers of the book, they will be pictured.

- F5035 **Jimmy Durante** 1952 cut-out coloring book
- F5036 **Suprise Cut-Out Book** 1952 cut-out coloring book
- F5039 **Hans Christian Andersen's Fairy Tales** 1953 paper doll/coloring book
- F5041 **Three Little Kittens** 1953 paper doll/coloring book
- F5044 **Minnie Mouse** 1953 paper doll/coloring book
- F5046 **Daisy Duck** 1953 paper doll/coloring book
- F5047 **Walt Disney's Dumbo** 1953 cut-out coloring book
- F5049 **Walt Disney's Three Little Pigs** 1953 cut-out coloring book
- F5053 **Winnie Winkle** 1953 paper doll/coloring book (dolls on covers)
- F5054 **Playtime Cut Out Book** 1953
- F5055 **Hopalong Cassidy** 1954 paper doll/coloring book
- F5056 **Color Bunny Cut-out Coloring Book** 1954
- F5058 **The New Baby** 1954 paper doll/coloring book
- F5061 **Walt Disney's Disneyville** 1954 paper doll/coloring book
- F5063 **Frosty The Snow Man** 1954 paper doll/coloring book
- F5064 **Jungle Animals Cut-Out Coloring Book** 1954
- F5066 **Annie Oakley** 1954 cut-out coloring book
- F5067 **Heidi** 1954 paper doll/coloring book
- F5068 **My Teddy Bear** 1954 paper doll/coloring book
- F5070 **Penny and Pete** 1955 paper doll/coloring book

Giant and Golden Funtime Books

- GF101 **Wild Animals Around the World** 1955 cut-out coloring book
- GF102 **Walt Disney's Pluto Pup** 1955 cut-out coloring book
- GF104 **Pinky Lee's Health & Safety Cut-Out Coloring Book** 1955 (pantin with hats, ties)
- GF105 **Cowboys of the Frontier** 1955 stand-ups
- GF106 **Career Girls** 1955 paper dolls
- GF107 **Birds Coloring Book** 1956
- GF108 **Walt Disney's TV Cut-out Coloring Book** 1956
- GF110 **Indians** 1956 stand-ups
- GF111 **Dogs Coloring Book** 1956
- GF113 **Knights in Armor** 1956 stand-ups
- GF114 **On the Farm** 1956 stand-ups
- GF116 **Mother Goose** 1957 cut-out coloring book
- GF117 **Trains** 1957 stand-ups
- GF118 **Soldiers** 1957 stand-ups
- GF119 **Walt Disney's Snow White and The Seven Dwarfs** 1957 cut-out coloring book
- GF121 **Cars and Trucks** 1958 stand-ups

GF122 **Wild West Wagon Train** 1957 stand-ups	GF157 **Birds, 12 Wild Birds to Punch Out** 1960 paper toys	GF194 **Eskimos and Other People of the North** 1962 stand-ups
GF123 **Black Beauty** 1958 cut-out coloring book	GF158 **Circus Parade** 1960 stand-ups	GF195 **Walt Disney's Pinocchio** 1962 stand-ups
GF125 **Baby Animals** 1957 cut-out coloring book	GF161 **Nurse Nancy** 1960 sticker book	GF196 **Walt Disney's The Toymaker "Babes In Toyland"** 1961 stand-ups
GF126 **Wyatt Earp** 1958 coloring book/stand-ups	GF162 **Wild Animals** 1960 sticker book	GF197 **Ludwig Von Drake** 1961 sticker book
GF127 **Airplanes** 1958 stand-ups	GF163 **Pollyanna** 1960 paper dolls	GF198 **Dick Tracy Jr. Detective Kit** 1962 punch-out toy
GF128 **Fire Engines** 1958 stand-ups	GF164 **Career Girls** 1960 paper dolls	GF200 **Astronauts** 1961 stand-ups
GF131 **Viking Ships** 1958 stand-ups	GF165 **Presidents of the United States** 1960 trading cards	GF202 **Horses** 1962 stand-ups
GF132 **Zorro** 1958 stand-ups	GF166 **Animal Trading Cards** 1960	GF204 **Games** 1962 paper toys
GF134 **Smokey the Bear** 1958 cut-out coloring book	GF167 **Augie Doggie and Doggie Daddy** 1960 stand-ups	GF205 **Picture Lotto** 1962
GF135 **Space Rockets To Punch Out and Assemble** 1958 stand-ups	GF168 **The Alamo** 1960 stand-ups	GF206 **Camping** 1962 stand-ups
GF136 **Dinosaurs** 1958 stand-ups	GF169 **Pixie and Dixie Stencil Book** 1960 some stand-ups	GF207 **Dr. Kildare Junior Doctor Kit** 1962 doctor kit and equipment
GF137 **Nursery Tales** 1959 cut-out coloring book	GF173 **Little Red Riding Hood** 1961 sticker book	GF208 **The Three Stooges** 1962 stand-ups
GF139 **Boats, 3 Dimensional Punchouts** 1959 stand-ups	GF177 **Popeye** 1961 stand-ups	GF209 **Doll House** 1962 stand-ups
GF140 **Steve Canyon's Interceptor Station** 1959 stand-ups	GF178 **Cars Old and New, 10 models to Assemble** 1961 stand-ups	GF210 **Country Fair** 1962 stand-ups
GF141 **Fishes** 1959 stand-ups	GF179 **Saddle Your Pony** 1961 paper dolls and stand-ups	GF211 **Cinderella** 1962 stand-ups
GF142 **Doll House** 1959 stand-ups	GF180 **Dress Your Doll** 1961 paper dolls	GF212 **Gay Purr-ee** 1962 stand-ups
GF143 **Christmas Manger To Assemble** 1959 stand-ups	GF183 **MGM'S Velvet & King** 1961 cut-out coloring book	GF213 **Airplanes Old and New** 1962 stand-ups
GF144 **Reptiles and Amphibians** 1959 stand-ups	GF184 **Puzzles & Games** 1961 (1 page of stand-ups)	GF215 **Birds** 1963 coloring book
GF145 **A.B.C. A Playtime Alphabet Cut & Paste Book** 1959	GF185 **Baba-Looey, Featuring Quick Draw McGraw** 1961 stand-ups	GF220 **Mr. Magoo's Christmas Carol** 1963 stand-ups
GF146 **Chris Jingle Cut & Paste Book** 1959	GF186 **Mr. Magoo cut-out coloring book** 1961	GF221 **Tammy Punch-Out Paper Doll** 1963
GF147 **Trucks and Tractors** 1959 stand-ups	GF187 **Rudolph the Red Nosed Reindeer** 1961 stand-ups	GF221 **Tammy and Pepper** 1963/64 paper dolls (Tammy from above book)
GF148 **Paper Dolls** 1960	GF188 **Fred and Wilma Flintstone** 1961 stand-ups	GF223 **The Clampetts in Hollywood** (Beverly Hillbillies) cut-out coloring book 1963
GF149 **Mr. Green Jeans** 1959 cut-out coloring book	GF189 **Dinosaurs** 1961 trading cards	GF225 **Baby Flintstone, Pebbles** 1963 cut-out coloring book
GF151 **Ben Hur** 1959 stand-ups	GF190 **Baseball Stars** 1961 trading cards	GF227 **The Lucy Show** cut-out coloring book 1963
GF152 **The War Between The States, Civil War Figures** 1959 stand-ups	GF191 **Goldilocks & the 3 Bears** 1961 sticker book	GF229 **Baby Flintstone, Pebbles** 1963 stand-ups
GF154 **I Love Lucy** 1959 coloring/tracing/stand-ups	GF192 **Hanna-Barbera Hokey Wolf & Ding-a-ling Cut-Out Coloring Book** 1961	GF230 **Walt Disney's Disneyland** 1963 stand-ups
GF155 **Walt Disney's Sleeping Beauty** 1959 stand-ups	GF193 **Trim the Tree** 1961 Christmas ornaments	GF231 **Supercar** 1964 Cut-Out Coloring Book
GF156 **Dennis The Menace** 1960 stand-ups		GF236 **Walt Disney's Mary Poppins** 1964 cut-out coloring book
		GF237 **Charmin' Chatty** 1964 paper dolls
		GF238 **Walt Disney's Mary Poppins** 1964 paper dolls

In the 1980's Simon and Schuster published three paper doll books shown here:

 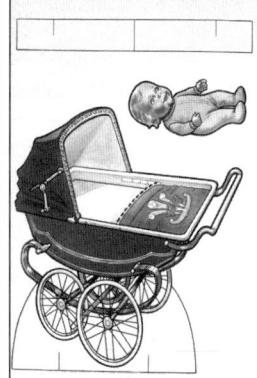  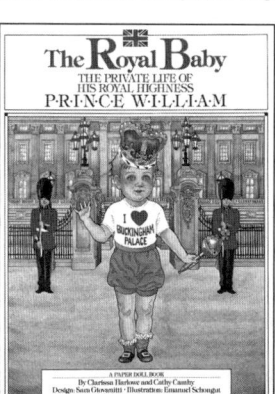 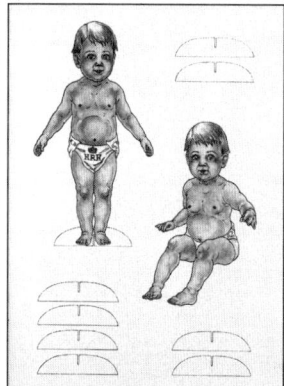

0482-480 Chuck and Di Have a Baby 1982 $25 - 50   0982-575 Cat's Closet 1982 $10 - 15   49892 The Royal Baby 1983 $25 - 50 (published by Pocket Books, a division of Simon & Schuster, Inc.)

Beginning in 1983 Western began publishing paper dolls with the Golden logo. Because these paper dolls were similar to their previous Whitman paper dolls and followed the same numbering system, they are listed and shown in the author's previous book that covered the Lowe and Whitman paper dolls.

Simon & Schuster • Pocket Books • Golden Press

Watkins-Strathmore Company

The Watkins-Strathmore Company began in Aurora, Illinois in 1923. They were the originator and designer of the Magic Slate. The company was purchased and made a subsidiary by Western in 1958.

1805-A Summer Fun 1963 $5 - 10

1805-B Fancy 1963 $5 - 10

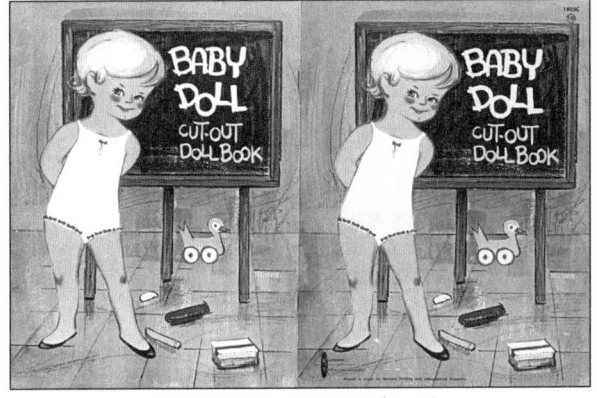

1805-C Baby Doll 1964 $5 - 10

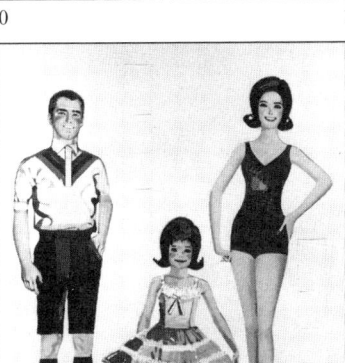

1805-D Sandy 1964 $5 - 10

1818 Bridal Doll Book 1963 $25 - 35

1818 Inside covers

1818-A   Cynthia Pepper 1963 $40-50   **1818-A   Inside covers**

1819-A   Elly May 1963 $40 - 50   **1819-B   Teen Time** 1963 $5 - 10

 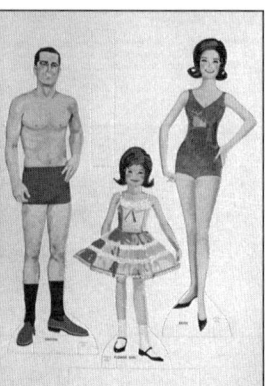 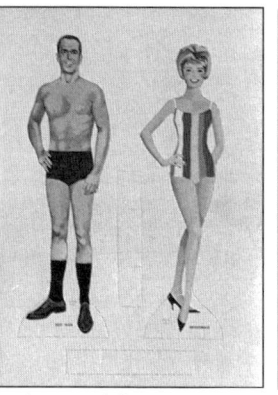

1820-5 Bridal Doll 1964 $20 - 30   **1820-5** Inside covers This book has the same dolls as 1818 except the men dolls are dressed differently in this book.   **1820-6 Miss World** 1965 $15 - 20

 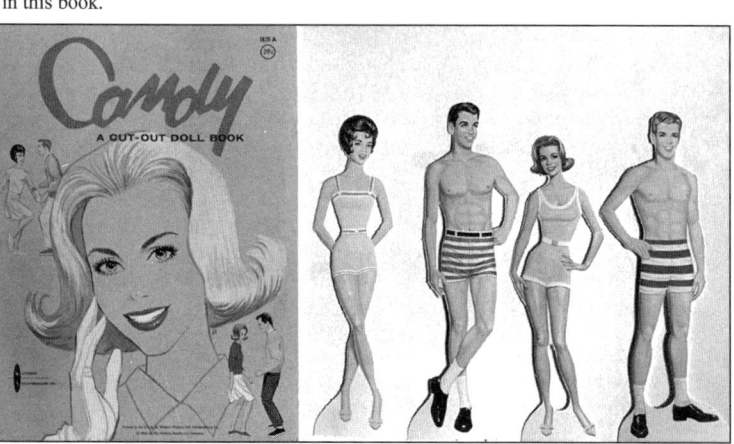

1820-7 The Twins Lance and Lorie 1965 $12 - 18   **1820-A   Candy** 1964 $18 - 25
This is a reprint of 1818-A Cynthia Pepper. The doll of Cynthia Pepper has been re-drawn.

Watkins-Strathmore

1870-4 PeePul Pals 1967 $5 - 10   1885-D Tammy 1963 $25 - 35

1885-E Tiny Thumbelina 1963 $18 - 25   1892-6 Walt Disney's Jane and Michael 1964 $25 - 40

4976 Peggy 1967 $12 - 15   4976 Modern Stick-on Dresses no date $12 - 15   4977 Teen Fun 1967 $15 - 20

Paper Dolls Published by the Watkins-Strathmore Company:

Many of the Watkins-Strathmore paper dolls are reprints of Whitman paper dolls, and such books are indicated by the Whitman number in the parentheses followed by the word "Whitman". These books can be seen in the author's previous book *Tomart's Price Guide to Lowe and Whitman Paper Dolls*. A few of the Watkins-Strathmore reprints have more pages than the original Whitman books. These books will be noted with an asterisk*.

1805-A	**Summer Fun** 1963	1805-D	**Sandy Cut Out Doll Book** 1964	1818-A	**Cynthia Pepper** 1963
1805-B	**Fancy Cut Out Doll Book** 1963	1817-A	**Bridal Doll** 1964 (1818)	1818-B	**Dolls of Other Lands** 1963/67 *
1805-C	**Baby Doll Cut Out Doll Book** 1964	1818	**Bridal Doll Book** 1963		(2074 Whitman)
	(some books not dated)	1818-A	**Teen Time** 1963 (1819-B)		

Watkins-Strathmore

1818-D	**Buttons and Billy** 1963/67 * (2071 Whitman)	1820-3	**Teen Time** 1963 (1819-B)	1885-D	**Tammy Cut-Outs** 1963
1818-E	**Cute Quintuplets** 1964/67 * (2071 Whitman)	1820-4	**Candy** 1964 (1818-A, Cynthia Pepper doll re-drawn)	1885-E	**Tiny Thumbelina** 1963
1818-F	**Bride and Groom Wedding and Trousseau Clothes** 1963/1967 *(2070 Whitman)	1820-5	**Bridal Doll** 1964 (1818)	1892-6	**Walt Disney's Jane and Michael** 1964 (includes "Mary Poppins" also.)
		1820-6	**Miss World** 1965	4943	**Happy Tot Dolls**, date not available. Dolls are Kay and Jay (4123 Whitman)
1818-G	**Baby Kim** 1962 (1969 Whitman)	1820-7	**The Twins Lance and Lorie** 1965		
1818-2	**School Pals**, date not available * (2075 Whitman)	1820-A	**Candy** 1964 (1818-A, Cynthia Pepper doll re-drawn)	4976	**Peggy** 1967 box
1818-3	**Dolls of Other Lands** 1963/67 * (2074 Whitman)	1821	**Here's The Bride**, no date (1953 Whitman)	4976	**Modern Stick-On Dresses**, no date, box
1818-4	**Buttons and Billy** 1963/67 * (2071 Whitman)	1822	**Annie Oakley** 1956 (1960 Whitman)	4977	**Teen Fun** 1967 box
1818-5	**Cute Quintuplets** 1964/67 * (2071 Whitman)	1870-4	**Peepul Pals** 1967	4977	**Bridal Party Cut Out Dolls**, no date, box (1818)
1818-6	**Bride and Groom Wedding and Trousseau Clothes** 1963/1967 * (2070 Whitman)	1873	**Christmas Manger** 1959 stand-ups (GF143)		
1818-7	**Baby Kim** 1962 (1969 Whitman)	1873	**Christmas Manger** 1959/1966 same as above, with new cover.		
1819-A	**Elly May** 1963	1883-B	**Barbie and Ken** 1962 Paper doll/coloring book. (1183 Whitman, pictured in the coloring book section of this book) Some copies have been found without the W/S logo and just Western Publishing Co. printed on this book.		
1819-B	**Teen Time** 1963				
1820	**June Allyson** 1955 (1956 Whitman)				
1820-2	**Elly May** 1963 (1819-A)				

Coloring Books With Paper Dolls On the Cover

Only Coloring books with paper dolls on the books covers are pictured. The coloring paper doll books for Saalfield and Merrill will be pictured in their sections.

Whitman/Golden (Pictured in Alphabetical Order):

1043 Baby Beans 1973 $8 - 10

1077 Baby Tenderlove 1971 $12 - 18

Watkins-Strathmore

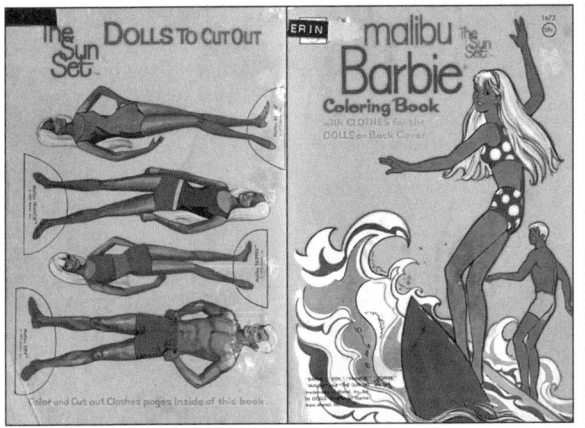 

1672 Barbie 1973 $18 - 25 (Malibu, The Sun Set) **1653 Barbie** 1977 $15 - 20 (Ballerina)

1637-1 Barbie 1978/1979 $10-15 (Photo Fashion) **3175-2 Barbie** 1988 $5 - 8

5522 Barbie 1988 $5 - 8 (doll like 3175-2, clothes new) **5522-1 Barbie** 1990 $4 - 6

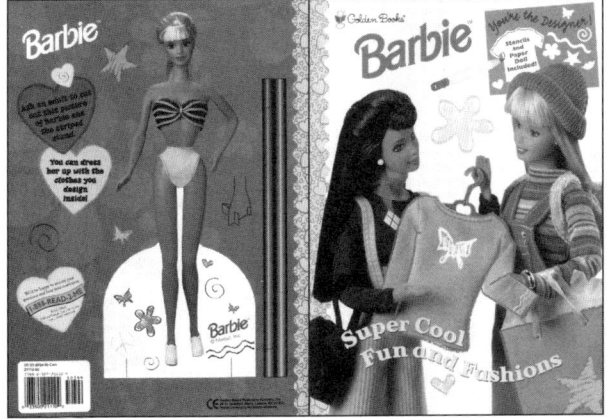 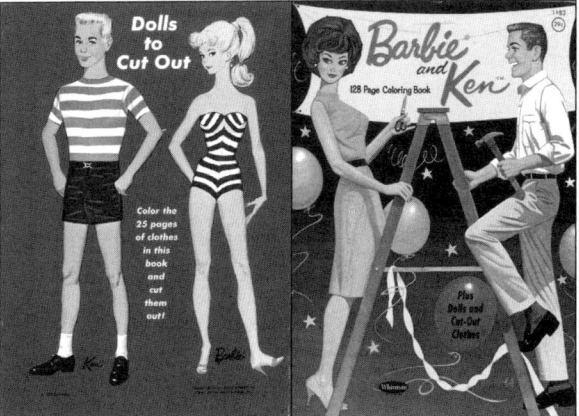

21110-00 Barbie 1999 $4 - 5 **1183 Barbie and Ken** 1962 $25 - 40

Coloring • Sticker • Activity Books

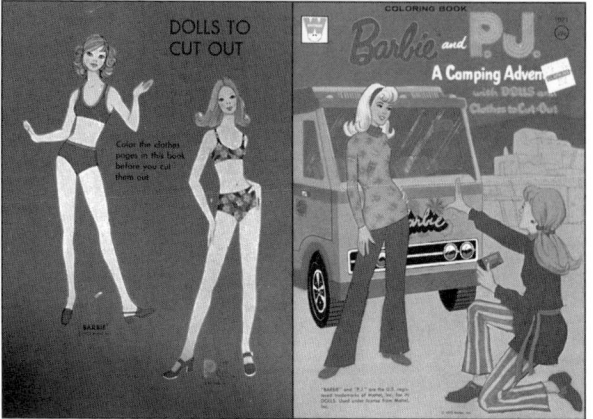

1071 Barbie and P.J.
1973 $15 - 20

This 1071 has been found in two editions. One has 4 pages of outfits, the other has 11 pages of outfits.

1637 Barbie and Ken 1970 $18 - 25

1640 Barbie and her little sister Skipper 1965 $20 - 35   **1130 Bridal Book** 1968 $18 - 25

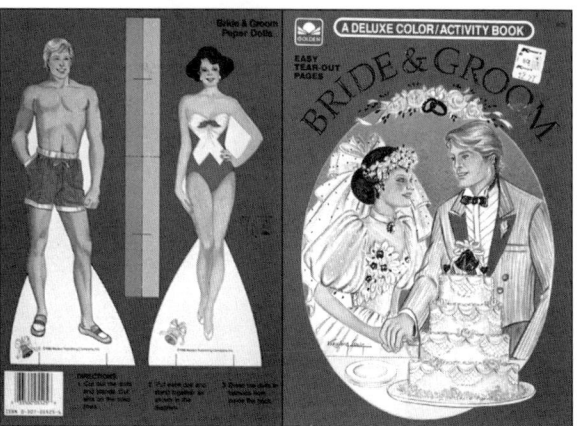

1139 Bride and Groom 1972 $12 - 15   **5525 Bride and Groom** 1988 $5 - 8

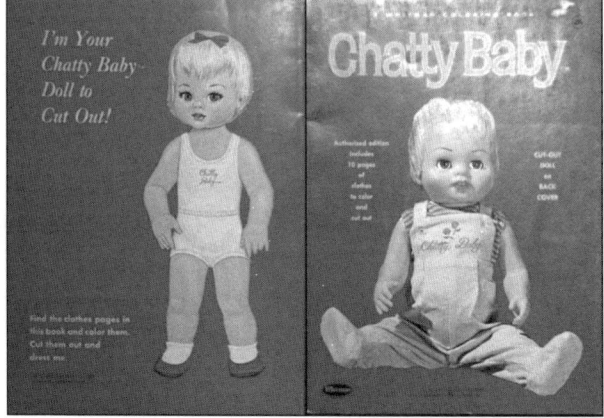

1087 Baby's Hungry! 1968 $20 - 35   **1141 Chatty Baby** 1961/1962/1963 $20 - 35

Coloring • Sticker • Activity Books

1643 Cheerful Tearful 1967 $20 - 30

1670 Dawn 1972 $10 - 12

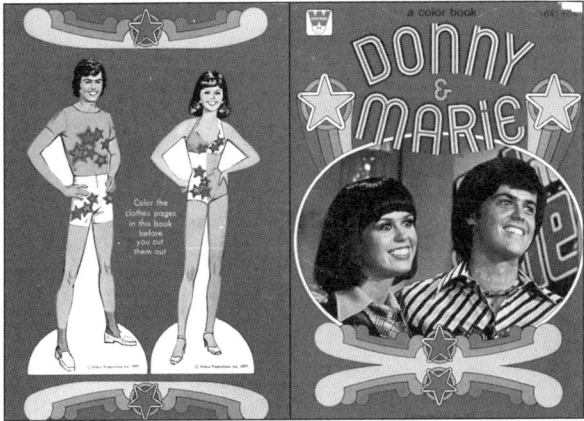
1641 Donny & Marie 1977 $20 - 30

1094 Francie 1967 $25 - 35

1068 Growing Up Skipper 1978 $15 - 20

1133 Carol Heiss 1961 $25 - 45

1043-1 Here Comes the Bride 1979 $5 - 10

1121 Little Dancers 1972 $4 - 8

Coloring • Sticker • Activity Books

1033 Mrs. Beasley 1972 $15 - 20

1053 Nancy and Sluggo 1972 $20 - 35

1662 New 'N' Groovy P.J. 1971 $10 - 12

3113-86 Punky Brewster 1986 $5 - 10

1650 Raggedy Ann 1971 $15 - 20

1650 Raggedy Ann 1971/1975 $10 - 18 The doll and clothes are new in this book but the regular coloring pages are from the 1971 book.

1138 Secret Sue 1967 $15 - 20

1061 Sweet Swingers 1971 $8 - 10

Coloring • Sticker • Activity Books

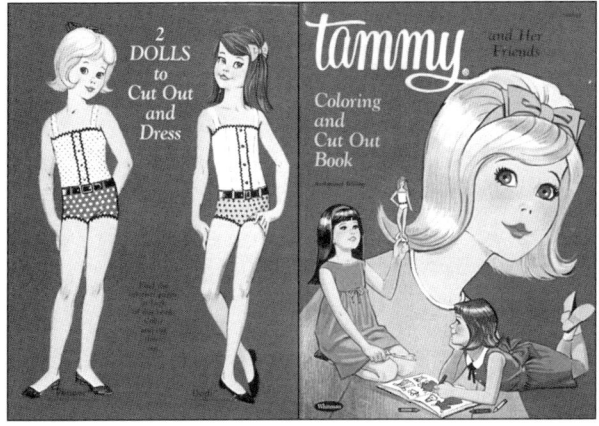
1650 Tammy and Her Friends 1966 $20 - 30

1667 Timey Tell 1972 $12-18

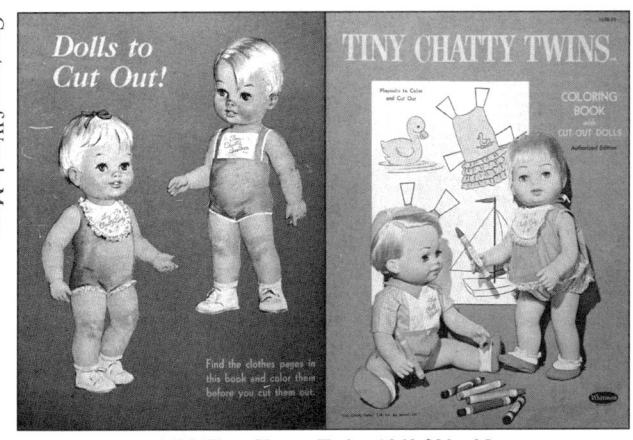
1638 Tiny Chatty Twins 1963 $20 - 35

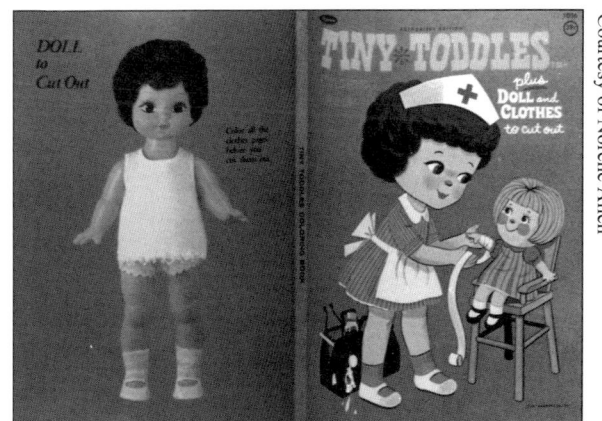
1056 Tiny Toddles 1970 $12 - 18

1085 Tubsy 1968 $12 - 18

1717 Winnie-the-Pooh 1978 $5 - 10

1646 Wishnik 1966 $18 - 25

1670 Wizard of Oz 1976 $12 - 18

Coloring • Sticker • Activity Books

Sticker Books With Paper Dolls on Back Cover:

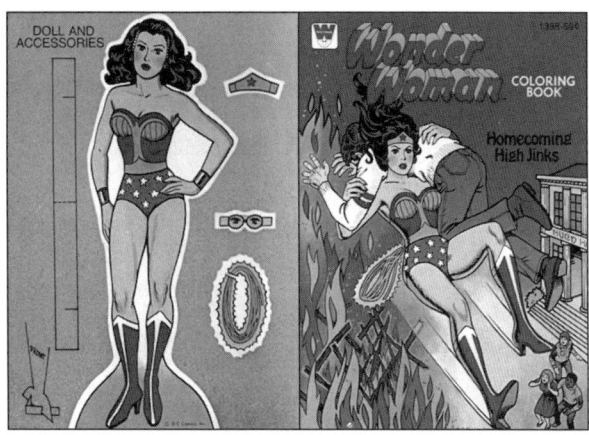
1398 Wonder Woman 1979 $15 - 30 (Coloring Book)

2135-12 Barbie 1989 $4 - 6

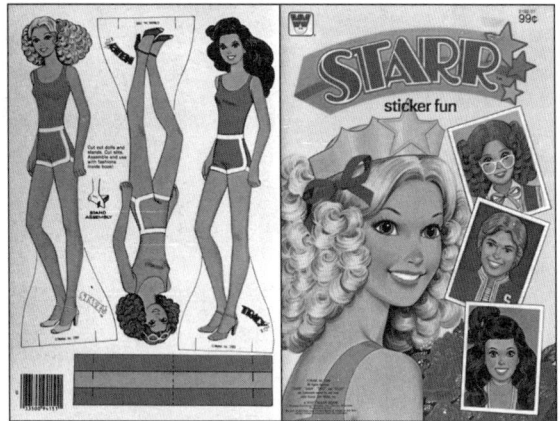
2192-31 Starr 1980 $5 - 8

1695 World of Barbie 1971 $15 - 20

Activity Book With Paper Doll Inside in color:

2169 Howdy Doody Fun Book 1951 $30 - 45 Paper doll is Princess Summerfall/Winterspring

Some Coloring Books by Other Companies:

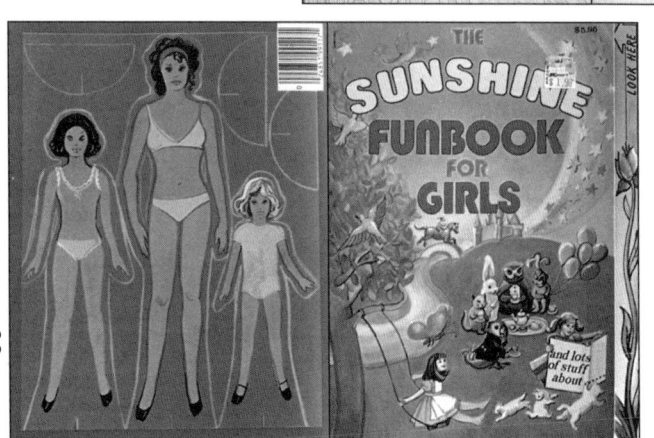
Sunshine Funbook for Girls 1983 $4 - 6 (Banner Press)

P4304 Mother Goose 1952 $10 - 15 (Playday Books) Book Associates

Courtesy of Louise Leek

2595 Rosemary Clooney 1956 $40 - 50 (Lowe) Doll from 2713 Rosemary Clooney Paper Doll book

EN1120 Santa's Christmas Fun 1984 $4 - 6 (Enrich Corp.)

2873 Duet Book 1958 $30 - 45 (Lowe) Dolls from 2411 Patience & Prudence Paper Doll book

2508 Pam and her Pram 1956 $10 - 12 (Lowe)

2639 Play Time $12 - 16 (Lowe) Abbott

2596 2 in One Color and Paper Doll Book 1953 $10 - 12 (Lowe)

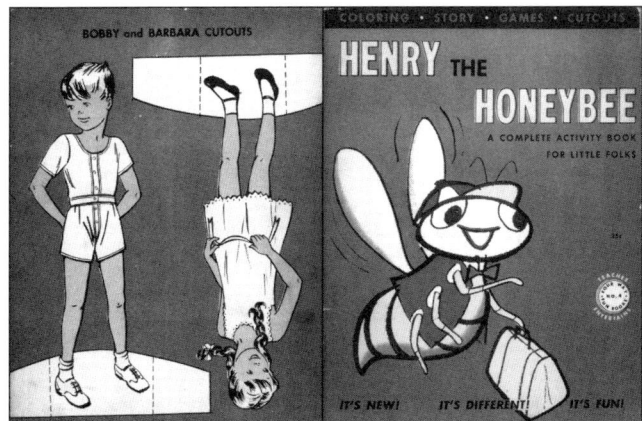

Henry the Honeybee 1953 $10 - 12 (Petco Press)

89-4 Go Team Go 1998 $4 - 5 (Playmore Inc.)

Coloring • Sticker • Activity Books

Courtesy of Louise Leek

Hello Kitty's Busy Book 1982 $4 - 6
(Random House Happy House Books by Sanrio Co. Ltd.)

Playskool Funtime 1984 $3 - 5 (Random House)

326 The Bobbsey Twins Doll Coloring Book 1958 $30 - 40 (Treasure Books)

353 Dolls Around the World 1960 $15 - 25 (Treasure Books)

370 Sing Along With Peggy Lee $40 - 50 (Treasure Books)

9544 Scissors and Coloring Fun 1957/1974 $4 - 6 (Treasure Books)

9600 Heidi 1971 $8 - 12 (Wonder Books)

9601 Alice In Wonderland 1971 $8 - 12 (Wonder Books)

Coloring • Sticker • Activity Books

9602 Little Red Riding Hood 1971 $8 - 12 (Wonder Books)   **9603 Cinderella** 1971 $8 - 12 (Wonder Books)

9604 Snow White and the Seven Dwarfs 1971 $8 - 12 (Wonder Books)   **9605 Bride and Groom** 1971 $8 - 12 (Wonder Books)

Activity Book With Paper Dolls on Back Cover:

2509 My Hansel and Gretel Story and Playbook
1955 $7 - 10 (Wonder Books)

This is a List of the Known Coloring Books that have Paper Dolls on the Covers for Whitman/Golden:

Listed in Alphabetical Order

- 1043 **Baby Beans** 1973
- 1077 **Baby Tenderlove** 1971 Also #1017
- 1087 **Baby's Hungry!** 1968
- 1672 **Barbie (Malibu, The Sun Set)** 1973
- 1653 **Barbie (Ballerina)** 1977 also #1653-1
- 1637-1 **Barbie (Fashion Photo)** 1978/79
  also #1637-33 & 1660-33
- 3175-2 **Barbie** 1988 (doll dated 1987) also #3175
- 5522 **Barbie** 1988 (doll same as above but dated 1988, 1987. The clothes and the rest of the book are completely different.)
- 5522-1 **Barbie** 1990 also 5522-3 dated 1990/91
- 21110-00 **Barbie** 1999
- 1640 **Barbie and Her Little Sister Skipper** 1965
- 1183 **Barbie and Ken** 1962
  also #1883-B (Watkins/Strathmore)
- 1637 **Barbie and Ken** 1970

- 1071 **Barbie and P.J.** 1973 (A Camping Adventure)
- 1130 **Bridal Book** 1968 also #1183
- 1139 **Bride and Groom** 1972
- 5525 **Bride and Groom** 1988 also 5525-1 dated 1988/1992
- 1141 **Chatty Baby** 1961/1962/1963
- 1643 **Cheerful Tearful** 1967
- 1670 **Dawn and Her Friends** 1972
- 1641 **Donny & Marie** 1977
- 1094 **Francie** 1967 also #1169 & 1167
- 1068 **Growing Up Skipper** 1978 also #1013-1
- 1133 **Carol Heiss** 1961
- 1043-1 **Here Comes The Bride** 1979 also #1061-31
- 1121 **Little Dancers** 1972 also #1131 & 1105-22
- 1033 **Mrs. Beasley** 1972
- 1053 **Nancy and Sluggo** 1972

- 1662 **New 'N' Groovy P.J.** 1971 also #1654
- 3113-86 **Punky Brewster** 1986
- 1650 **Raggedy Ann** 1971
- 1650 **Raggedy Ann** 1971/1975 also 1650-1, 1660-32 & 1830. The doll and clothes are different from above but other coloring pages are the same as 1971 book.
- 1138 **Secret Sue** 1967
- 1061 **Sweet Swingers** 1971
- 1650 **Tammy and Her Friends** 1966
- 1667 **Timey Tell** 1972
- 1638 **Tiny Chatty Twins** 1963
- 1056 **Tiny Toddles** 1970
- 1085 **Tubsy** 1968
- 1717 **Winnie-The-Pooh** 1978 also #1136-3, 1206 & 1640-1
- 1646 **Wishnik** 1966
- 1670 **Wizard of Oz** 1976 also #1661-33
- 1398 **Wonder Woman** 1979 also #1398-2

Sticker Books With Paper Doll On Back Cover

2135-12 **Barbie** 1989 also #2135-16
2192-31 **Starr** 1980
1695 **World of Barbie** 1971

Also Pictured is the Following Activity Book with a Paper Doll Printed Inside in Color: (Princess Summerfall/Winterspring)

2169 **Howdy Doody Fun Book** 1951

The Following Three Whitman Coloring Books with Paper Dolls on the Covers Are Shown in the Lowe/Whitman Guide:

2107 **Doris Day** 1953
674 **Judy Garland Fashion Paint Book** 1940
2104 **Mary Hartline** 1952

The Following Activity Book with Paper Dolls Inside the Book, Printed in Color, can be Found in the Lowe/Whitman Guide:

1035 **Roy Rogers Double-R-Bar Ranch** 1955

Some Coloring Paper Doll Books By Other Companies:

Banner Press, Inc.
Sunshine Funbook For Girls 1983

Book Associates (printed by Western)
Playday Books -
    P4304 **Mother Goose** 1952

Enrich Corp.
EN1120 **Santa's Christmas Fun** 1984

Lowe Publishing Co.
2595 **Rosemary Clooney** 1956
2873 **Duet Dolls** 1958
2574 **Paint Betsy's Sunday Best** 1955
    (can be seen in the author's
    Lowe/Whitman Guide by Tomart)
2508 **Pam and Her Pram** 1956
2639 **Play Time** (The dolls in this book
    are from two Lowe paper doll
    books; 1283 Cuddles & Rags and
    1252 Rockabye Babies.)
2596 **Two in One Color and**
    Paper Doll Book
    (The dolls in this book are from
    two Lowe Paper doll books:
    4207 Penny & Sue and
    1057 Playhouse.)

Petco Press
Henry the Honeybee 1953

Playmore Inc.
89-4 **Go Team Go** 1998

Random House
Hello Kitty's Busy Book 1982
    Happy House Books
Playskool Funtime 1984
    Happy House Books

Treasure Books
326 **The Bobbsey Twins Doll**
    Coloring Book 1958
353 **Dolls Around The World** 1960
370 **Sing Along With Peggy Lee** 1961
9544 **Scissors and**
    Coloring Fun 1957/59/74

Wonder Books
2509 **My Hansel and Gretel Story**
    and Play Book 1955
9600 **Heidi** 1971
9601 **Alice In Wonderland** 1971
9602 **Little Red Riding Hood** 1971
9603 **Cinderella** 1971
9604 **Snow White and**
    The Seven Dwarfs 1971
9605 **Bride and Groom** 1971

Photo Index

A
A Day with Diane 51
A Party of 6 Paper Dolls 104
Air Hostess 42
Air, Land and Sea 38
Airliner Paper Dolls 99
Airliner Pilot and Stewardess 92
Alice 8
Alice Faye 109, 116
Alice In Wonderland 146
Alice's Trousseau 16
American Beauty Paper Dolls 90
Amy Jo 54
Angel Baby Dolls 108, 117
Angel Paper Dolls 50
Animal Paper Dolls 43
Ann Blyth 94, 109
Ann Sothern 29, 58
Anne 21
Arlene Dahl 56
Army and Navy Wedding Party 30
Army Nurse and Doctor 100
Around the Clock with Sue and Dot 90
Around the World With Connie and Jean 51
Artist Models 32

B
B is for Betsy 93
Babes in Toyland 112, 131
Baby's Hungry! 140
Babs 52
Baby Album 111, 123
Baby Beans 138
Baby Brother 40, 51
Baby Dear 24
Baby Dears 59
Baby Doll 110, 135
Baby Dolls 22
Baby Mine 118
Baby Paper Dolls 18
Baby Sandy 100
Baby Sister and Baby Brother Dolls 94
Baby Sisters 102
Baby Sitter 49
Baby Sparkle Plenty 41, 105, 125
Baby Tenderlove 138
Baby's First Year 108, 118
Badgett Quadruplets, The 27
Ballerina, A Paper Doll Story Book 112, 130
Ballet 54
Ballet Dancers 103
Ballet Paper Dolls 44, 61
Barbara Britton 57
Barbie 139, 144
Barbie and her little sister Skipper 140
Barbie and Ken 139, 140
Barbie and P.J. 140
Beautiful Models 37
Beauty Queen 49
Belle of the Ball 39
Bessie 9
Best Friends 44
Betsy McCall 69, 112, 131
Betsy McCall's Paper Doll Story Book 112, 129
Bette Davis 109, 116

Bettina And Her Playmate Rosalie 12
Betty and her Play Pals 17
Betty Blue and Patty Pink 92
Betty Field 30
Betty Grable 92, 95, 109
Betty Jane 12
Big 'N' Easy 101
Big 'N' Little Sister 90
Big Moment 39
Blondie 63, 107, 111, 124
Blue Bonnet Paper Dolls 102
Boarding School 115
Bob and Betty 32, 106
Bobbsey Twins 110, 146
Bonnets and Bows 17, 61
Bonnie Bows 56
Bonny Braids 47
Bonny Paper Dolls 34
Boots and her Buddies 30
Boy And Girl Cut-Out Doll Book 12
Brand-New Baby 47
Brenda Starr 64, 107
Bridal Book 140
Bridal Doll 110, 136
Bridal Doll Book 135
Bridal Party 18, 49
Bride and Groom 91, 140, 147
Bride and Groom Military Wedding Party 99
Bride Doll Book 121, 124
Brothers Grimm 17, 106
Bubble Party 37
Bugs Bunny 125
Butterfly Ballet 35

C
Calico Cut-Outs 47
Calypso 38
Campus Sweethearts 60
Candy 136
Candy Queens 38
Candy Stripers, The 68
Career Girls 37, 111, 131, 132
Carmen Miranda 47, 105
Carmen Paper Dolls – Rita Hayworth 46
Carnival 32
Carol Heiss 141
Cat's Closet 134
Cathy goes to Camp 93
Champion 34
Charlie Chaplin and Paulette Goddard 27, 105
Charmin' Chatty 111, 132
Charming 19
Charming Paper Dolls 50
Chatty Baby 140
Cheerful Tearful 141
Children 'Round the World 96
Children in the Shoe 93
Children of America 27
Chuck and Di Have a Baby 134
Cinderella 36, 42, 130, 147
Circus Paper Dolls 43
Classic Boutique 68
Classmates 35
Claudette Colbert 5, 30, 41, 105
Coke Crowd 102, 108

College Style 97
Colonial America 52
Comics Paper Doll Cut-Out Book 22
Connie Darling and Her Dolly 73
Corinne 70
Coronation Paper Dolls and Coloring Book 56
Cover Girls 108, 117
Cowboy and Cowgirl 103
Cradle Baby 70
Cradle Tots 103
Curiosity Shop 58
Cutting Up with Ramona! 126
Cynthia Pepper 136

D
Daddy's Girl 52
Dainty Dolls for Tiny Tots 41
Daisy Mae & Li'l Abner 27, 28, 105
Daisy's Cut-Out Dolls 12
Darling Dolls with Wavy Hair 33, 71, 73, 75
Date Time 40
Dawn 141
Deanna Durbin 109, 113, 116
Debbie Reynolds 111, 125
Debra Paget 111, 124
Debs & Sub-debs 27
Dell Dolls 111, 122
Dell Twins, Dick and Dot 111, 121, 124
Deluxe Mounted Dolls 45
Diana Lynn 48
Dick and Dot 122
Dionne Quints Paper Dolls 109, 114
Dionne Quintuplets 109, 114, 115, 116, 124
Dodie from My Three Sons 69
Doll House 45
Doll I Love Best 10
Dollies To Paint Cutout and Dress 16
Dolls and Toys 112, 129
Dolls Around the World 146
Dolls From Storyland 91
Dolls We Love 99
Dolls You Love to Dress 39
Dolly and Me 64
Dolly Jean - Her Paper Doll House, Furniture and Clothes 13
Donna Reed 59
Donny & Marie 141
Donny Double 14
Dora Grows Up 43
Dotty Double 14
Double Date 50
Double Wedding 62, 104, 109
Dream Girl 103
Dress Your Doll 111, 132
Dresses Worn by the "First Ladies" of the White House 24
Drum Major and Majorette 99
Duet Book 110, 145
Dutch Treat 46

E
Elaine Stewart 125
Elizabeth 9
Elizabeth The Beautiful Bride 72
Elizabeth Trousseau 11, 16
Elly May 136

Esther Williams 93, 95, 109
Eve Arden 56, 107
Evelyn Rudie 60, 65, 105

F

Family of Dolls 123
Family of Paper Dolls 42
Fancy 110, 135
Fashion Land 40
Fashion Plate 36
Fashion Shop 24
Fashion Show 123
Fashion Whirl 72
Fashions for the Modern Miss 51
Fave Teens 55
Faye Emerson 47, 107
Festival Paper Dolls 29
Fiesta 35
15 Puppy-Kitty Cut-Outs 101, 108
50 Paper Dolls 26
Finian's Rainbow 63
First Date 118
First Family 126
Five Baby Paper Dolls 35
Five Dionne Quintuplets 124
Five Dollies to Cut Out and Dress 10, 11
5 Little Belles 52
Flower Girls 61
Flying Nun, The 69
For Miss America – Henrietta Hippo 52
4 Ballerina Cut-Out Dolls 121
Four Cousins 36
4 Great Big Paper Dolls 107
Four Hi-Heel Standing Dolls, 74
Four Little Dolls, The 15
14 Good Little Dolls 27, 107
Francie 141

G

Gale Storm 122
Gene Autry Ranch Cut-Out Book 114
Gigi Perreau 43
Gina Gillespie 17, 105
Ginger Paper Doll 129
Girl Friend – Boy Friend 49
Girl Pilots of the Ferry Command 117
Girlfriends 55
Gisele MacKenzie 60, 105
Gloria Jean 19, 105
Go Team Go 145
Golden Girl 90, 108
Golden Record "Paper Doll" 112, 131
Goldilocks and the Three Bears 25, 53, 106
Gone with the Wind 89, 98, 109
Good Neighbor 32
Greer Garson 109, 118
Growing Up Skipper 141
Grown-Up Paper Dolls 98
Gulliver's Travels 17, 124

H

Hansel and Gretel 130
Happiest Millionaire, The 67
Happiness is Babyland 34
Happy Birthday 40, 44, 104, 108
Hat Box 44
Heavenly Blue Wedding 96
Heavenly Twins 91
Hedy Lamarr 43, 105, 109, 114
Hee Haw 70, 106

Heidi 146
Heidi and Peter 53
Helen 8, 21
Helen's Trousseau 16
Hello Kitty's Busy Book 146
Henry and Henrietta 24
Henry the Honeybee 145
Here Comes the Bride 51, 59, 107, 141
High School Dolls 91
High School Paper Dolls 35, 108, 113
Holiday 37
Holiday Twins Betty and Bobby, The 72
Holly 54
Hollywood Fashion Dolls 25, 107
Hollywood Fashions 34
Honey Kitten 42
Hootenanny 64, 106
Hour of Charm 31
Housekeeping with the Kuddle Kiddies 23
Howdy Doody Fun Book 144

I

Ice Festival 50
In Old New York – Colonial Paper Dolls with Pictures to Color 58
In Peter Pumpkin's House 94
Indian Paper Dolls with Pictures to Color 58
Indian Princess 35

J

Jack 8, 9
Jack And Jill Painting Book 12
Jack's Trousseau 16
Jane 9
Jane and Jack 111, 124
Jane and Michael 110, 137
Jane Arden 28, 107
Jane Fonda 66
Jane Russell Paper Dolls and Coloring Book 57
Jane Withers 125
Janet Leigh 95, 109
Jeanette MacDonald 104
Jeannette 70
Jill and Her Trunk Full of Clothes 117
Joan Carroll 29
Joan Caulfield 47
Joanne Woodward 63
Johnny, Janey and Judy in Storybook Land 90
Judy 20
Judy and Jim 112, 128
Judy Doll – Miss Teenage America 64
Judy Holliday 48
Judy Paper Dolls, The 91
Juke Box 33
Julia 40, 63, 107
Julie Andrews 60
Juliet Jones Paper Dolls and Coloring Book 57, 107
June and Stu Erwin 48, 105
Juniors 36

K

Karen 18
Karen goes to College 94
Kathy and Sue 74
Kelly Sisters, The 36
Kewpie Dolls 73
Kewpie Kin 68
Kewpies – A Coloring and Cut-Out Book 75
Kewpies 17, 106
Kiddie Circus 61

Kim Novak 60, 105
Kim Novak Paper Dolls with Pictures to Color 58
Kissy Paper Doll 17
Kissy – Coloring and Cut-Out Book 75
Kitchen Play 24
Kitty goes to Kindergarten 90

L

Laraine Day 47
Laugh-in Party 72
Leading Ladies 34
Let's Play Doctor 24, 107
Let's Play House with the Dionne Quints, Annette 115
Let's Play House with the Dionne Quints, Cecile 115
Let's Play House with the Dionne Quints, Emilie 116
Let's Play House with the Dionne Quints, Marie 116
Let's Play House with the Dionne Quints, Yvonne 116
Let's Play Wedding 25, 107
Let's Play with the Baby 91
Liberty Belles 109, 113
Li'l Abner 27, 28, 105
Lilac Time 51
Linda Darnell 48, 101
Lindy-Lou 'n' Cindy Sue 96, 108
Little Audrey's Dress Designer Kit 71
Little Ballerina 89
Little Dancers 141
Little Fairy, The 90
Little Family and Their Little House 92, 108
Little Girls are Everything Nice 70
Little Golden Paper Dolls 112, 128
Little Lulu 125
Little Mary Mixup And Her Friend Peggy 13
Little Miss Alice Paper Dolls – Pictures to Color 58
Little Miss America 27, 106
Little Miss Christmas and Holly-Belle 97, 108
Little Orphan Annie's Paper Dolls 29
Little Playmate 10
Little Princess 98
Little Rascals – Spanky and Darla 50, 107
Little Red Riding Hood 130, 147
Little Toddlers 48
Little Women 18, 65, 106
Loretta Young Paper Dolls and Coloring Book 58
Lost Horizon 68
Lots of Little Paper Dolls 39
Lovely Dolls with Real Cloth Dresses 71
Lovely Lady 36, 39
Lucille Ball 31, 105
Lucky Paper Dolls 5, 37

M

Magazine Cover Girls 108, 117
Majorette 50
Make Believe and Play Stewardess 73
Make Clothes for Patsy 104
Many Things To Do 14
Mardi Gras 36, 58
Margaret 8
Margaret's Troussaeu 16
Marie Osmond 70
Marilyn Monroe 55
Martha Hyer 60
Mary 9
Mary Lou 71
Mary Martin 29, 32
Mary Poppins 111, 132
Mary, Mary Quite Contrary 54
Mary's Troussaeu 16
Melissa 20

Melody Four, The 38
Merry Teens 44
Mickey Mouse and Minnie Mouse 14
Midi-Mod 40
Mike and Melissa 112, 129
Mini Mods 64
Mini Moppets 64
Miss World 136
Mitzi and Sissy 36
Mod Fashions – Featuring Jane Fonda 66
Model Paper Dolls 39
Modern Miss in Paper Dolls, The 28
Modern Stick-on Dresses 137
Molly 19
Mommy and Me 28
Mother and Daughter 17, 34, 73
Mother Goose 33, 110, 144
Mother Goose Land with Judy and Jim 129
Mother, Dad and Us Kids 39
Mrs. Beasley 142
My Bonnie Lassie 53
My Book Of Paper Dolls - Ready To Cut-Out
    And Dress 15
My Four Dollies 10
My Hansel and Gretel Story and Playbook 147
My Little Margie 48
My Sweet Dollies 10
My Twins 21

N
Nancy & Her Dolls 31
Nancy and Sluggo 142
Nanny and the Professor 53
Navy Girls and Marines 108, 117
Navy Scouts 100, 108
New 'N' Groovy P.J. 142
New Baby 117
New Quintuplet Dolls 98
New Shirley Temple in Paper Dolls, The 29
New Zoo Revue, The 25
Nurse and Doctor 44

O
Oklahoma! 112, 128
Old Woman Who Lived in a Shoe 65, 106
Once Upon a Wedding Day Coloring and
    Cut-Out Book 76
Our New Baby 100
Our Soldiers 124
Outdoor Paper Dolls 38
Ozzie and Harriet 57

P
Pageant 37
Pals and Pets 43
Pam and Her Pram 110, 145
Paper Doll Ballet 74
Paper Doll Family 23, 106
Paper Doll Family and Their House 22
Paper Doll Family and Their Trailer 101
Paper Doll Party 28
Paper Doll Patsy and Her Pals 49
Paper Doll Playmates 39, 49, 66
Paper Doll Wedding 117, 128
Paper Doll's with Early American Costumes 34
Paper Doll-Little Golden Record 112, 131
Paper Dolls 34, 38, 111, 132
Paper Dolls - 180 Pieces To Cut-Out - Ten Dolls
    With Hats, Dresses And Playthings 14
Paper Dolls and Wardrobe Box 31

Paper Dolls and Dresses 40
Paper Dolls Around the World 23
Paper Dolls from Mother Goose 50
Paper Dolls of All Nations 35
Paper Dolls On Parade 26
Paper Dolls To Cut-Out - Ten Dolls With Dresses,
    Hats And Playthings 12
Paper Dolls with Costumes of 21 Nations 35
Paper Dolls With Glamour Gowns 49
Paper Dolls with Lace-On Costumes 73
Paper Dolls, Bob and Judy 77
Parade of Paper Dolls 34
Partridge Family 40, 69
Pasting Without Paste Paper Dolls 46
Pasting Without Paste – Little Dressmakers 46
Patchwork 72
Patchy Annie 35, 72
Patty and Sue 36
Paulette Goddard 27, 105
Pearl 9
PeePul Pals 137
Peggy 52, 110, 137
Peggy Lee 110, 146
Peggy Lou 33
Penny 73
Penny and Her Pets 48
Pepe 38
Pert and Pretty Paper Dolls 45, 91, 108
Pete and Peg 111, 124
Petticoat Girls 51
Petunia and Patches 24
Picnic 44
Pier Angeli 111, 124
Pig-Tails 102
Pink Prom Twins 97
Pink Wedding, The 92
Piper Laurie 95, 109
Platter Party 123
Play Time 145
Playmates 54
Playskool Funtime 146
Playtime Pals 37
Playtime Paper Dolls 36
Polka Dot Darlings 35
Polly and her Playmates 91
Polly and Molly and Their Dollies 74
Polly and Molly in Fancy Dress 40
Polly Bergen 62
Polly Dolly 77
Polly Pepper Paper Dolls 23, 106
Pollyanna 111, 132
Posy Pals 33
Preschool 71
Pretty as a Picture 36
Pretty as a Rose 18
Pretty Bride Wedding Party 122
Prince & Princess 45
Prince Valiant and Princess Aleta 57
Princess Paper Doll Book 25, 105
Prints and Polka Dots 55
Punky Brewster 142
Push-Out Paper Dolls 42

Q
Quintuplets 18, 106
Quintuplets, The Dionne Babies 109, 114
Quiz Kids 29

R
Raggedy Ann 142
Raggedy Ann and Andy 41, 106
Ranch Family, The 97
Real Baby Paper Dolls 113
Rhonda Fleming Paper Dolls and Coloring Book 57
Ride a Pony 118
Riders of the West 46
Rita Hayworth 46, 113
Robin Hood and Maid Marian 34, 49, 107
Rock-A-Bye Baby 31
Roller Rhythm 118
Romance Paper Dolls 33, 41
Rosemary Clooney 110, 145
Round the Clock 34
Royal Baby, The 134
Ruth E. Newton's Paper Doll Cut-Outs 25

S
Saalfield, Albert George 7
Saalfield, Henry Robinson 7
Saalfield Paper Doll Assortments 7, 8
Saddle Your Pony 111, 132
Sally 21, 52
Sally Lou 14
Sally Twinkletoes and Peggy Twirl 59
Sally's Silver Skates 90
Sandra Dee 59
Sandy 48, 110, 135
Santa's Christmas Fun 145
School Girl 28
Schoolmates 40, 42
Scissors and Coloring Fun 146
Scootles and Kewpie Doll Book 23, 107
Secret Sue 142
Seven and Seventeen 101
Shamrock 54
Shari Lewis 65, 107
Shari Lewis and her Puppets 72
Sheree North 59
Shirley 19
Shirley Temple 7, 21, 22, 63, 68, 105, 106
Shirley Temple Dolls and Dresses 21
Shirley Temple Play Kit 76
Shirley Temple Playhouse 21
Shirley Temple Standing Doll 20
Shirley Temple Standing Dolls 20
Shirley Temple – Dolls and Dresses 23
Shirley Temple – Her Movie Wardrobe 22
Shirley Temple – In Masquerade Costumes 22
Shirley Temple's Birthday Book 125
Short-Stop Sue & Her Wardrobe 52
Sing Along with Peggy Lee 110, 146
Six Dollies to Cut Out and Dress 11
Six Little Steppers, The 103
6 and Sweet 16 96
6 Grown-up Paper Dolls 103
6 Standing Dolls with Lace-On Costumes 75
16 Paper Dolls 42
Skating Party Paper Dolls 26
Sleeping Beauty 112, 130
Sleepy Doll 55
Slumber Party 117
Smart Paper Dolls 39
Snow White and the Seven Dwarfs 125, 147
Soldiers and Sailors House Party 114
Sonja Henie 99, 109, 113, 115
Southern Belles 44
Spanky and Darla 50, 107

Photo Index

Square Dance 46
Stage Door Canteen 31
Stand-Together Dolls 42
Stand-Up Dolls – Honey and Bunny 97, 108
Star Babies 101
Star Bright 38
Starr 144
Story of the Ballet 76
Story Princess 50, 107
Storyland 51
Sub-Deb Paper Dolls 98
Sugar 'n Spice 51, 64
Sugar Plum Pals 66
Summer Date 38
Summer Fun 135
Summertime Sue, Wintertime Wendy 71
Sunbeam 55
Sunshine Funbook for Girls 144
Superman Cut Outs Book 19
Susan Dey 34, 54
Susan Doll Book 102
Sweet 16 Dolls 108, 118
Sweet Swingers 142
Sweetheart Dolls 72, 74
Sweetheart Paper Dolls 30, 43

T
Tammy 110, 112, 130, 132, 137
Tammy and Her Friends 143
Tammy and Pepper 111, 132
Tammy Marihugh 62
Teen Boutique 55
Teen Fun 137
Teen Shop 45
Teen Time 136
Teen Town 101

Ten of Us 37
Terri and Tonya 39
Texas Rose 66, 106
That Girl – Starring Marlo Thomas 67, 106
The Doll I Love Best 10
3 Darling Dolls 75
3 Paper Doll Books 28
Through the Year with 3 Paper Dolls 33
Through the Year with Cindy 66
Tillie The Toiler 125
Timey Tell 143
Tina 33
Tiny Chatty Twins 143
Tiny Thumbelina 110, 137
Tiny Toddles 143
Tiptop Paper Dolls 26, 106
Toodles the Toddler 59
Tote Bag 111, 121
Town and Country 45
Tressy Fashion Model 76
Tricia 55, 105
Trudy in Her Teens 117
Tubsy 143
Tuesday Weld 61
12 Baby Dolls 104
27 Dancing School Paper Dolls 102, 108
Twin Babies 100
Twins Lance and Lorie 110, 136
2 in One Color and Paper Doll Book 145
Two Marys, The 103
Tyrone Power and Linda Darnell 101

U
Umbrella Girls 95
Uncle Sam's Little Helpers 30
United Nations 62

United We Stand 12, 106

V
Vanity Paper Dolls 35
Victory Paper Dolls 29, 106
Victory Volunteers 100, 108
Virginia Mayo 60

W
Walking Paper Doll Family 14, 106
Walt Disney's Babes in Toyland 112, 131
Walt Disney's Jane and Michael 110, 137
Walt Disney's Mary Poppins 111, 132
Walt Disney's Sleeping Beauty 112, 130
Walter Lantz Cartoon Stars 18
Watch Me Grow 118
Wedding Day 34
Wedding of the Paper Dolls 115
Wedding Party 47
Well Dressed Girl 5, 37
Western 33
White House Paper Dolls 67, 107
Wiggie the Mod Model 67
Winnie Winkle 111, 131
Winnie-the-Pooh 143
Winter Girl Wendy, Summer Girl Sue 43
Wishnik 143
Wizard of Oz 143
Wonder Woman 144
Wonderful World of the Brothers Grimm, The 17
World of Barbie 144

Y
You Are a Doll 74

Z
Ziegfeld Girl 104

About the Author:

Picture Courtesy of Jean Polus

Mary Young was born in Lake Forest, Illinois, and lived in the Chicago area most of her early years before marriage. After marriage to George Young, they moved to Maryland for four years and then to Dayton, Ohio, where they have lived ever since. They have five children and 16 grandchildren.

Paper dolls were always Mary's favorite pastime as a child. As soon as her last child started school in 1970 she began to start a collection of paper dolls. After four years of collecting she became interested in learning about the artists who drew these paper dolls, so she set out to find them! This venture evolved into her first book on the subject in 1977. In 1980, she published her first price guide on paper dolls, which was met with instant success. She has gone on to write other books covering paper dolls. This is her eighth book on the subject.

Mary also collects children's school readers and other children's books and toys.